From The Inkwell.

""As a lifelong Chicagoan and a [...] the 1969 Cubs still hold a very special place in my heart. That team captured the city of Chicago's imagination and some 50 years later they still do! Fergie Jenkins was not only a Hall of Fame baseball player but he is an even better person. To hear him tell the inside stories of that team and that season returns me to my childhood again and again!"
-David Kaplan, Sportscaster - ESPN 1000/NBC Sports Chicago

"Fergie Jenkins is a man I greatly admire on many levels. He is the greatest pitcher in Chicago Cubs history. He was one of the players I followed as a teenager. I was always amazed at how easy he made it look, yet I know it's not easy as I've been around baseball for my entire 36-year broadcasting career. In Fergie's extraordinary life he has experienced tremendous highs and the 1969 season was one of those. I'm sure you will find it compelling to read about his amazing 1969 season. Fergie is smart, intelligent and humble with a great sense of humor. He is a great guy to spend time with and hear the stories. This will show in this amazing inside stories book."
-Pat Hughes, Chicago Cubs Radio Broadcaster

"Fergie Jenkins tossed 267 complete games during his Hall of Fame career, which is a testament to his strong work ethic, remarkable mental toughness and uncanny ability to get out of jams. Similarly, he has been able to overcome incredible challenges off the field to finish strong with his head held high. I have the utmost respect for him as a pitcher and a person."
-Fred Mitchell, Chicago Tribune Sportswriter (41 Years)

"Fergie Jenkins was as good a Cubs pitcher as there's ever been. He was a workhorse, pitching complete games, never complaining, always a team guy, always a sportsman. This book gives you a rare insight into this great man's life, which was neither as simple or easy as it looked to outsiders. A fine read."
-Rick Telander, Sports Columnist, Chicago Sun-Times

THE 1969 CHICAGO CUBS
LONG REMEMBERED.
NEVER FORGOTTEN.

Some of the 1969 family —
The way the fans collected us.

By Hall-of-Fame Pitcher Fergie Jenkins
with George Castle

For information about special discounts for bulk purchases,
please contact John Schenk & Associates, LLC at:
314-384-4171
info@johnschenkassociates.com

The 1969 Cubs
Authors: Fergie Jenkins with George Castle

Library of Congress Control Number: 2018963752
ISBN-13: 978-0-9995298-5-0
ISBN-10: 0-9995298-5-4

Book Cover Design & Interior Graphic Elements: John Hanley
Managing Editor: Howard Schlossberg
Associate Editor & Interior Layout: Reji Laberje
Photos are from 1966 to present, courtesy of Fergie Jenkins, and provided through the generosity of friends, family members, and MLB colleagues.
Photo of Fergie Pitching (Page 60) courtesy of Kel Kissamis / Kelcub Studio.

The Signature Strength Speakers Bureau can bring authors, athletes, and other motivational speakers to your live events. For more information or to book an event, contact the Signature Strength Speakers Bureau at 314-384-4171 or visit its website at www.SignatureStrength.org.

Published by John Schenk & Associates, LLC d/b/a Signature Strength®

Signature Strength® trademark is owned by Schenk Intellectual Property, LLC

First Printing: 2018
Printed and bound in the United States of America.

Dedication

For my late mother, Delores Louise Jenkins,
my late father, Ferguson Holmes Jenkins,
and my mentor, Gene Dziadura.
And for three of the greatest women in my life:
My first wife Cathy and our three daughters
Kelly, Kimberly and Delores.
My late second wife, Mary-Ann
and our son Raymond and late daughter, Samantha Marie.
My late third wife, Lydia C. Jenkins.
For my grandchildren Kaleb, Ian, Nathan and Allison.
For my great grandchildren Terry Jr., Logan, and Lilly.
All of you have touched my heart and my life
in so many ways and on so many levels.

FERGUSON JENKINS

Fergie Jenkins (Left)
Randy Hundley (Below)

1969 Chicago Cubs
Batterymate

RANDY HUNDLEY

A Note from Fergie...

Everyone on the mound needs to locate his pitches. No excuses if you don't. But having a great catcher in tune with your mindset always helps. I had one from the first pitch I made for the Cubs on April 23, 1966, through the end of my first tenure on the North Side. During that time, I won 20 games, six years in a row, and a Cy Young Award. Randy Hundley, take a bow, you kept me level-headed and got me back on track if I strayed.

I've asked Randy to be leadoff man for this monster of a book, and he was glad to oblige. He's one of the greatest catchers in Cubs history and a man who cared about his teammates very deeply. His eyes glisten when he talks about our teams, the era in which we played, and the special support of Cubs fans. So please enjoy a few of the Rebel's thoughts about my work and a time in baseball history of which he was a centerpiece.

~ Fergie Jenkins

Once a teammate, always a teammate. At left: Fergie Jenkins and Randy Hundley. The pair became batterymates in their rookie season in 1966.

Below: Three Hall-of-Famers (Billy Williams, Ernie Banks, Jenkins) ironman catcher (Randy Hundley) reunite at a Wrigley Field ceremony decades later.

By: Randy Hundley

I was batterymate of Fergie all but my first 10 days with the Cubs in 1966 – before his trade from Philadelphia – and with time out due to injuries in 1970-1971. He did not need a lot of my help, even when he worked out of the bullpen in our rookie year. I never had to get on him much. He developed pinpoint control like few other pitchers. To play the game with Fergie . . . what an honor.

I don't take much credit for much of what Fergie has done. He was his own man on the mound. I'd give him a fastball and give him all the signs and go back to the fastball. Sometimes I'd try to get him to do something, but he knew what he wanted to throw. He just kept improving his control to the point he walked just 37 batters against 263 strikeouts in 325 innings in 1971. That's 1 walk every 9 innings. I don't think we'll ever see that kind of razor-sharp control and certainly over that many innings *ever* again.

Pitchers today care how many guys they walk. They don't realize the potential in scoring runs by putting runners on base with free passes. It's made worse when managers pull starters in mid-game. If you pitch 6 innings now, you're a good starter. Fergie was on cruise control in many games after 6 innings, with plenty left in the tank to go all the way.

Fergie pitched his own game.

I'd call a fastball low and away, but he might throw me a bloomin' slow fastball. Next time he'd get 2 strikes on a guy, he might hump it when the guy doesn't expect it. He controlled it; I could not control it. I did not go out and rag on him. Once I learned how he was going to pitch, shucks, you think I'm going to change it? Fans and writers might rag on him for giving up a lot of home runs, but I never remember getting on his case after he served one up.

Location, location, location. It applies in real estate and even more so in pitching. Fergie was the best at it. Early in his career he'd throw up and in on guys. You must do that to survive. You had to keep the hitters honest no matter how good your control was. Hitters knew that, even as Fergie was painting the strike zone, he was using his hard-breaking slider elsewhere in the zone to baffle them.

Later, he got away from that. He did not want to throw in on hitters and did it less and less later in his career. When I was traded to Minnesota in 1973, we played Fergie, who was with the Rangers, and I told the guys don't look "in." But how he survived in the American League without going in on hitters was stunning. Every pitch was low and away. But that's how good he was. His Hall-of-Fame plaque proves it.

Many say I had a good cop/tough cop reputation, tilted toward the latter. I did not have to necessarily get "tough" with Fergie. We went pitch-by-pitch, as I held the tough-cop attitude in reserve, simply because Fergie could pinpoint the fastball and the slider so well. Once in a while he threw a big curveball. Better yet, he did not have a funky windup motion. Fergie was compact and smooth. That allowed his arm to survive as long as it did – 18 full big-league seasons until he was 40.

Fergie was compact and smooth.

Once Fergie starting winning 20 games every year, we did not put that number as our goal as a battery, even if Fergie himself projected 20. You could not think of numbers start by start. *I wanted quality games every time out.* That's all I ever thought about. If I had ever been worried about numbers, you'd think I'd be protecting my batting average a little better catching as much as I did.

But when you go years beyond the heat of trying to win each game, when you have time to look over Fergie's numbers, they're incredible. He racked up all those complete games – the peak being 30 in 39 starts in 1971, with 6 complete-game defeats – and led the National League in starts. He threw 267 complete games and won 284. And he pitched every fourth day. Pitchers today work in five- or even six-man rotations and are often on pitch counts. The game is so much different now. And yet some common concepts about pitching transcend the generations.

Some years back, Fergie and I were eating at an establishment that was being frequented by a lot of young pitchers. A friend asked if I could get those guys over there to talk to Fergie. I talked to Fergie first to ask if he'd gab with them. You know Fergie will talk to anyone in baseball. So they come over. Do you know who one of the first ones was to go to Fergie and take bloomin' notes on everything he said? Fella' named Jake Arrieta. Fergie was telling how he'd pitch in long sleeves and pitch every four days. Well, Jake did not wear long sleeves and worked every five days. But in his Cubs' Cy Young Award season in 2015, Jake walked just 48 in 229 innings. He was tough enough to hit, but he realized you also don't tempt fate to beat yourself. What worked for Fergie would also work 45 years later. Quality strikes, one after another, give you the big edge.

Jake also worked quickly, emulating Fergie. Keeping a quick pace was as important as any other factor of Fergie's success. As soon as Fergie was ready, I'd give him the pitch – no wasting of precious seconds. Let's strap it on. The pitcher dictates the pace, the hitter does not have time to think and get comfortable and our fielders mentally stay in the game with the ball coming to them at any second. Fergie could not strike out everybody and certainly credited his fielders for his wins.

Now, one angle in this book is how Fergie's gray flannel road uniform did not seem drenched at all in his July 4, 1969 duel against Bob Gibson in tropical St. Louis. We're all sweating to death in those heavy uniforms, but the TV images apparently showed Fergie as a dry guy. Well, outside appearances sometimes are deceiving. Fergie was still sweating like a pig. Perhaps his cool, laid-back demeanor threw off those watching the game. You couldn't walk on that field without sweating. If Fergie said he didn't sweat, he's full of crap! I was with him, so you couldn't avoid sweating with that long-sleeve bloomin' jersey on. Kiss my bloomin' . . . . but, cool under pressure? Yeah, that was Fergie.

Just like we didn't figure numbers as we went along, I didn't think I caught a potential Hall-of-Famer. To win today, you have to. I don't give a flip about anything else. You do everything you can to win THAT day – and then I'd go home to dream about winning the next day.

I had to do a lot of dreaming in 1969, with Fergie by now well-established as our ace. All we knew to do was to go on the field to win the game that day. And we were fortunate to have the fans at our back. Do you know what a thrill it was to play for those fans, and the fans stayed in the ballpark after the game. I get choked up now thinking about it. To see 40,000 people staying in the stands and not leaving. How can it get better than that? We couldn't wait to get to the ballpark every day.

Check the record book. The guys who played the game at that time are in the record book. The era was one of baseball's best. The visiting gate attractions of Hall of Fame-caliber players were now joined by a winning, charismatic team that younger Chicagoans at the time had never experienced. Except for a wartime pennant, the Cubs had not won since Gabby Hartnett was on the team (1922-1941). And there was that great 1969 Opening Day with Willie Smith hitting that pinch-hit, game-winning homer was a big thing for us. But as we found out over the long run, winning is not easy. It's a tough, stinking game.

Fourteen years later, I founded our Fantasy Camps to bring together former players and fans who are eternal kids. A great side benefit is the annual reunion of our team. The 1969 veterans were the first major group to continually show up in the 1980s, joined later by Cubs from the rest of the 20th century. And now we've completed our 36th season. The tales get taller by the year, the home runs reaching the first row are now out on Waveland Avenue. But that's the magic of baseball and the impact of our 1969 Cubs team.

I think we learned something a lot of young players have yet to experience. They don't know what's ahead of them. I just want to shake these guys to say, '*This is going to be a fleeting moment for you - 10, 15, 20 years in a lifetime! You're going to be out of the game and needing to find another job or hopefully you have enough money not to need to do so. You won't be a part of Major League Baseball and it'll be frustrating. Hold onto this!*'

I wanted to be in Major League Baseball all my life.

I can't even begin to describe what it's like to go to that ballpark, put that uniform on, go on the field, and try to win a stinkin' ballgame. I am so thankful I had that privilege of being able to do that. I know many believe we created the base for all the success the Cubs would enjoy as one of Chicago's top attractions. But that was just the end result of having a job to do; being paid to play baseball and win stinkin' ballgames. The No. 1 thing is winning. So it was a tremendous thrill to see the 2016 Cubs come from behind to win the World Series. Tremendous and so incredibly hard.

Forget everything else, what they call bread and circuses. When I went on the field, I wanted to whomp your fanny. And then do it all over again the next day. That's the only way you could play baseball the right way.

Was I disappointed at the final result in 1969, with the Mets winning it all and taking over the city of New York? You better believe it. But you know what else? We gave every bloomin' thing we had to win those ballgames that year. Many decades later, people say to me that I shouldn't have played so much. I agree with them now, as the body has gotten older. But at the time, I didn't think about it. All I wanted to do was win that game. You can't play any other way.

Randy Hundley in his playing days and today.

Why Am I Time-Tripping to 1969?

I am extremely well-motivated to depict the events and personalities surrounding the 1969 Cubs, a half-century later and with the welcomed assistance of baseball historian, sports journalist, and author, George Castle.

Better late than never . . . and better for this insider to share what he knows about the unforgettable group of guys who truly gave birth to the *modern* Chicago Cubs.

I want to give full credit to three teammates with whom I'm honored to share enshrinement in Cooperstown. Four Hall-of-Fame players on any Cubs squad is, for now, the most in team history. Beyond this quartet, I am throwing my best fastball to provide just due to some of the most adept players at their positions since the Cubs began as a National League (NL) franchise in 1876, as well the most little-used benchwarmer and reliever, the four coaches, and, yes, to manager Leo Durocher, who—for all his faults—was the sparkplug to get us to our level of competence in 1969.

We were all winners; we were all World Series worthy, no matter what the final result says in the record books. Without that 1969 Fall Classic entry, we still won over a sprawling city and a baseball-loving heartland in a manner that continues to positively impact the Cubs today. Harry Caray is given a ton of credit for boosting the Cubs and Wrigley Field into a summer tourist attraction, starting in 1982, when I began the last of my two pitching stints in Chicago, but before he was belting out *"Take Me Out To The Ballgame!"* we laid the groundwork.

John McDonough, the Chicago Blackhawks' president and CEO, was closely identified with boosting the Cubs profile and appeal during and after the Caray era. As the North Siders' marketing boss, McDonough conceived the Cubs Convention – granddaddy of all team off-season fan fests – that began in 1986. But in 1994, 25 years after our season in the sun, he gave full credit to our team for planting a seed that grew into a bumper crop of Cubs interest over the decades.

"We still live off the legacy of what happened on that April day in 1969," McDonough said of Willie Smith's walk-off pinch homer on Opening Day that touched off our run. "I really am a firm believer that (they) helped to ignite and start the engine of the great popularity the Cubs enjoy right now. That 1969 team...led off the season in such a dramatic fashion. That might be a team that is held in the highest regard of any team in Cubs history, despite some other teams that won divisions (in 1984 and 1989)."

Building on our upsurge in 1967-1968, an absolute mania swept through Chicago and hundreds of miles in every direction in the Midwest after Smith's homer and our 11-1 start. The cry of "Cub Power" on bumper stickers, buttons ,and a record album permeated the senses everywhere. Proportionally, I believe the intensity of interest was as great as for any Cubs team that succeeded us. Maybe even bigger, because the sports and entertainment world was much smaller then, and with the internet just in the laboratory, overall distractions were much simpler.

The fans and players may have had the closest relationship of any team in Cubs annals. I waved to the famed Bleacher Bums as I walked to the bullpen to warm up for home starts. Ron Santo walked out to left field on September 5, 1969, to regretfully announce to the fans he would not start that day due to a knee injury. Pitcher Dick Selma led cheers with a towel from the bullpen. Fans and players could rub shoulders on the street, in grocery stores, in bars home and road and in so many personal appearances. The fans identified with a team whose core remained together for the bulk of a decade, longer than any other similar group in Cubs annals since the 1930s and into the 1940s.

"I think everybody focuses on that one year, 1969," said lefty Ken Holtzman, who threw the first of his two Cubs no-hitters on August 19, 1969. "The Cubs from 1967 to 1973 were a pretty good ballclub. I think we were a better team than the Mets in the following years (after 1969) and probably immediately before '69. [The] Cubs were probably the best team not to have won for a number of years. That's probably why people remember that set lineup, players who were here for a long time, and that's why they kind of identify with all those players.

The Cubs were probably the best team not to have won for a number of years.

Free agency was still years into the future, putting a lid on salaries. We could not leave the Cubs unless we were traded, were released, or we retired. What we lost in income, though, we gained in fan loyalty.

"It's team identity," said second baseman Glenn Beckert. "...today, fellas (play) one or two years and they're gone. With free agency, there's no time period where fans out there can get to know the player on a daily basis."

"A lot of people focus on the '69 club, we got so close," added Williams. "They felt sorry because we didn't win. The surroundings we were in were the key. We were a household name in Chicago. We stayed together for so long. People sensed the fun we were having on the field. After ballgames, many, many people stood outside to get our autographs. We were involved with the fans because we had to walk to the other side of the street to our cars. Normally, every day we would give out 20, 25 autographs to fans. They'd shake our hands, congratulating us for making a nice summer for them."

The core hitters of Williams, Santo, and Ernie Banks typically batted in positions 3-4-5 from 1963 to 1970, when Banks' age and battered knees forced him out as a regular. Beckert and shortstop Don Kessinger were the Cubs' longest-running double-play combo for almost nine seasons, from 1965 to 1973. Randy Hundley was our regular catcher from 1966 to 1973, with time lost to injuries in both 1970 and 1971. Our Big Three starting rotation of myself, Bill Hands, and Holtzman had the shortest run, from 1968 to 1971, but Hands and Holtzman were still important cogs in the pitching staff in 1966 and 1967.

The season was like one big party. Players gladly posed in yellow Bleacher Bum helmets. The fans and players often mixed as if they were one group.

Kessinger called the 1969 experience "phenomenal."

"There was such a great chemistry among the group of guys who played together for so long," he said. "The fans probably realized we enjoyed each other and had a lot of fun playing. There was a great relationship between the players and the fans. Nothing I ever experienced before. Maybe the fact we had such a great summer for five months (in 1969) and then all went through some adversity together, maybe that drew us together even closer between the fans and the players. Whatever it is, we certainly love it and appreciate it."

With many of us living year-round in Chicago, we became accessible to the long-suffering fans and fulfilled a yearning for a competitive team that no longer would be the National League's doormat. When we pulled off an instant turnaround in the late spring of 1967, we *finally* gave the fans a reason to play hooky from work or school, or plan part of a vacation around flocking to Wrigley Field. The fans began filling up Wrigley Field on summer weekdays instead of just a few Sunday games or the odd weekday doubleheader with the Giants or Dodgers as the gate attraction. They came early and often.

Holtzman recalled, "You used to have a crowd watching the pitchers take batting practice (BP). You were excited right out of bed. It was pretty hard not to get excited and pumped up to see pitchers take BP. It was like a summer-long carnival."

Wrigley Field drew just 7,936 for a Friday, August 20th, 1965, home doubleheader against the Houston Astros. A turnout of 6,000 or 7,000 was typical for a weekday summer afternoon in those years, but on Friday, August 27, 1965, the Cubs drew 20,723 to a 7:30 P.M. night game 90 miles to the north at Milwaukee's County Stadium. It was the final Cubs' visit to a Milwaukee Braves home series before they moved to Atlanta and before the Brewers filled their cleats. It attracted 77 busloads of fans from Chicago! When Williams, my Hall-of-Fame mate and fishing buddy, slugged a grand slam, a large portion of the crowd roared with delight. Back then, the fans would only come out in numbers for TGIF at week's end. Other than brief upticks in midweek crowds when the Cubs flirted with contention at mid-season in 1958 and 1963, the Friendly Confines just were not a summertime destination in a world-class city, until a fortuitous series of events brought us all together as the Sixties ebbed.

With the last season attendance of one million taking place in 1952, owner Phil Wrigley should have put in lights decades earlier, but that's an issue for an entire book itself.

As we turned the season around on a dime – the amount of money our Bleacher Bums often tossed at us in the outfield during batting practice began nudging past 20,000 for an early August weekday series against the archrival St. Louis Cardinals. The fans simply thirsted for a winner, or even a hint of one, willing to twirl the turnstiles for a Cubs team that would spark their passion.

The demarcation line for the franchise for that era and many decades to come was the 40,000 who watched us beat the Reds, 4-1, on Sunday, July 2, 1967, and refused to leave the ballpark until the grounds crew hoisted the Cubs flag atop the scoreboard to first place. Some 10,000 more were turned away from that landmark game. Two weeks later, when nearly 35,000 showed up for a Sunday doubleheader against the San Francisco Giants; with all the box seats sold out in advance, fans showed up as early as 1:00 A.M. to get in line for tickets. The early arrivals played catch on the sidewalk. One young woman napped on a car's back seat that her date had removed from his vehicle. Even as we faded out of the race behind the eventual world champion Cardinals during the final six weeks of 1967, the impression was made for future in-person Cubs loyalty.

And despite our mediocre first half in 1968, wrecking our pennant shot against the Cardinals, the fans still made early reservations to see us. We drew an amazing 42,261-person crowd, the biggest Wrigley Field attendance in 20 years, for a July 28 twin bill against the Dodgers. That meant more than 6,000 fans could only get in via standing-room-only tickets. A hot July and early August in 1968 stoked capacity crowds against the Cards for a Monday-Thursday series in mid-August.

George Langford, a then-30-year-old Chicago Tribune baseball writer in his second stint covering us in 1969, believed he had a finger on the pulse of why we clicked so quickly with the populace. "I am no social or cultural anthropologist, but I firmly believe the Cubs were just another entertainment franchise in a big city until July 2, 1967, when a perfect storm of circumstances propelled them into a compelling entity people wanted to identify with. I covered lots of stuff and that was a truly feel-good, landmark event. The era had Vietnam, assassinations, street riots, seismic shifts in race relations, and rebellion against moral and social mores. Tumultuous times. So it really mattered not over the next year or so that they were not in first place (in 1968). They were good, entertaining, and a fabulous escape, and they had a chance. Even shut-ins could participate because it was free on TV. And the lead characters were embraceable or, if not, ornery in a spirited way. Even though they did not win it all until almost 50 years later, the Cubs enjoyed a new standing in Chicago."

They were good, entertaining, and a fabulous escape, and they had a chance.

We did serve another important purpose at the time. The social upheavals of the day created division, fear, and tension among the general populace. Only the uplifting Apollo XI moon landing on July 20, 1969 (my teammates and I, alongside our opponents ,the Phillies, lined the baselines in tribute on the same day) and the Woodstock music festival a few weeks later seemed to counterbalance the constant flow of bad news. Baseball was a welcome diversion, a trip to the toy factory for the world-weary.

As the beloved Jack Brickhouse said, "Pack up your cares and let (names of Cubs and opposing managers) do the worrying for you."

Pundits in Detroit said the world champion Detroit Tigers brought a torn city together in 1968, a year after 43 were killed in the worst of the urban riots. I don't know if we had a similar effect in Chicago, where dozens of blocks of the West Side burned down in riots after the assassination of Dr. Martin Luther King Jr. Only 4 ½ months later, televised police-protestor clashes on Michigan Avenue during the Democratic National Convention gave many middle-Americans that the idea the revolution was on . . . but not at Wrigley.

"Baseball was continuing to be an escape," said Holtzman. "People looked to that. There really wasn't a lot going on in 1984 and 1989 to compare with those days, and that's why you see the identification with those teams, that even though they won the division, might not be as lasting as the '69 Cubs."

The two-year interest buildup crested in 1969 and our season attendance was a Chicago-record of 1,674,000. Opening Day, Tuesday, April 8, we drew more than 40,000 fans. We had some 17 crowds of at least 30,000 on weekdays. During the 1969 season, Cubs broadcaster Vince Lloyd told General Manager John Holland (1957-1975) that if we won that year, the Cubs would draw more than 2 million the following season. In his old-school thinking, Holland did not believe him. Future events proved Lloyd right – and then some. No Chicago baseball team would draw as many as the 1969 Cubs until the 1983 White Sox. And even though we had more bad decades to come – such as no winning seasons from 1973 to 1983 – the Wrigley Field atmosphere would never slip back to the pre-1967 levels with summertime crowds of 7,000. Eventually, Cubs season attendance moved over 2 million (2,491,242 in the division-winning 1984 season) and continued increasing. The all-time season record of 3.3 million, set in 2008, would double that of 1969 – a virtual sellout every game.

We gave the fans what they wanted – exciting baseball amassed by personable players.

Banks was long the beloved "Mr. Cub" by now, the franchise's greatest-ever player enjoying a career revival with his 500th homer not far off. Williams was the reliable sweet-swinging left and sometimes right fielder who simply would not miss a game. Santo could have been classified as the NL's best all-around player in the mid-1960s, a 30-homer, 100 RBI hitter and a Gold Glover at third. Hundley quickly established himself as a durable catcher and team leader.

I went from a long reliever in 1966 to a 20-game winner in 1967 for the first of what could be an unsurpassed six seasons in a row. Holtzman had promise as the NL's best up-and-coming lefty this side of Steve Carlton. Hands matched me for control and became our rotation's enforcer – *do not mess with him*. And, by 1968, we had the NL's Fireman of the Year in Phil Regan – did he or didn't he throw the wet one? Coming over from the Dodgers with Regan was a spare outfielder named Jim Hickman, who developed into one of the best clutch hitters in Cubs history.

You could reach out and almost touch a Cub in cozy Wrigley Field. As the 1969 frenzy reached a crescendo, we all took turns in a pre-game autograph booth in the third-base concourse behind our dugout. You could bump into a Cub in the grocery store or local deli year-round. Banks, Santo, Williams, Kessinger, Beckert, and Hundley made their year-round homes in the area, while I was just a short flight away in Chatham, Ontario, Canada. On the road, you might even belly up to the hotel bar with a Cub.

We showed how much fun winning was, in a simpler era less complicated by a mass of distractions and $20 million salaries. Sure, we wanted to get paid, and fairly as the Major League Baseball Players Association began to realize we had labor rights we had forever left on the table. But the game itself was the main attraction and focus.

The slogan "Cub Power" inundated Chicago and surrounding areas. We touched off a mania for winning baseball at Wrigley Field that has been scarcely duplicated since in Chicago or in other big-league cities. We were mobbed like rock stars when we left the ballpark after games to walk to our cars, with some players' shirts being torn in the frenzy. Some fans even waited at intersections west of Wrigley Field to greet players as they drove home. We were sent off and greeted again as we flew in and out of O'Hare Airport. The fans went absolutely nuts at dramatic moments, storming the field by the hundreds after a no-hitter or ninth-inning comeback victory. I'm convinced if we had gone on to win the World Series, thousands would have poured onto groundskeeper Pete Marcantonio's carefully-tended acreage and tried to carry off anything that wasn't nailed down.

No.

We did not win it all.

Or even finish first.

Baseball is the cruelest sport of all, an endurance and good-fortune test, where the batting champion fails two of every three times at-bat. Teams rise and fall with no provocation, no prelude. The Mets, expected to perhaps flirt with .500 due to their good young pitching, staged one of baseball's greatest-ever stretch runs with a 37-11 finishing kick. New York's magical core of players never got near the 90-win mark ever again, sneaking into a World Series appearance in 1973 after winning the NL East with a slender 82 victories.

Most seasons, our 92-70 record would have been good enough to finish first, and maybe much more. Unfortunately, our timing – so crucial in baseball – was off. We only had four head-to-head games against the Mets down the stretch. We would have needed to be as hot as we were in the first week of April to fend off the Mets; they finished 8 games ahead of us.

Fast and furious finishes are part of baseball history. Most famous was Durocher's 1951 New York Giants club that wiped out a 13 1/2-game Brooklyn Dodgers' lead and forced a pennant playoff, decided by Bobby Thomson's "Shot Heard 'Round the World." Among other memorable stretch runs, the same Giants in 1937 went 41-19 from August 1 on to wipe out the Cubs' peak 6 ½-game lead on August 13, the same date in 1969 we had our top 10-game edge over the Mets. The '37 Cubs finished 93-61, winning more games than their pennant-winning successors in 1938, but also ending up 3 games out at the finish.

Baseball is dramatic, cruel and unpredictable, all wrapped up in one riveting package.

Recriminations about 1969 have been debated since before the final out that season. I will stick up for one factor just as strongly as I advocate for many of my teammates as true game-changers in Cubs history. We were not a *cursed* team. There was no billy-goat curse that kicked in, supplemented by that black cat I believe was turned loose by the Shea Stadium grounds crew on September 9, 1969, in a game I pitched. Not one Cub believed the team was hexed by other worldly powers.

The concept of curses is thrown around too liberally. Even after the 2016 Theo Epstein-assembled team seemingly put the 71-year-old goat-hex angle to bed for all time, author Rich Cohen came out with his own memoir: "The Chicago Cubs: The Story of a Curse."

Other teams had to deal with the catchy concept. The Boston Red Sox suddenly seemed under a whammy traced back to Babe Ruth, the big guy they let get away in 1920, when columnist Dan Shaughnessy penned the "Curse of the Bambino" book in 1990. Ruth never cursed the team for which he starred both on the mound and as a record-breaking slugger. Yet for the next 14 years after that book's publishing, the mythology quickly grew that the Red Sox were also under a spell. The Boston fans could have had it much worse – their favorites played in four World Series between 1945 and 2004, compared to the Cubs' zero.

Almost every Cub of the final three decades of the 20th century and first 16 seasons of the 21st had to deal with crazy questions about a barnyard-animal hex. I was at the front end of all of that nonsense.

♋ ♋ ♋ ♋

Media accounts of the 1945 World Series curse story involving William Sianis, who then operated a bar frequented by sportswriters across from the old Chicago Stadium, began circulating with our failure to win in 1969. Our successive runner-up finishes prompted more recollections of "Billy Goat" Sianis and his mascot beast getting kicked out of the 1945 Series at Wrigley Field. In response, Sianis supposedly put a curse on the Cubs that the team would never win another World Series until another goat was admitted to the ballpark.

The whole thing was the work of a goat keeper-turned-publicity hound. The hex angle only got legs from 1969 going forward. Meanwhile, we were only cursed by what I believed was sub-standard management that was finally fixed by the present Ricketts family ownership.

Top Chicago columnists Mike Royko and Dave Condon, regulars at a Billy Goat Tavern that moved across the street from the Wrigley Building on Michigan Avenue in 1964, began running humorous accounts of the curse. Sam Sianis, William's nephew who took over the bar upon William's death in 1970, actually shipped his goat to Wrigley Field in a limousine on July 4, 1973, when we held a first-place lead, but security guards barred the goat's entry. Condon wrote a Tribune column on the goat's arrival. The story simply gained more traction when we had a 6-29 pratfall in the rest of July through mid-August. We again did not finish first . . . and I did not win 20 for the first time in my career as a full-time starter.

Sam Sianis finally got his goat admitted to Wrigley Field on Opening Day 1982, first for new owner Tribune Company with yours truly on hand. That frigid day was the first time I crossed paths with a Sianis mascot. A good luck charm? I don't know about that, but I did go 6 2/3 shutout innings to beat the Mets, and later in the season I logged my 3,000th strikeout, but still no pennant as the Cubs finished fifth, at 73-89.

Sam Sianis brought the goat onto the field for the 1984 National League Championship Series, but apparently the animal helped only in Chicago; the Cubs blew a 2-0 advantage and the 5-game series altogether with 3 losses in a row in San Diego. Then, copycats entered the picture. A bunch of seminarians from Wisconsin enlisted Banks to admit their goat through the Wrigley Field wagon gates in right field to try to end a 12-game home losing streak in May, 1994. Amazingly, Steve Trachsel, whom I coached the next two years as a Cub, did just that with a 5-2 win over the Reds. Fans even brought their own goat to Houston's Minute Maid Park late in 2003 to supposedly jinx the Astros, competing in the NL Central race with the Cubs.

The brutal truth according to Chicago Daily News baseball writer Jack Kuenster was that, between 1945 and 1969, no sports scribe wrote about the 1945 curse to explain away the Cubs' long wanderings in baseball. William Sianis had alleged barfly Condon as his newspaper conduit going way back.

In a May 29, 1962 column, Condon detailed how Sianis tried to smuggle his goat into the top newsmaking venues in Chicago. Sianis followed up on the 1945 World Series by renting a hearse, after he was denied tickets, to get into the Republican National Convention at the South Side International Amphitheater in 1952.

"I rode in the back with my goat," Sianis told Condon. "A very good hearse, although my goat nearly died because it was so hot. We got to the Amphitheater, and I told a policeman, "Emergency! Emergency!" He opened the gates so we could put in the hearse, and right on the main floor I held up my goat so everyone could see it." Today, this might qualify as animal abuse.

Seven years later, in 1959, Sianis bought two tickets from White Sox owner Bill Veeck for the World Series against the Dodgers at old Comiskey Park. Veeck warned Sianis he knew the seat locations and thus to not sneak in the goat, but Sianis traded the tickets for ones in another location to admit the beast.

Veeck again found out, and vowed, "I'd never get the goat in again," said Sianis. "But I went to suburban Aurora and paid $150 to a helicopter pilot to drop me and my goat at second base just before the seventh game." T

hat seventh game was never played, with the Dodgers winning it all in Game 6.

In the column reference to the original 1945 incident, Sianis told of wiring Phil Wrigley after his ejection: "My goat wants to know who smells now."

Yet there was no mention of a curse, consistent with Kuenster's recollection. The hex simply developed a life of its own; too many people believed in it, too many media wrote about it; a beer company even used a goat on a commercial aired on Cubs telecasts.

But, once and for all, there was no curse and no connection to our team. If recent events haven't put it to bed, I'll close out the ninth as in my prime and retire it for good.

Once and for all, there was no curse.

It isn't the curse, but the team that lifelong fans remember, and painfully, as with Illinois Governor, Bruce Raunerwho watched us mostly on TV as a teenager at his north suburban Deerfield home.

"I still can't watch a Mets game," Rauner said. "The Mets drive me nuts. They overtook the Cubs. I was so depressed. My favorite memory was watching Ronnie (Santo) running down the left field line clicking his heels. Fergie Jenkins and Bill Hands and Ken Holtzman and Hundley. Billy Williams was my personal favorite. What a class guy, an incredible athlete. Center field and right field were not the same caliber. I didn't handle it well. I was emotionally scarred. I was 14, lived and breathed every game. The cratering that started in August. You started to get a bad vibe in August. It was so painful. We were the best team in baseball, no question. They just ran out of gas. The Mets got lucky."

Many similar sentiments to Rauner's about the 1969 race have been expressed in the last half-century. Baseball people not from Chicago simply did not get it.

I know the baseball mentality from having pitched more than 18 seasons. Players and managers live in the here-and-now. History is a nice sideline, but it cannot impede trying to win that day's game. If anything, our bunch was like a ghost team, always present around Wrigley Field. The ghosts sometimes would filter into the Cubs manager's office. The often-acerbic Jim Frey, my last manager in spring training 1984 before I retired, seemed bothered the most by references to 1969 . . . some 15 years later.

"To be asked questions about it (1969) on a daily basis is a waste of time," Frey said. "I wasn't here then. I didn't know the makeup of that Cub team. Nobody on this year's (1984) team gives a shit about 1969."

Then Frey employed the f-bomb to describe 1969. He used the magic word in so many other situations, it was like his introduction. But as manager and general manager, like so many others, Frey came and went from Wrigley Field.

But we're still here.

We did not get the big prize, yet we did something right in the masses' eyes. As we move along into our senior-citizenship, veterans of the 1969 team feel a special bond with each other and to that season. It is our un-severed umbilical cord to the *Cubs Experience*, to which we helped give birth.

The best example of the 1969 Cubs Experience came one night in August, 1989, at the Darien, Illinois, home of Doak Ewing, owner of the Rare SportsFilms firm. Ewing had discovered a kinescope – a film taken off a TV monitor – of the July 12, 1969 telecast of the NBC Game of the Week with Curt Gowdy and Tony Kubek. I pitched that humid afternoon against the Phillies at Wrigley Field, and won, sans a vintage performance. Once the Ewing find became known, George Castle arranged for Williams and Hundley to watch the kinescope shown on the wall of Ewing's apartment.

My batterymate never went off duty from 1969:

> *Watching plate ump Ed Sudol not call one of my sliders a strike, Hundley barked at the one-dimensional images of the ump and his 20-year-younger self.*
>
> *"How can you miss that pitch, for cryin' out loud?" the Rebel proclaimed.*
>
> *Then Gowdy described Hundley as the "youngest player rep in the majors."*
>
> *"Not for long," the present-day version of Hundley laughed.*
>
> *Regan relieved me on the kinescope. His pitches performed their telltale dip.*
>
> *"It was a little slider, a little cut fastball," Hundley said with a straight face.*
>
> *As the film proceeded, he clapped or pounded his fists together for every positive achievement on that flickering image, like it was happening for the first time. The 1969 and 1989 versions of Hundley were one and the same.*
>
> *Williams was not as demonstrative, as befitting of his personality. He was more analytical and reflective.*
>
> *"We're still friends today," he said. "We didn't win that year, but I guess we suffered together. We were all ready to really enjoy winning the pennant."*
>
> *Hundley admitted feeling melancholy as the kinescope wrapped up.*
>
> *"About the eighth inning, I started getting sad," he said. "I looked out on the field and saw we had a super ballclub. We didn't win the pennant."*

Three months later, after he engaged in a memorable hitter's duel with Will Clark in the NL Championship Series, it was Cubs Mark Grace's turn to peer back in time. All through the surprise "Boys of [then-manager Don] Zimmer" NL East title season in 1989, .314-hitting first baseman Grace and his teammates were peppered with questions about 1969 on its 20th anniversary – and its connection to the striving Cubs team of his current day. The first book about the 1969 Cubs, by former Chicago Tribune sportswriter Rick Talley, had just come out.

"I told them, 'Honest to God, I don't know what happened in 1969,'" Grace said at Ewing's apartment. 'I was 4-years old and living in St. Louis.'"

One of the first things that struck Grace was the change in field dimensions in Wrigley Field. The basket still was one season away in 1969. Grace was surprised to hear Bleacher Bums danced and tooted a bugle atop the leftfield wall.

"Fall onto the field?" he said, puzzled. "I think that basket was a good invention. It kept a ton of people healthy. There's some major brawls over home runs out there, and people would be spilling onto the field trying to get a ball going to the wall."

Grace's left-handed contact style would have been a challenge for me. He returned the compliment. I'd later be in the same clubhouse as Grace as pitching coach in 1995-1996.

"Sliders," he said of my 1969 black-and-white image. "I'm glad I'm not hitting. His stuff is nasty." But he claimed I balked on another pitch, due to a change of rules interpretation through the decades.

Grace also saw why Williams hit at a level higher than him.

"This is my first look at live coverage of Billy," he said of the man who served as his hitting coach for about half his Cubs career. "This is neat. He's never been so young. Nice stride. His swing was a little longer than mine and he can get more power into it."

After watching the kinescope, Grace was far more understanding than Frey of the continuing fascination with 1969.

"It gave me a chance to finally realize what the hype was all about," he said. "It gave me a chance to see what the fans were like on a mid-July day, with the fella' (pitcher Selma) out in the bullpen going crazy, getting the fans going. I think that's what helped the city fall in love with the Cubs in 1969. And it (enthusiasm) has been carried over. I think 1969 is a magical moment in Chicago history that will never die. It will be like No. 715 for Hank Aaron down in Atlanta. The fans will never forget it the rest of their lives, even if we go to a World Series."

I certainly appreciate "Gracie's" comments when he was a second-year big-leaguer. He was spot on, predicting the future 27 years going forward. I am thankful that one of the all-time Cubs from another era really got it.

We were winners as ballplayers with only the big prize in our sights.

"The 1969 Mets are wearing my World Series ring," said Kessinger.

We were never "lovable losers." Lovable, for sure. Many of us were matinee idols to one of the highest percentage of female fans in the majors . . . a big deal in that day. We gave the Cubs Universe a daily passion play. We were not cursed nor did we view our season fate that way. Instead, we're thankful to be a kind of Eternal Cubs.

Dirt from the fans...

"We'd arrive early by the bleachers and played catch on the streets bordering the park, waiting for the players to arrive to snag autographs. Fergie Jenkins was my favorite '69 Cub. Autographs had no monetary value to us. Just to have your hero's John Hancock was cool. I recall Jenkins would come out to acknowledge us on days he did not pitch."
-Jim Zenner, Morton Grove, Illinois

1969 Talent Jumped Through
Hoops To Land At Wrigley Field

We were very fortunate to enjoy the assemblage of talent in 1969 at Wrigley Field. Four Hall of Famers suited up – me, Ernie Banks, Billy Williams, and Ron Santo – more than any other Cubs team in history. We were all later voted in 1999 by fans as starters on the Cubs All-Century Team. Despite his considerable controversies in his entire career, the manager also made it to Cooperstown. A pair of 20-game winners, myself ,and Bill Hands, took the mound for one of the very few times in Cubs annals. We also fielded one of the top three shortstops in team history in Don Kessinger, and certainly one of the better catchers in Randy Hundley.

All converged in spite of the considerable obstacles of the post-war Cubs organization management, full of eccentricities and truth-is-stranger-than fiction moves that had the baseball world baffled. Fortunately, the franchise's most memorable team into the 21st century came together to re-establish the Cubs' appeal for even bigger and better things to come.

The 1969 Cubs were born out of three great signings in the 1950s, a trio of uncommonly adept trades, a tragedy that took away one great talent while bestowing another at second base and, a handful of more recent graduates from a farm system that never quite reached the level of baseball's most productive talent chains.

You might say the 1969 Cubs started their building process back on dusty fields in segregated Dallas in the late 1940s. A kid with a quick bat named Ernie Banks was noticed by Negro League legend Cool Papa Bell and signed by the Kansas City Monarchs. Army service interrupted Banks' fledgling baseball career from 1951 to 1953. After his discharge, Banks returned to the Monarchs, where he attracted the attention of big-league scouts.

A common story had Bill Veeck, then the financially-strapped owner of the St. Louis Browns, first on the trail of Banks. Veeck could not afford Monarchs owner Tom Baird's asking price, reportedly $30,000. Having grown up in the Cubs organization thanks to dynamic father and team president William L. Veeck Sr., the younger Veeck put the Cubs onto Banks. The White Sox ,and apparently the New York Yankees, also were aware of him, but the Cubs were quicker on the trigger, purchasing Banks' contract for $20,000 in early September, 1953. The payment was perhaps the greatest bargain in Cubs history. Banks became the Cubs' first African-American player, immediately taking over the regular shortstop job in the final weeks of 1953.

Escorting Banks to Wrigley Field for his signing was Monarchs Manager Buck O'Neil, who would make history himself, becoming the first black coach in the majors in 1962, also with the Cubs. He had already worked as a scout, touring through the African-American schools of the South, for a previous seven years. Buck's talent-procurement abilities and counsel played an unheralded factor in our 1969 fortunes.

Just as Banks was establishing himself as the National League's most dominant power hitter in the latter half of the 1950s, including back-to-back MVP awards in 1958 and 1959, outfielder Billy Williams began filtering his way to Chicago. He was signed for a song by scout Ivy Griffin in 1956 out of Whistler, Alabama, near Mobile. Oddly enough, O'Neil was not initially involved in Williams' procurement.

"Our scout went out to watch another boy," General Manager John Holland recalled for Chicago Tribune columnist David Condon. "Billy Williams, who was really filling in for his brother, caught the scout's eye and it was recommended we sign him."

Williams was actually brought into the organization, starting at Ponca City, Oklahoma, by the predecessor regime of Wid Matthews, prior to Holland's promotion to general manager after the 1956 season. He worked his way up to Double-A San Antonio by 1959. But Williams was put off by the rank Jim Crow discrimination in the historic Texas city and jumped the Missions to return home. Credit O'Neil with a big save. Holland dispatched O'Neil to reel Williams back into the fold. Buck showed Williams how much fun the kids had playing baseball at a local park in Whistler.

Williams returned to San Antonio without any penalty assessed by the front office. He was first called up to the Cubs in August, 1959. He finally stuck at Wrigley Field in September, 1960, after a season in Triple-A. In 1961, Williams won the NL Rookie of the Year award with a 25-homer output, making up a bit of the power loss when Banks dropped to 29 homers due to a knee injury.

Joining Williams in San Antonio in 1959 in his first pro season was Ron Santo. He already had a connection to Banks. While in high school in Seattle as a catcher, Santo was enthralled with watching Banks' slugging feats on the network Game of the Week telecasts on weekends. Despite higher bonus offers from other teams, Santo signed with the Cubs for about $18,500 in an attempt to make his dream of playing with Banks come true.

A natural hitter converted to third base in the pros, Santo's offensive output was regarded even more highly than that of Williams. When both were analyzed in spring training by Hall-of-Famer Rogers Hornsby, then a Cubs hitting coach, Williams and Santo were proclaimed the only two out of all minor leaguers who'd make it to the majors.

Santo also found out he suffered from Type 1 Diabetes as he broke into the pros. Keeping the diagnosis secret from the Cubs, Santo first tried to manage his disease via diet, but he had a fast track to the majors. Santo was keenly disappointed not making the team out of spring training under manager Charley Grimm in 1960. You could not keep this emotional man down. Still just 20, Santo made his debut in a doubleheader in Pittsburgh in June, 1960 and would hold down the third-base job for the next 13 ½ seasons.

When Santo enjoyed a breakthrough 99-RBI season in 1963, he pushed Banks – enduring a subpar year due to more physical problems – one spot down from the cleanup position which Santo locked up for the next seven years. Meanwhile, Williams took over the No. 3 spot. The eventual Hall-of-Famers would comprise the 3-4-5 hitters with only temporary lineup shifts all the way through 1969. Sometimes they were the only legit hitters in the lineup. Frustrated Cubs fans could only imagine how productive the trio could be if they'd been surrounded by more-productive talent.

But a .239-hitting rookie second baseman named Glenn Beckert, with just 30 RBI, often led off in 1965. Beckert, almost 30 years later my best man in my marriage to Lydia, took an unlikely route to the job. Holland recalled to Condon that the Cubs tried to sign Pittsburgh-native Beckert for a nominal bonus out of Allegheny College in 1961. Instead, the Red Sox snared then-shortstop Beckert. Boston did not protect Beckert in the November 26, 1962, minor-league draft. This time, the Cubs paid $8,000 to snare Beckert.

When Beckert's shortstop arm and range weren't perceived of big-league quality, fate sadly and suddenly intervened with the death of Cubs second baseman Kenny Hubbs, the 1962 NL Rookie of the Year. He died in a crash of his private plane just before spring training of 1964, and Beckert was immediately moved to second. Beckert dramatically improved to .283 in his second season in 1966, his inside-out swing and hit-and-run talents to right field a lineup staple at the No. 2 spot going into 1969.

After the mercurial Dominican Roberto Pena had fumbled away a ton of grounders at shortstop in the spring of 1965, the Cubs recalled 1964 signee Don Kessinger to take his place. A basketball and baseball star at Ole Miss, Kessinger and a high-school shortstop in the area were being considered by the Cubs. They chose right when Kessinger was offered $25,000 to sign. But the lean, lanky kid barely cracked the future Mendoza Line of batting averages at .201 in 1965. His career blossomed, though, when he learned how to switch-hit in 1966, boosting himself to .274. He was first used as leadoff man in 1966, helping Beckert set the table for Williams, Santo and Banks.

Another 1965 arrival was lefty Ken Holtzman, the Cubs' fourth-round pick out of the University of Illinois, earning about a $65,000 bonus in the inaugural 1965 draft. He made the Illini as a freshman in 1964 under coach Lee Eilbracht, impressing with his stuff from the outset. "My dad went up to the pitching coach and said, 'Don't teach him anything,'" Ann Eilbracht said of his father's initial impression of Holtzman at 18.

After only two months in the minors and still just 19, Holtzman was called up for several relief appearances in September. He threw batting practice to simulate a hard-throwing southpaw two hours before Sandy Koufax took the mound in Dodger Stadium on September 9, 1965. Holtzman's serves did not help much, though. Koufax threw a perfect game, the second time the Cubs were no-hit in three weeks.

A year later, Holtzman – pitching above his rookie 11-16 record, almost turned the tables on Koufax. On September 25, 1966, in Wrigley Field, Holtzman took his own no-hitter into the ninth before hanging on for a 2-1 victory.

With Holtzman and Kessinger already at the big-league level, Holland made a trio of trades that ranked as among the best in Cubs history, and certainly the top three in the general manager's checkered 19-year history at the Cubs' helm. The deals rounded out the nucleus of the '69 Cubs.

The first good move was dispatching outfielder Don Landrum and former closer Lindy McDaniel to the San Francisco Giants on November 2, 1965, for a well-regarded young battery – right-hander Bill Hands and catcher Randy Hundley.

"We could have made a deal for Hands much earlier in (1965), but decided to let him have more time at Tacoma," Holland said. "We were ready to deal for Hands when Leo came in as manager, and we arranged a more complicated swap. Actually, they didn't want to give up Hands, They offered other pitchers. We held out. (Giants manager) Herman Franks became sold on Landrum the day we sent Don in as a pinch hitter to beat the Giants with a homer."

Control-pitcher Hands shuttled between the rotation and bullpen in his first two seasons in 1966 and 1967, with a 2.46 ERA in the latter season. Hundley seized a wide-open catcher's job as a rookie, and hardly let go, with the exception of knee injuries the next seven seasons. Hundley, nicknamed the Rebel for his Virginia roots, could not bear to watch a game from the dugout. He caught tons of doubleheaders – probably to his detriment – by choice and set a big-league record with 160 games played in 1968. Taking note of Santo's status as team captain, lefty Rich Nye has said Hundley was the Cubs' real on-field leader.

I was up next in a blockbuster deal on April 21, 1966, less than two weeks into the season. My Philadelphia Phillies still regarded themselves as an NL contender in need of veteran starting pitching. Little did I know that the famed Fred Martin had noticed me in the Phillies chain, telling *As good a prospect as we could find.* Holland and Co. I was "as good a prospect as we could find" in the minors. Thus the Cubs knew about me for a while. Among other feats, Martin was Cubs pitching coach when the staff had a 3.08 ERA in 1963, second to the Koufax-Don Drysdale Dodgers. As Cubs minor-league pitching coordinator a decade later, Martin salvaged Hall-of-Famer Bruce Sutter's flagging career by teaching him his trademark split-fingered fastball. And he helped me with my breaking pitches during spring training.

Originally, the Cubs tried to pull another deal with the Giants, via talks in their opening 1966 series in San Francisco and when the Giants came to Chicago on April 19. Holland and Durocher stayed up until 2:00 A.M. in one instance talking to Franks. Unable to cut a deal, the management was all ears when Phillies General Manager John Quinn called them while the Giants were still in town on April 21. Seeking veteran starters to complement Jim Bunning and Chris Short, Quinn wanted 36-year-old Bob Buhl, a 13-game winner in 1965.

The Cubs sweetened the deal to get me, center fielder Adolfo Phillips and first baseman John Herrnstein. Holland threw in fellow veteran starter Larry Jackson, a 24-game winner in 1964.

"Sure, we were gambling in trading Jackson," Holland told Condon," but everything in baseball is a gamble. Jenkins was a relief pitcher for the Phils, but we did not have relief pitching in mind for a guy so strong."

Even after the trade was made, I stayed in the bullpen until August 25, getting a no-decision against the Pittsburgh Pirates. Fittingly, my first big-league win as a starter was against the Phillies at Wrigley Field on September 6, 1966, before just 3,218 fans. I retired 19 in a row from the first through the eighth while striking out 9 in a 7-2 victory.

Five-tool player Phillips had his moments in center, led by a 4-homer doubleheader burst on June 11, 1967, in Wrigley Field. But Phillips lost his job in spring training 1969 due to a broken hand, and was traded two months later, as less-regarded talents in Don Young and Jimmy Qualls earned playing time, almost by default, at our most unstable 1969 position.

The final big deal that shaped the 1969 Cubs was another April transaction, this time in 1968 with the Los Angeles Dodgers. Holland knew the bullpen in our breakthrough 1967 season was under par and he could not fix it in the offseason. But the Dodgers were breaking up their 1965-1966 pennant winners. Available was Phil "The Vulture" Regan, slapped with his avian nickname for swooping down to snatch starters' victories in the late innings via a 14-1 record in '66. Regan picked up where he left off, winning NL Fireman of the Year honors for us in 1968 before taking on a similar heavy workload the next season.

Holland and Dodgers General Manager Buzzie Bavasi talked shop in spring training, 1968, and Regan's supposed arthritis put a hold on the deal. So Bavasi looked at sometimes 1967 Cubs right fielder Ted Savage in the proposed swap. If he lost Savage, Holland needed a right handed-hitting replacement. Bavasi was not with the team when they played us in Scottsdale in the spring, so Holland asked Vin Scully, probably the greatest baseball announcer in history, for a scouting report. Scully said veteran Jim Hickman, ticketed for demotion to Triple-A, probably could be had.

On April 23, 1968, Holland and Bavasi finally shook on the deal, and Hickman – an original 1962 New York Met – was dissuaded from quitting due to the short detour to Triple-A. Hickman was soon called up to the Cubs, spent the next season-plus as a spare part in the outfield, and then took off like a rocket in August 1969 with 10 homers that month. Over the next several seasons, the Gentleman from Tennessee proved one of the best clutch hitters in Cubs history. Meanwhile, Regan plugged up a bullpen hole with 25 saves, winning NL Fireman of the Year honors in 1968. Regan started out equally effective in 1969, but eventually, I believe, was overworked by Durocher.

The trio of trades that brought me, Hands, Hundley, Regan and Hickman rounded out the core of the 1969 Cubs. They were by far Holland's best trades.

Given the combination of Wrigley and Holland as the one-two men on the management food chain, we were lucky to have assembled a pennant contender going into 1969. But we did not have the additional necessary talent – an impact outfielder, another young position player knocking on the door, nor adequate pitching depth – to go further, given the direction of the Cubs.

Early in his tenure, Holland became a proponent of making trades to build a team. He was an enthusiastic dealer, including with the archrival St. Louis Cardinals, who – from the 1980s onward – rarely transacted business with the Cubs. Loyalty and fealty, as with Holland's relationship with Wrigley, kept many on the job.

"Many of the scouts wanted to please John Holland," said 1969 Traveling Secretary Blake Cullen, who was gradually evolving into a de facto assistant general manager. "Everybody had to be loyal to the organization. John could be intimidating in person. He could get irritated and mean. You'd be afraid of telling him, 'You're full of shit.' We didn't have too many guys being contrary to him."

Plenty of "what-ifs" surround 1969. We launched an all-time memorable season with a powerful front line, but also with holes in two outfield positions and the 7th through 10th pitchers on our staff. What we didn't know until it was too late is we could not afford to go wire-to-wire with those holes.

Building Blocks

I would not recommend a player go through a 103-loss season when he is looking up at all the other nine teams in the National League. There's only so much that can be said for character-building.

Numbers don't always tell the entire story in baseball, the ultimate numbers game. The first Cubs team on which I played in 1966 may have made Leo Durocher's first prediction, "This is not an eighth-place team," comically inaccurate. I arrived in an April 21, 1966 trade from the Philadelphia Phillies amid an orgy of losing. Yet by August, the first embryonic seeds of a contending team were firmly planted.

I got a taste of starting-pitching dominance while numerous teammates were placed in lineup positions in which they would thrive for years to come. We may have finished in 10th place with 103 losses for the second time in five seasons. Yet, with gathering confidence and the feeling that Durocher gave us respectability, we had gotten the franchise out of the rut in which it existed.

That better feeling, along with tastes of success, carried over to our breakthrough season in 1967 that truly energized Cubs fans. That was another building block. And after a big pratfall near the midpoint of the 1968 season, we recovered our equilibrium in July that carried over directly into the positive start of 1969.

Then and now, I could say I was fortunate Durocher insisted on throwing former 24-game-winner Larry Jackson, the Cubs' 1966 Opening Day starter, into the deal built around right-hander Bob Buhl, to assure he'd land me, Adolfo Phillips and John Herrnstein. Although I was originally a Phillie and made my debut on September 10, 1965, I felt I could have been called up a year earlier and maybe could have helped prevent the Phillies' infamous season-ending collapse under manager Gene Mauch, as they would finish 1 game behind the eventual world-champion St. Louis Cardinals.

I hit the ground running and doing a home-run trot in my first Cubs game on Saturday, April 23, 1966, against the vaunted Los Angeles Dodgers at Wrigley Field. The Cubs had started 1-8 in Durocher's managerial debut and looked totally lost. They needed a spark from anywhere. Lefty starter Bob Hendley, who lost 1-0 and allowed just one hit in Sandy Koufax's perfect game on September 9, 1965, had allowed 5 hits and 4 walks in the first 2 2/3 innings. Somehow, none of the baserunners had scored. Durocher, who had a quick hook with his starters in 1966, summoned me with the bases loaded and 2 outs. I got out of the jam by inducing shortstop John Kennedy to fly to right.

I settled down to keep the Dodgers at bay. But somehow, I knew how to make I made my entrance even grander and somehow talked about for decades to come. In my second at-bat in the bottom of the fifth, I homered off future Hall-of-Famer Don Sutton, who began a four-year track of bad luck against the Cubs. Then, in my next at-bat in the seventh, I singled in batterymate Randy Hundley, who had singled and advanced to second on a bunt. Fergie Jenkins 2, Dodgers 0.

I'd pitch one more inning, finishing with a yield of 4 hits while striking out 3. Durocher figured I had enough excitement for the afternoon, and I admitted I was gassed, so he summoned closer Ted Abernathy to work the ninth. I sweated out my first Cubs win as Abernathy put on the tying runs with 1 out before finishing it. Between starting the game and throwing 8 shutout innings, my introduction to the Cubs Universe could have hardly been more pleasing.

I enjoyed reading about my debut. My full name, Ferguson Arthur Jenkins, was too long for most published descriptions, so I quickly was referred to by my nickname, Fergie. However, for years to come, the Chicago Tribune could not get the spelling right, going with "Fergy," which was okay as long as they got the score, my pitching line and my quotes right.

⚾ ⚾ ⚾ ⚾

Prior to arriving in Chicago, I had the image of being a relief pitcher, from the way the Phillies had used me. I had finished 6 of the 7 games (2-1 record) in which I had appeared in 1965. Yet, in my minor-league background, I also had success as a starter, which the Cubs had picked up on. Early in my Cubs tenure, Durocher came out to left field one day as I was shagging fly balls during batting practice and queried me about the starting-relieving issue. My long-relief appearance and overall stuff had put the idea in the back of his mind that I might be able to be in his rotation in the near future.

And 'Leo The Lip,' as he was known, left that door open when he told reporters after my debut: "Don't say I won't start him, though. You may be wrong." He'd eventually be right, but he also revealed a part of my repertoire that I swear I did not throw. For some reason, Durocher claimed I threw a few knuckleballs against the Dodgers.

I subsequently gave the curious reporters a quick biography of myself and my family, such as being forced to give up hockey by the Phillies and my father's work as a chef at the William Pitt Hotel in Chatham, Ontario. Meanwhile, I'm fortunate Chicago Tribune beat writer Richard Dozer did not jinx my career when he wrote of that outing, "If it turns into a lingering saga of baseball exploits, 6,974 fans can always tell their grandchildren, 'I was there on the day Jenkins first pitched for the Cubs.'"

20-win seasons and Hall-of-Fame exploits were not really on anyone's minds. Winning a job was paramount as the Cubs' losing ways hit rock bottom. Durocher was almost working from a blank slate as the 1966 Cubs fell 30 games under .500 (25-55) by July 7. He was in the middle of "backing up the truck," his tried-and-true phrase for getting rid of players held over from the previous regime that he did not want. When hired on October 25, 1966, he vowed to get the best of any trade he and General Manager John Holland would agree to make. That was impossible, but Durocher's brashness and braggadocio were just what the somnolent franchise needed.

Backup catcher Chris Krug, a 1965 holdover, was banished by Durocher by mid-season because the manager for some reason suspected he was trying to get the phone number of Alison Wrigley, the first wife of Bill Wrigley, son of owner Phil Wrigley. Krug was spied chatting with Alison, sitting in the first row, while catching a pitcher who was warming up in the bullpen along the leftfield line. Durocher called a team meeting to denounce Krug, claiming in his colorful life he had sex in any number of situations, but never with the owner's wife.

A Krug replacement working behind Hundley was 6-foot-5 catcher Don Bryant. Paired with September call-up Rich Nye, Bryant insisted the rookie clear out of their hotel room for a few hours' bloc of time.

"He said, 'Hey, rook, I got a date tonight, find something else to do,'" recalled Nye.

So Bryant, called up in mid-July, got into just 13 games. And after he departed for the Giants' organization at the start of the 1967 season, he did not see the big leagues until resurfacing as an Astros backup in 1969.

Meanwhile, George Altman finished out his final full Cubs season in 1966. Plagued by injuries, the fan, team favorite, and once a productive lefty-hitting run producer and All-Star in 1961 and 1962, could never get untracked in his second tour in Wrigley Field. As a Cubs newcomer, I was sometimes mistaken for Altman. We were almost the same height and, of course, the same skin color.

Other shopworn veterans briefly on the roster as pinch hitters were 1965 Phillies Wes Covington and Frank Thomas. The latter had gained undue notoriety in the City of Brotherly Love for a batting-practice fight with star slugger Dick Allen, my former minor-league roommate.

The pitching staff was something else though. Durocher ran through 23 pitchers in that lost season. The eventual Big Three of 1969 – me, Ken Holtzman and Bill Hands – were green rookies then. But Holtzman, as promising a lefty as existed in baseball in 1966, wasn't even with the Cubs full time in April and May. Holtzman had an arrangement with the University of Illinois-Chicago to continue his classes on weekdays, then join the Cubs for weekend series. Holtzman had been drafted off the University of Illinois' Champaign campus after his sophomore year in 1965. Hands was shuttled between the rotation and bullpen.

Veterans Dick Ellsworth and Ernie Broglio still held rotation spots opening the season. Only three years after his 22-victory, 2.11-ERA peak season, lefty Ellsworth allowed 31 unearned runs while permitting 321 hits in 269 innings. He tied a Cubs record with 22 losses, compared to just 8 victories. Even with some of the downer numbers, Ellsworth had more than his fair share of tough luck on a tail-ender team.

Meanwhile, Broglio was finally full-time in the rotation after his elbow "locked" in his hotel room in New York on the morning of August 23, 1964. When roomie Joey Amalfitano heard Broglio complain of being "locked," he jokingly tossed the pitcher the room key to remedy the situation. Broglio would require elbow surgery in November, 1964, and tried to come back too quickly the following spring.

He was barely a batting-practice pitcher in brief appearances in 1965. Broglio finally had a decent spring training under Durocher in 1966, making the rotation out of camp in Long Beach, California. But the damage to his elbow and control had been done. Broglio was 2-6 with a 6.35 ERA in 15 games (11 starts). He was released July 6, his career over at age 30.

Other pitching teammates included lefty Curt Simmons, a former Phillies "Whiz Kid" of 1950, and Chuck Estrada, an ex-"Baby Bird" on the Baltimore Orioles. Future two-time Cubs pitching coach Billy Connors got into 11 games (7.31 ERA) in relief, proving you don't always have to "do" in order to "teach."

On July 13 though, Simmons would be re-united with his fellow "Whiz Kid" mound star. After being waived by the Houston Astros, Holland signed future Hall-of-Famer Robin Roberts as a combo fifth starter-assistant pitching coach. Springfield, Illinois native, Roberts was supposed to supplement efforts of Durocher's pitching coach, "Fat Freddie" Fitzsimmons, with "counsel." Roberts' arrival and addition to the coaching brainpower quotient was part of a mini-shakeup. Former Durocher-era Brooklyn Dodger "Pistol" Pete Reiser was also promoted from Double-A Dallas-Fort Worth to work as batting coach.

As for me, I found myself benefiting greatly from Roberts' arrival. Our pitching styles were somewhat similar. Like Roberts, I was a control pitcher who served up more homers than average, but they did not hurt either of us because we did not issue free passes in front of the clouts. Roberts' advice was not only welcome, but timely, as Durocher was about to allow me to make a great leap forward.

Even on a team where the rotation was somewhat in flux and pitchers were moving in and out via the Durocher-truck-in-reverse, I was deemed too valuable to just come out of the bullpen for long outings. Five weeks after my arrival, I got two consecutive starts. On May 29, 1966, I went 8 1/3 innings, giving up 2 runs with 9 strikeouts in a no-decision. Four days later, on June 2, I'd suffer what would be an uncommon loss against my old team in Philadelphia. I yielded 5 runs and 5 walks with just a lone strikeout in 6 1/3 innings. After that, I was back in the bullpen for almost all games until the season's dog days. By mid-August, Durocher began tossing around his early-season suggestion that I could be a starting pitcher.

I was deemed too valuable to just come out of the bullpen for long outings.

A year later, in 1967, he recalled, "I told him to go sit in the bullpen for three days and not move, and on the fourth day I went up to him and said, 'Here's the ball, you're a starting pitcher now.'"

On August 25, against the New York Mets at Wrigley Field, I was in the rotation to stay for the rest of my career. In our six weeks together, Roberts had advised me well as I would allow just 1 earned run in 8 1/3 innings in a no-decision. Then I racked up another no-decision in Atlanta on August 29, also in 8 1/3 innings with a 2-run yield, as Roberts recorded his final big-league victory with 2 innings in relief in the eventual 4-2, 14-inning Cubs victory.

I finally got my first Cubs win as a starter on September 6 in Wrigley Field with what would fortunately become a familiar line for me – 8 1/3 innings and 2 runs allowed, with 9 strikeouts. The Phillies were the opponents, and I was certainly motivated to show them they had let a good one go. In coming years, I'd have gone all the way in the 7-2 victory, but Durocher did not yet have a bead on my endurance and psyche. He called on lefty Hendley to nail down the final two outs.

I'd go on to a 4-2 record in my September starts and now Durocher did not have to worry about one rotation spot. The only downer was Roberts, as knowledgeable about pitching as anyone with 286 career victories, did not get along with Durocher. He was released after the season and was not offered the pitching coach's job for 1967.

Durocher's other decisions that molded us were less conflict-ridden. As I entered the rotation, the top five positions of our lineup were locked down for years to come. Finding himself as a switch-hitter, Kessinger hit around .300 in the second half of 1966. With Phillips out of the lineup in mid-August, Durocher needed a leadoff man, selecting the slender shortstop, who had typically batted eighth. He now batted in front of Beckert, who had a breakout season with 188 hits, a .287 average and 59 RBI on just 1 homer. When Phillips returned to centerfield, Durocher dropped him to eighth due to his prodigious strikeout totals. Phillips did steal 30 bases in 1966, but the manager no doubt believed the thefts were less effective if you couldn't steal first base.

You could flip to another side of the coin, though, with Kessinger's promotion to leadoff man. While a faster-than-average baserunner, Kessinger was no prolific base stealer – he could typically get 10 to 15 steals, but was no master thief. We had lost Brock in that infamous trade two years earlier. The lack of the ability to manufacture runs beyond the newly perfected Kessinger-Beckert hit-and-run tactic would take something away from us at the top of the lineup for years to come. Durocher had been an aggressive manager on the base paths in his previous managerial incarnations. But from about 1968 onward, he was a station-to-station skipper.

After a 9-22 July, the more stable lineup and rotation permitted us to begin coalescing into a competitive team. We were 27-30 in August and September, losing our final 2 games in St. Louis in October. The fans weren't yet sold, though.

"When you looked up in the stands, all you saw were vendors. You didn't see fans," observed Nye, getting his first taste of Wrigley Field as a last-month call-up. The Chicago Sun-Times ran a Joe Kordick photo of the sea of empty box seats behind the Cubs dugout with the caption: "Seventy-seven of the 530 paying customers are shown in first-inning shot. Of course, some figures are hard to distinguish, and it might be easier to count the empty seats. There were 36,114 of them."

A far bigger crowd – 21,659, excellent for a September Sunday – showed up for Holtzman's next start on September 25. The big draw was Koufax and the Los Angeles Dodgers, battling their archrival San Francisco Giants in another frantic pennant-race finish. The dramatic outcome proved we could play with anyone.

The Holtzman-Koufax duel ended up the only time they were matched against each other. The duel was set up by Koufax's start pushed back one day due to Yom Kippur, the most holy day in Judaism, taking place on September 24. Holtzman was often compared to Koufax, not only because of his also being Jewish, but also because of his own good fastball.

"I understood the media trying to compare us and it was certainly flattering," Holtzman recalled. "But Sandy was a one-of-a-kind pitcher.

"I wasn't nervous once the game started, but I was a little anxious the night before," Holtzman recalled. "I was extremely apprehensive about finally getting to bat against him, however. I was going to see that blazing fastball up close!"

Amazingly, Holtzman out-pitched Koufax as the innings piled up. He allowed just a third-inning walk to Dick Schofield, who was wiped out by a double play. And he had been given a 2-0 lead in the first on a Beckert triple and an error.

The home crowd and the Cubs broadcasters were excited going into the ninth. Holtzman had not allowed a hit. But Schofield broke up the no-no with a single to center. A walk and Maury Wills' single helped break the shutout with one out. With the winning run on base, Durocher let Holtzman go lefty-lefty against Willie Davis, who wound up lining out to Beckert for an unassisted double play, nailing down the memorable 2-1 victory.

Koufax and the Dodgers would go on to the World Series, but we went into the offseason knowing we were no longer patsies, no longer Bad News (Baby) Bears. Durocher told me, Holtzman, Nye, and Hands would compete for the rotation spots in 1967. Motivation to improve on a good base was a priority going into a new season. Durocher and Holland largely went with the young talent on hand.

Durocher later would have little confidence in young pitchers. But for his Opening Day starter on Tuesday, April 11, 1967, against the Phillies, 'The Lip' picked me, despite just 12 big-league starts so far. Writers noted that I had just 196 *innings* in the big leagues going up against fellow future Hall-of-Famer Jim Bunning with his 175 *victories* and a perfect game to his credit.

"The inning vs. victory comparison dramatizes Jenkins, 24-year-old gangling Canadian right-hander, as one of the chief new props in the Cubs' youth program," wrote the Chicago Tribune's Ed Prell.

The Cubs had not yet totally flushed away remnants of their College of Coaches and pre-Durocher era players. My Opening Day batterymate was Dick Bertell, the regular catcher from 1961-64, subbing for an injured Hundley. Infielder-outfielder Jimmy Stewart and pitchers Bob Hendley and Cal Koonce were still on the roster. A Sixties sized-opener crowd of just more than 16,000 was in the house, held down somewhat by frigid temperatures.

It was not easy to sleep the night before, having learned of the Opening Day assignment only on Sunday. Managers typically did not announce their first-game pitchers weeks ahead of time in spring training back in the day. I stayed up until 1:00 a.m. watching TV, trying to keep busy.

I'd get further inspiration from the presence of my parents, Deloris and Ferguson Jenkins, Sr., watching me play in the majors for the first time. I revealed to the media that my mother was almost fully blind with just 4 percent vision in one eye and 6 percent in the other. She probably could not see the baseline coaches, but she surely soaked up the positive atmosphere, despite being bundled up.

My mom and dad picked the right game to scout me. In a pattern that I would be fortunate to establish for much of my career, I got stronger as the game went along, locking down the Phillies once I got a 4-2 lead. I finished with a 6-hitter and the praise of Durocher, but I knew I still had a lot to prove under the circumstances.

"I said to myself that if I was going to prove I was a starting pitcher, now was the time," I told reporters afterward. I also posed for photos with my mother kissing me and my father proudly beaming.

Two new features were evident at the '67 opener. The National Anthem now would be sung before each game, as a patriotic nod to the ongoing war in Vietnam. And a new organ manned by Jack Kearney would entertain fans from its perch in the football press box above third, from which General Manager Holland also watched games.

And there'd be no sad-sack start as in 1966. We finally emerged with a winning record in May. Although I initially bumped along at .500, Holtzman was sizzling. He was 5-0 with a 2.33 ERA on May 20 at Wrigley Field, after winning a *statement game*. We got notice all throughout baseball by thumping the defending NL champion Dodgers, 20-3.

We got notice all throughout baseball by thumping the defending NL champion.

Ace Don Drysdale hoisted a white-towel-wrapped bat in his dugout as he and his teammates mockingly shouted, "We surrender now!"

For good measure, Beckert slashed an inside-the-park homer while newly acquired right fielder Ted Savage stole home. The only downer was Holtzman's departure after the game for six months of National Guard duty at Fort Polk, Louisiana. Amid the Vietnam draft, age-eligible athletes typically avoided active duty and possible combat by enlisting in the National Guard or for Army Reserve duty. As a result, they often missed weeks or more at a time during the season rather than being lost for an entire season for full-blown military service, as took place with Ted Williams and later Willie Mays 15 years earlier during the Korean War, as well as many platoons of star players during World War II.

Still another landmark event which convinced fans that the bad days were receding was Phillips' career afternoon during a Sunday, June 11, doubleheader at Wrigley Field. Five-tool Phillips, who had come over with me in the trade with the Phillies 14 months earlier, slugged a homer in the opener while we beat the New York Mets, 5-3. Savage stole home again while I batted, but moments later Phillips had his only failure of the long afternoon, knocking himself silly for a second in his own unsuccessful steal attempt of home.

Then, amid a massive slugfest in the nightcap, Phillips belted 3 homers out of the 7 the Cubs clouted in an 18-10 victory.

Broadcaster and Cubs voice Jack Brickhouse tried to top his own signature "Hey! Hey!" call on each Phillips homer.

Adding two great catches, Phillips had the nearly 20,000 fans eating out of his hands as they repeatedly chanted, "Ole! Ole!" as if he was a dashing matador. He raised his hands over his head in salute to the fans, who up to that point never had a Latin hero in Cubs pinstripes. Phillips was so thrilled with his unforgettable day he actually told reporters afterward he was just fine with batting eighth. Unfortunately, nothing ever approached June 11, 1967 again for Phillips and he would not be a central part of our most memorable season as a group.

Very soon we took off and set up another building block toward 1969. With a 29-26 record on June 15, we ripped off 16 wins in our next 19 games to tie the Cardinals for first place. The fans began making Wrigley Field appointment viewing in person or on TV. Almost 32,000 showed up for a Sunday doubleheader with the Houston Astros, an unattractive draw. But weekday crowds doubled from 1966's modest totals. Finally, one of the most astounding scenes in Wrigley Field history took place Sunday, July 2, when I mastered the Cincinnati Reds 4-1 for my 11th victory against five losses. I was glad I conserved my effort on the mound with a 3-hitter in just two hours, seven minutes. On the bases, I had a workout with an RBI triple to dead center and a double.

The main story was the crowd. Some 10,000 were turned away as some 40,000 packed the park. All tickets, including standing room, were sold a half-hour before the game. In a preview of a daily sight a generation later, many rooftops across Waveland and Sheffield avenues, affording clean looks into the park, were jammed with well-connected rooters.

Fans ran onto the field after the final out. I needed a cordon of Andy Frain ushers guarding my back to reach the clubhouse in the left-field corner as the fans romped all around me. They were overjoyed by a simple fact: the Cubs had temporarily seized first place this late in the season for the first time since 1945. None of the mob left the ballpark, chanting for the grounds crew to lift the Cubs flag to the top of the pole when news of the St. Louis loss reached the ballpark.

"Look at 'em, 40,000 people and they won't leave," exclaimed Hundley. Phillips, Boccabella, and Joe Niekro all squeezed into the clubhouse doorway leading to the field, gaping at the sight of the crowd that refused to go home.

The Cardinals beat the Mets though in the nightcap, forging a deadlock for the NL lead. We won still another game in Atlanta the next night, preserving the tie. Even though baseball is cyclical, and we'd go on to lose 9 of the next 10 games on a punishing road trip, the country was excited by Chicago baseball. Meanwhile, crosstown, the pitch-and-putt White Sox under 'Durocher-lite' manager Eddie Stanky led the American League. TV talent-meister Ed Sullivan suggested he'd bring his popular Sunday night show to Chicago if the Cubs and Sox squared off in the World Series.

Meanwhile, a future Cubs figure cut himself a piece of our new-found celebrity out at Candlestick Park. Twelve-year-old Pat Hughes and brother John, three years older, were both baseball fanatics living down the freeway in San Jose and had made a habit of trying to sneak into the visitors' locker room whenever they made a visit with their father, a college professor. When the Cubs came to Candlestick for a Sunday, July 16, doubleheader, with Durocher in a dour mood due to the post-July 3 slump, the brothers found a weak spot and slipped through the door.

"Invariably, the guard said take a hike, get lost," recalled Pat Hughes. "We'd head back to our seats. We were not bad kids, we just wanted to hang out. After batting practice this day, we got the idea we might be able to sneak into the clubhouse and follow players like we were their kids or hide behind their bodies. We did just that."

"The first person we see was Ernie Banks. He could not have been nicer. He had his big beautiful smile and said, 'Nice to see you.' We could see how strong his wrists were. We were enough of fans to know that was his reputation. Then we wandered into the clubhouse. We saw Billy Williams having coffee and the paper. He was reading about his game the day before in Los Angeles against the Dodgers. We asked Billy what's it like hitting Don Drysdale, what to think about Juan Marichal. He was friendly, but not as much as Ernie."

"Finally, after about five or six questions, Billy asked, 'How did you guys get in? Who's your father?' John said our dad is a professor at San Jose State. Billy did not look overly impressed by his academic status. I still laugh with Billy because anytime he could have blown our cover, and he was nice enough to not get rid of us. I did see Ron Santo across the room. He actually looked kind of scary. Huge, big legs and arms. His uniform was tight. He looked almost like a bear in uniform."

But the gig was soon up for the Hughes boys. "We also saw Leo Durocher. He came around a corner, and was kind of frowning. He looked like he was in a bad mood and we skedaddled shortly."

Hughes did marvel at the talent on the field, though. The Cubs and Giants each had four future Hall-of-Famers on their rosters. Maybe the Hughes boys were our good-luck charm that day in the City by the Bay. The Cubs swept the doubleheader, but those were not the most impactful Cubs wins Hughes ever witnessed. After teaming for 21 seasons with Santo in the Cubs' radio booth, Hughes earned the all-time distinction as the only Chicago broadcaster to ever call Cubs World Series championship-clinching wins on November 2 and 3, 2016. He also has served longer continuously than any other full-time Cubs radio announcer.

The sweep, meanwhile, touched off another hot streak – 8 wins in 9 games going into a showdown at Busch Stadium on Monday, July 24. Phillies expatriate Culp survived a muddy mound and an hour-long rain delay to stifle the Cardinals 4-1. We were again tied for first place. Many dared to dream the impossible dream as Red Sox fans did the same season in Boston and the momentum soon stopped. The Cardinals got hot, winning 5 of the next 6 against us through the first week of August, and soon had a 10-game lead. The archrivals swept a 3-game series in mid-August in St. Louis for the icing on their cake. The fans still were hyped even as we dropped to third place. During the greatest marathon schedule in my career – four consecutive doubleheaders at Wrigley Field over the Labor Day weekend in 1967 – good crowds turned out. On Labor Day, September 4, with the Dodgers in town, despite our standing 12 games behind, many cheered when the Pirates scored in their doubleheader sweep over the Cardinals, fantasizing we could rally for the pennant.

The re-charged fans, enjoying the team's most successful season since 1945, had a rooting interest in Holtzman's unique return. Holtzman was given weekend leaves from Texas' Fort Sam Houston's National Guard six-month commitment to pitch for the Cubs, starting August 13. The team arranged for a catcher to work with Holtzman in his off-hours to get his arm back into shape. He did not disappoint, winning 4 more games without a loss, including one of the spree of doubleheader contests on September 3. Again, Holtzman was the talk of the town with a 9-0 record and 2.53 ERA even with his fractured season.

Fortunately, we played competitively and finished with an astounding 28-game improvement over 1966. Meanwhile, I reached the coveted 20-win mark for the first time on September 29 with a 4-1 win over the Reds in Cincinnati's Crosley Field.

Owner Phil Wrigley was ecstatic over the greatest season-to-season improvement by the Cubs since the 1920s, handing out generous raises in the offseason. Fans began dreaming of a pennant in 1968. They had been waiting unfulfilled for decades and finally seemed to have a team racing toward the light at the end of the tunnel.

Other young pitchers joined me and Holtzman in dramatic improvements. Nye was 13-10 as a rookie. Shuttling between the rotation and the bullpen, Hands sported a team-leading 2.46 ERA. After making the Cubs as a non-rostered player and not starting a game until May 24, Joe Niekro was a surprise 10-7 with a 3.34 ERA. Culp acquitted himself well despite a losing record, while stocky Bill Stoneman was impressive in late relief.

Durocher, though, did not like Culp's propensity for full counts. Allowing just 3 runs in 36 innings going into his clutch victory over the Cardinals July 24 was not enough to lock in the manager's loyalty. So with other young pitchers establishing themselves, Culp was shipped off to Boston in the offseason for obscure hitter Bill Schlesinger, a move that would not bode well for us.

Our lineup seemed solid for the future, factoring in expected maturity from Phillips, who tailed off in the second half after his late-spring power outburst. But one gaping hole remained – right field. Rather than promote from within, the Cubs went outside to get a player Holland had been familiar with. "Sweet Lou" Johnson had originally come up with the Cubs in 1960, playing his way onto the team after a sensational spring. But he was traded the next year to the Braves, and wandered throughout baseball until the Dodgers brought him up in 1965 to replace an injured Tommy Davis in left field. Johnson turned out to be a clutch hitter and great clubhouse guy for back-to-back pennant winners and got the only hit in the famed Sandy Koufax-Bob Hendley all-time pitching duel that concluded with Koufax's perfect game in 1965.

Trading promising infielder Paul Popovich – a move opposed by Kessinger and Beckert – to LA for Johnson, the Cubs thought they had the missing piece of a real contender with Johnson, a 33-year-old journeyman, but the deal went bad after Johnson had another great spring training. Normally an affable guy described as "baseball's leading smiler" by Chicago Sun-Times columnist Bill Gleason, Johnson said decades later that African-American players in the Sixties had to hold their tongues about controversial topics, such as civil rights, for fear of endangering their livelihoods. The assassination of Dr. Martin Luther King, Jr. on April 4, 1968 was too much for Johnson as we arrived in Cincinnati five days later for the season opener, delayed as the country mourned King.

Johnson and Hundley were in a hotel elevator together. Already incensed, Johnson was put off by Randy's Virginia drawl. Not realizing that Hundley was totally absent of prejudice, dealing with me and other black Cubs, Johnson exploded in anger. Although Johnson became the regular right-fielder off the bat, he never found his stroke, hitting .244 with 1 homer, and he did not mesh with Durocher, either.

ᔕ ᔕ ᔕ ᔕ ᔕ

My own 1968 season debut was delayed until the second game, as Niekro took the ball in the opener. I was injured falling off a horse when I went riding with Santo during spring training in Arizona, (agitating Durocher to no end). Fortunately, I healed by the time the season began.

Attempting to get their minds off King's death and the resulting riots that devastated Chicago's West Side, nearly 34,000 showed up for our April 13 home opener, the largest first-day Wrigley Field crowd since 1946. The 1967 turnaround carried right over into the fans' pre-game demonstrations. Santo and Banks were loudly cheered as they launched batting-practice homers.

As we came back out onto the field for infield practice, the leftfield bleachers, populated by an unorganized band soon to be known as the Bleacher Bums, chanted "We're Number 1!"

None of the bleacher fans seemed upset that their admission charge increased to $1 from 75 cents in 1967, reflecting the new popularity of the Cubs and the owners' offseason pay raises to the overachievers.

A self-identified loyal South Sider and White Sox fan, columnist Gleason, noticed the sea change in his April 14 Sunday column: "Wrigley Field Now "In" Place To Be" was the headline that drew in readers. He wrote how the town had shifted to the Cubs after the White Sox had an overall 16-year attendance advantage.

"At 11:15 a.m., there were more spectators in the seats and aisles of Wrigley Field than the 7,000-plus who watched the White Sox open against Cleveland (on Wednesday, April 10)," wrote Gleason.

He described how Andy Frain ushers and Burns security men did not prevent younger fans from crowding the box seats to watch batting practice close-up and yell for our autographs:

"Somebody in the Cubs organization understands that those kids jamming against the railing, waving scorecards, banners, and signs, generate enthusiasm. Their interest is infectious and it convinces adults that Wrigley Field is the place to be. After all, if teenagers appreciate baseball, it has to be the "in" thing…This Cubs team and the kids belong to one another."

Not everyone under 18 in the Cubs backyard was sold. Then-Bleacher Bum Jay Vershbo, in the spring of 1968, a sophomore at Mather High School, five miles northwest of the ballpark, recalled how seemingly only a small group of he and his chums were caught up in the growing mania for the team. Mather's middle-class and upper middle-class teenagers "would rather watch hair grow than a triple into the right-field corner," as Gleason termed the stereotype of late 1960s young people believing baseball was slow, old-fashioned and out of date. "Sex, drugs and rock 'n roll," was the tag line for the youth culture's prevailing interests at the time. So was an anti-establishment protest attitude. Both applied to Vershbo's Cubs-apathetic classmates. Even with the distractions of a non-baseball youth culture, enough kids jumped on our bandwagon to became paying customers, building the Cubs into a 2 million-, then 3 million-strong gate attraction over the next four decades.

Unfortunately, we did not give the counter-culture crowd much impetus to switch to traditionalism in that first half of 1968. Our lineup sputtered, its collective performance worsening in what would be termed the "Year of the Pitcher," in which baseball-wide offensive production dropped precipitously.

Perhaps the toughest-luck example was my astounding five defeats by 1-0 scores amid amazing shutout streaks by fellow future Hall-of-Famers. One loss was to the Dodgers' Don Drysdale during his then-record 58-inning scoreless skein. Another was to archrival Gibson, who hurled 13 shutouts out of his 22 victories, smack dab in the middle of his own 47-inning blanking spree that was the impetus to his record-low 1.12 season ERA. Gibson, in fact, had a stretch of 99 innings where he gave up just 2 earned runs and had two complete-game victories in which the only run he allowed was unearned. But Gibson had some tough luck of his own in the stingy pitching duels. Outside his baker's dozen shutouts, three short of Grover Cleveland Alexander's all-time record, he was 9-9 with a 1.83 ERA. I was not helpless though in fighting fire with fire. I'd go on to toss 3 shutouts of my own, with a career-low 2.63 ERA.

The Cubs' own record-tying offensive scoreless streak wrecked our pennant-contending chances. From June 15, which we opened with a 30-29 record, 5 games out, until June 21, we could not eke a run out through 48 consecutive innings. even with three future Hall-of-Famers as our heart of the order. We literally went 0-for-St. Louis in a 3-game series, crippling us in the standings. A lone win in Crosley Field where we finally scored punctuated 10 road losses and a drop to 13 games behind the Cardinals by the time we returned to Wrigley Field. In a June 26 game at Houston, Durocher tried a radical shakeup of the order by dropping cleanup hitter Santo to seventh while backup first baseman Dick Nen took his place at No. 4 and sent Banks to the bench.

The lineup demotion was the bottom of Santo's season. The team captain particularly felt bedeviled in 1968. Coming out of a five-season span in which the third baseman was one the game's best all-around players, annually flirting with .300 with 30 homers and the Gold Glove, Santo struggled in the .250 range all year.

Meanwhile, reserved seats for weekend games were in scarce supply. On July 26, an overflow crowd of 42,261 packed the ballpark for a doubleheader with the Dodgers. The remnants of the mob lustily cheered Holtzman as he sought the final out in his 1-0, 10-strikeout victory that swept the twin bill and finally put us back over .500 at 52-51.

The fans appreciated winning baseball, even if the Cardinals were not in hailing distance, barring an all-time miracle. We spun off a 33-14 run, including a stirring 3-game sweep of the Cardinals in front of huge crowds in St. Louis, as the home team dedicated a statue to Hall-of-Famer Stan Musial. The final two games of the run took place at Wrigley Field, August 12-13. The fans treated the four-game series like a pennant showdown, even though we came in 14 games behind.

For the opener on a Monday the bleachers filled more than 90 minutes prior to the 1:30 game time. Cubs officials never could recall a non-holiday Monday drawing so well.

On August 13, ticket lines started forming at 7:00 A.M. I was certainly motivated and went the distance to beat the Cardinals, 10-3, for my 13th victory. After being dominated throughout 1967 and the first half of 1968, we had beaten the archrivals seven in a row. We had re-established one of baseball's hottest rivalries. The Chicago Tribune's Ed Prell even compared the 1968 Cubs to the Hack Wilson/Rogers Hornsby-paced 1929 pennant winners. Reality then hit, as the Cardinals took the final 2 games to send us into another slump.

We slid back to a game above .500 with a week to go in the season. Williams provided a highlight during the skid with a career-best 3-homer burst in an 8-1 win over the Mets on September 10. Durocher then appealed to our pride in finishing above .500 two years in a row for the first time in Cubs annals since 1945 and 1946. We did manage to win our final 5 games, 1 in particularly dramatic fashion, at home, to end up at 84-78. On September 25, losing 1-0 to Bill Singer of the Dodgers going into the bottom of the ninth, Santo slugged a walk-off grand-slam homer with none out. What he did not reveal at the time was he was undergoing a severe diabetic reaction as Singer pitched to him. Santo later claimed he actually saw three baseballs, swung at the one in the middle and tried to round the bases as quickly as possible to consume his sugar fix in the dugout to staunch the diabetic onslaught.

I won my 20th in a struggle against the Pirates on Saturday, September 27, at Wrigley Field, as the first Cub since Lon Warneke in 1935 to amass consecutive 20-win seasons. The mediocre mid-August-to-end-of-September record did not dampen the enthusiasm that had gathered in our hot streak. The final 2 games were described by the Tribune's George Langford as roaring like a 40,000-strong throng, caught up in the "electric excitement" over the good play of the second half.

Late summer was not too early to project what the Cubs would need to finally match the Cardinals in 1969. On August 17, radio color analyst Lou Boudreau said we needed three commodities for the next season: a legitimate backup catcher to Hundley; a lefty reliever to take pressure off overworked closer Regan; and a top bench guy. The Good Kid, as Boudreau was known, also felt Phillips was a key to 1969 and believed Durocher had been patient with him in a far-less productive 1968 season, even with the late-June fine.

Boudreau turned out to be prescient. Hundley had set the big-league record for a catcher with 160 games played, as Durocher did not discourage Hundley from catching doubleheaders. The backup catcher would not be obtained. In the offseason, Holland re-acquired submariner Abernathy and lefty Hank Aguirre for the bullpen and we'd eventually add backup infielders Popovich and Nate Oliver alongside popular returnee Willie Smith. How these players would be deployed would affect the outcome of 1969 and prove Boudreau correct.

The right-field hole remained unfilled going into 1969, though. Again, no impact, home-grown outfielder was in sight from Triple-A Tacoma or below, unless a 19-year-old Oscar Gamble with only a half-year's pro experience was that man, whom the brass almost breathlessly trumpeted as another Opening Day approached.

⁂

The new season would feature major changes to the structure of the game. I quickly adapted to the lowering of the mound from 15 to 10 inches, a major change to reverse six seasons of increasing pitcher dominance culminating in 1968's "Year of the Pitcher." And we'd play in the first-ever divisional format in which the addition of the expansion Montreal Expos and San Diego Padres necessitated creation of East and West divisions. Along with our friends in St. Louis, we were placed in the East.

That in good part came about because, well, who says the Cubs and Cardinals couldn't cooperate? Owners Phil Wrigley and Gussie Busch, respectively, evidently put their clout together to keep the archrivals in the same division – and out of the West. They were geographically incongruous. Cincinnati and Atlanta, both considerably east of Chicago and St. Louis, were placed in the West. But their ownership did not have the influence of Wrigley and Busch. No way was Wrigley and his longtime business partners at WGN going to tolerate a whole mess of road games beginning at 10 p.m. Chicago time and the prospective drop in fan interest and broadcast ratings. As Marvin Miller and the Players Association found out in ensuing years, ownership often was every man for himself. So what if Reds and Braves fans had to lose sleep listening to night games from the West Coast starting at 11 p.m. local time – if they tuned in at all? Well, that's their problem.

The start of the '69 season finally arrived. On his "Durocher in the Dugout" pre-game show prior to the April 8 season opener, the manager told Boudreau about prospective trades: "They want all our front-line players, give them four or five for one. We didn't tear this club down and start from the bottom and build it up to where we have it now to give these players away. We have a good ball club. I'd like to be a little stronger, possibly in the pitching department or in right field."

Minutes later, Holland told Boudreau on the radio Leadoff Man show: "This is the best frontline we've ever had during the period I was here. In 1960, we brought up Santo and Williams. They were just babies then. They're ready to really contend for the championship….Making a deal with other ball clubs is the most difficult thing in the world. We knew we were being short in some positions especially on the bench. Expansion clubs do have some players in time that will be available. Now they're asking too much for them."

Dirt from the fans...

I was part of a distinctive platoon of ushers in old-school, blue-and-white uniforms and caps that strained to keep fans off the field at crucial times in that memorable summer. Once the park opened on game day, it was all business, as the bleachers were the first to fill up. No reserved seats out there back then. It was on a first-come, first-serve basis and most of the regular bleacher fans sat in the same seats every game. The crowds formed very early at the bleacher gate and working that gate was always a challenge. If assigned to the bleachers, some of us had to be there at 6:00 A.M. to handle the early crowd out on Waveland and Sheffield avenues. No bottles or cans were allowed in, and it was our job to enforce this rule. By the end of the home stand, there would be a room off to the side that was full of beer, wine, and booze bottles that had been confiscated. Never knew what happened to all of it, but the ushers' parties were always a lot of fun!

-Jim Budka, St. Augustine, Florida

Chapter 4

This Ace Was Set-Up Man For
Wonderful Willie's Heroics

I had been a full-time starter for two-plus seasons by the time Opening Day, April 8, 1969, rolled around. On this unforgettable afternoon, I reverted to setup man for a former lefty pitcher, Wonderful Willie Smith.

The baritone-singing pinch-hitter and sometimes first baseman-left fielder was one of the most popular men on the 1969 Cubs. Never more so than when he muscled up for one of the most famous homers in Cubs history – his two-run, 11th-inning, pinch-hit. walk-off blast against Philadelphia Phillies reliever Barry Lersch. That clout capped off one of the more-memorable season openers in franchise history and set the tone for our season in the sun that proved to be the genesis of the modern Cubs.

Smith may not have had the chance to provide broadcasters Jack Brickhouse and Vince Lloyd with two of their most impactful home-run calls if I had been 100 percent truthful with manager Leo Durocher in the ninth inning. I take full responsibility for the hanging slider to Phillies rookie Don Money which tied that game 5-5 with 3-run homer onto Waveland Avenue and provided the right situation for Wonderful Willie to do his thing.

I was probably gassed when I went into the ninth inning leading 5-2. By that point in a game, I always had the mindset of finishing what I started. I had retired 9 in a row, 3 via strikeouts, since Money homered leading off the seventh. The first sign that maybe I had crossed a bridge too far was when Johnny Callison and Cookie Rojas led off the top of the ninth with singles. I had not gone more than 7 innings in spring training games before this outing. Managers then often did not count pitches no matter what point of the season. Both Sandy Koufax and Gibson logged 190 or more pitches in starts in their careers.

When Leo Durocher asked me about my stamina and mindset on the bench in the bottom of the eighth, as was his usual move later in my starts, of course I told him I was fine.

"He said he felt great, but I should have taken him out," he would say afterward.

What I was not aware of at the time was a published report stating 'Leo The Lip' had a $500 fine for any pitcher who did not truthfully tell him he was tired. That was a chunk of change, a week's salary for many players. And I had never heard Leo fine a pitcher for lobbying to stay in, then giving up the lead. Two years later, Durocher was so afraid to employ his bullpen that we led baseball with 75 complete games, 30 by me.

Additionally, I did not have buddy Billy Williams' hitting philosophy ringing around in my head. Williams professed to be like a patient cobra ready to strike, gauging the complete game-hunting starter's stuff over his first three at-bats, then lowering the boom on a diminished fastball the fourth time up.

Absolved of most guilt by a victorious 7-6 final score, I mused afterward that, "I guess I didn't feel that great."

Perhaps I would have had my first victory of the year if closer Phil Regan had come in to start the ninth and no Phils rally would have been consummated. Then the glory would have gone to Ernie Banks for his season-opening two homers that excited the crowd, and secondary credit to me for a workmanlike 8 innings of 2-run baseball.

That would have "wrecked the Hollywood script," according to Chicago Tribune veteran writer Ed Prell's description. If not for my pride in going the distance, Wonderful Willie would have been a small footnote in Cubs annals, simply an extra man from 1968 to 1970 upon whom Durocher called to pinch-hit and spot-start.

Seeing as I'd go on to win 284 games and earn induction into the Hall of Fame, I'm still thrilled at this late date to have given the glory to Smith for one shining day.

He capped what to us came off as a playoff atmosphere. The largest Opening Day crowd in Cubs history to date packed all standing-room only (SRO) nooks and crannies. Lured by a slew of pre-season Cubs pennant predictions and our two-year competitive buildup in 1967 and 1968 Lloyd told his WGN-Radio audience: "You tell me baseball's dead…Hah!!" Even the weather, usually stoked with leftover winter chill in early April, cooperated with a 65-degree game-time reading.

The action was more than lively after Durocher yanked me immediately after the second Don Money homer, because Durocher never feared extending Regan to three innings, or even more. Sure enough, in Regan's third frame, the 11th, Money put the Phillies ahead, 6-5, with a double to left off of Regan., which put a pending pall on such a promising afternoon.

Randy Hundley begged to disagree. He singled off Lersch with one out in the 11th and Durocher decided to play percentages, using a lefty to pinch hit for the right-handed swinging Jim Hickman.

He had two choices – Smith and Al Spangler, a part-time right fielder the past two seasons. Wonderful Willie thought "Spanky" would get the call.

"Al was an established pinch-hitter, more known than I was," Smith recalled in a 1994 radio interview from his hometown of Anniston, Alabama. "(Coach) Joey Amalfitano picked me out over Spangler. During the time, Spangler was down in the runway (where the one-urinal dugout bathroom was)."

Another Durocher hunch was that Lersch, working in his fifth inning of relief, would have a fastball that would be diminished his third time through the Cubs order.

Wonderful Willie just wanted to get it done quickly.

"I really wasn't too happy going up to pinch hit," he said of waiting 11 innings. "You're trying to keep warm. It felt like a shock (being called up). Well, the best thing I can do is go up and swing hard and hope I can (hit), and I can get out of there."

Then Smith swung a little bit too hard in the on-deck circle.

"I kind of pulled a muscle a little bit," he recalled. "I said, 'Oh my God, now what's going to happen next?'"

What happened was, despite the nagging muscle, he caught a Lersch meatball and powered it in the middle of the right-field bleachers as the SRO crowd's remnants went nuts, Brickhouse and Lloyd got as down-to-the-gut as possible on their calls and the celebrating WGN-TV camera operator shook his image of Smith's homer settling into a crowd of grasping fans.

And if Wonderful Willie felt tugs from his muscle pull, then he was yelping in some pain as half the team mobbed him at home plate.

"At home plate, I think I had 9 or 10 spike wounds in my foot, my ankle. Willie had a big puncture in his right toe." He took it for the team, though: "I would have done it 50 more times if necessary."

I don't think I contributed to the puncturing of Smith that day. I trailed the pack coming off the bench and did not get squarely in the scrum. We then retired back to our cubbyhole clubhouse and were in no hurry to leave. We roared our approval again when a radio replayed Lloyd's call of Wonderful Willie's homer. Each game is supposed to be compartmentalized in baseball, but if there was an afterglow from the late-afternoon outcome, it shined on the rest of our home stand. Best of all, his homer basically bought three more seasons for Smith in his journeyman's career.

He was the positive end result of the near-disastrous Lou Johnson trade of late 1967. When Sweet Lou did not work out, he was flipped to the Cleveland Indians in an inter-league waiver deal in late June 1968 for Wonderful Willie. The surprisingly sullen outlook of Johnson gave way to an 'Ernie Banks-lite' in Wonderful Willie, an instant hit with us in 1968. He pinch-hit, played some outfield, and even went back to the mound for a 2-2/3-inning scoreless stint in one outing. A year later, the replays of the Opening Day homer and his deep voice on celebratory "Cub Power" vinyl records and the like were some of the great soundtracks of the summer of 1969.

Wonderful Willie did not have to be paid chump change to sing on "Go-Cubs-Go" recordings. He sang for free for our edification and kept us loose in the clubhouse and the road. He always was singing "Sitting on the Dock of the Bay," probably one of many soulful Otis Redding songs that were part of Smith's repertoire before Redding was lost too soon.

Offering his distinctive baritone to us was Smith's latest incarnation. He started out pitching, then he proved he could hit a bit. An original Detroit Tigers product, Smith was a well-regarded lefty pitcher coming up. In 1963, he led the International League in winning percentage with a 14–2 record along with a 2.11 ERA. I was considered a good-hitting pitcher, but Smith was ridiculous the same year, in addition to having 30 hits in 79 at-bats (.380) and 13 RBI. The Tigers traded Smith to the Los Angeles Angels early in 1964 for pitcher Julio Navarro, father of future Cub Jaime Navarro. You just couldn't hold a good hitter down. Angels manager Bill Rigney shifted him to the outfield and Smith batted .301 with 11 homers and 51 RBI. He could not break the mold of a platoon player, though, and thus he made his way to us in 1968.

While Spangler got the majority of early-season duty in right field, Smith became Durocher's favorite pinch hitter. But as Spangler cooled as the weather warmed, the manager had to find another corner outfielder. He shifted Williams to right field, his former regular position in 1965-66, and inserted Smith, no glove man, in left. An immediate response though was perhaps the longest Cubs homer of 1969.

Jim Hickman launched some real missiles onto Waveland and Kenmore avenues. But I think Smith's "Southern Nights" performance beat them in distance. In the Cubs' first visit to Atlanta on June 10, right-hander Ron Reed held a 1-0 lead into the top of the eighth. But Smith blasted an offering into the fourth row of the upper deck down the right-field line. The first row of the deck was 52 feet from the ground. The blast was estimated at 475 feet as the longest to that date in the four-year old Atlanta Stadium (later renamed Fulton County Stadium). Never one for understatement, Ron Santo said the homer was 600 feet. Durocher, who had witnessed the Sultan of Swat's distance classics first-hand 40 years previously, called the clout "a Babe Ruth shot." More importantly, Smith's big belt sparked a 3-run Cubs uprising to cement another win, No. 10 for starter Ken Holtzman.

Wonderful Willie had hits in 14 for his first 44 at-bats to this point, including 3 homers. Durocher gave him most of the corner outfield at-bats against right-handers for the next six weeks. He responded well, especially against the Cardinals. On June 28 and 29, he amassed game-clinching homers in consecutive victories against our arch-rival on the 'Billy Williams Day" weekend at Wrigley Field. Smith also was the left fielder on duty in the July 12 game against the Phillies at home in which the complete NBC Game of the Week telecast had been preserved on kinescope.

Smith became as much a remembered name from 1969 as anyone else. He played one more season with the Cubs in 1970, then was traded for catcher Danny Breeden. Durocher, however, could not soon forget his near-automatic call for a pinch hitter when he wanted a power threat against a right-hander.

One day after Wonderful Willie's departure, the story went how the aging manager dozed under a blanket on the bench. Suddenly, he woke up and shouted: "Willie Smith, get in there and pinch-hit." There was dead silence on the bench. Hickman then came to Durocher and said, "Skip, we traded Willie Smith, but if you want me to go get him, I'll do it!"

Even though he moved home to Anniston, Alabama, for work and did not stay in baseball, Wonderful Willie never left us spiritually.

"Nobody will let me forget it," he said in a 1994 radio interview. "I will agree wholeheartedly that one hit sparked the whole ball team. I still don't think the best team won that division.

Smith's big swing sparked something more long-lasting than our fast start. Ditching work and school en masse now became fashionable for Cubs home openers.

Tribune Company management eventually limited standing-room tickets starting in the 1980s and the subsequent early morning lines by the bleachers disappeared. Unfortunately, so did all-time characters like Wonderful Willie Smith. But the ability to shake the lens of that 300-pound WGN camera and the entire Cubs Universe with the combo of power and charisma would prove to be difficult to duplicate.

Dirt from the fans...

"When the 1969 season began, I was 12-years old. That's an age at which you first begin to have a real understanding of baseball, the intricacies of how it's played, and the history behind the sport and your favorite team, without being jaded by losses. That's why that season was so exciting. I knew it had been 24 years since the Cubs had been in the World Series and 63 since they'd won it. Those numbers seem quaint and small now, especially with the World Series drought finally busted in 2016. But in 1969, there was still something of an innocence about them, and it seemed to all who loved the Cubs that the players we loved -- future Hall-of-Famers Ernie Banks, Ron Santo, Billy Williams and Fergie Jenkins, plus the rest of their talented teammates -- would bring the team that had been so bad for two decades to the World Series."

-Al Yellon, Chicago

Fergie vs. Gibby
Pitching Duel For The Ages

I t's tough enough to throw your best game matched up against Bob Gibson.
You can't make early mistakes or walk anybody. Almost every game in baseball is low-scoring and decided by 1 or 2 runs. If I gave up 2 or 3 runs, I was a loser. You were pitching for your life. A whole class of Hall-of-Fame pitchers were my opponents in 1969,but Gibson was my toughest competitor. I was the easy-going Fly in the clubhouse, but I had to be all business to a tee on the mound to match Gibson's laser-focus intensity. Plus Gibson doubled as a "barber," shaving close pitches uncomfortably inside to the likes of Ron Santo and Ernie Banks. He avoided knocking down Billy Williams, though, as "Whistler" connected for 10 career homers against Gibson.

Gibson's feeling about me was mutual. We staged some of the most classic pitching duels in baseball in the late 1960s and early 1970s, although Gibson, confident almost to a fault, knew I would match him pitch for pitch.

"I was aware, of course," Gibson said a generation later, when we were both big-league pitching coaches. "He was the enemy pitcher. The problem (was) everyone thought I loved to pitch against Fergie and I liked the competition. But not really. You'd rather pitch against somebody you know you're going to get 4 or 5 runs off him. We weren't going to get more than 1 or 2 runs off him, and that made him tough."

Gibson worked up a good sweat when he threw 95 mph-plus heaters. Me, less so. So when you throw the elements into the equation in a Gibson-Jenkins duel, I gained an advantage. That was one of the more astounding sights of the summer of 1969, the defending Cy Young Award winner throwing off waterfalls of perspiration while I appeared to be dry as a bone in a memorable afternoon holiday matchup in old Busch Stadium.

Oh, I was warm, too, but you had to adopt a mind-over-matter stance on top of careful physical preparation to go 10 innings in 100-degree St. Louis heat and humidity back on July 4, 1969. I outlasted Gibson in the second of back-to-back wins over the man who sported a record-low 1.12 ERA the previous year. I'm jumping ahead here in the 1969 narrative a bit, just to call attention to how tough pitching was in an era when Hall-of-Famers would duel each other on a regular basis.

I never called myself a cool cat or possessor of ice-water in my veins, but maybe it was deflating to the opposing Cardinals to look out at the mound on that steamy afternoon in the ballpark Casey Stengel once said held the heat well. In its fourth season, Busch Stadium was not yet carpeted with heat-retaining Astroturf —thank goodness for small favors. Meanwhile, thoroughly damp Cubs and Cardinals players, nearly 30,000 steaming spectators, and those watching around the Midwest on TV, witnessed me sporting an almost-dry gray *flannel* road uniform.

George Langford summed up the damp surroundings in the next day's Chicago Tribune. In the dugout in the 10th, my uniform was "light and dry with hardly a bead of perspiration evident" as I held ice to my back. In contrast, shortstop Don Kessinger, lean and limber with hardly any body fat to sweat off, had a uniform "thoroughly soaked and caked with dirt."

My teammates were astonished.

"I've never seen anything like you," Willie Smith told reporters after the game while looking at me. "It's 100 degrees and you pitched 10 innings and don't even break a sweat.

"Look at your uniform. It's not even wet. There were eight guys playing behind you and their uniforms were so soaked with sweat they weighed 10 pounds."

I told the scribes, sweating themselves from a press row exposed to the steam bath, that it was a matter of attitude and focus.

"I told myself it wasn't hot, honestly," was my analysis. "I just told myself it's a real nice cool day and to go out there and try to win."

Whether it was flirting with a tropical sauna climate or a Canadian-Chatham crisp at 39 degrees, as were the wind chills for a different 10-inning duel with Gibson in 1971, you had to put the elements out of your mind. You needed tunnel vision focused on your catcher and the plate umpire so the latter could give you the calls on the black of the plate. Fortunately, I did just that in an amazing five-day span in mid-season 1969. Any matchup like ours makes it a huge accomplishment for one to beat another in back-to-back starts.

Omaha-native Gibson had the same attitude about me. In the first radio interview we did together, in 1996, Gibson said a start against me was arduous. He couldn't afford any mistakes in the same manner. If I had to scout him, the process would be his pitching and mechanics, not his personality. We did not fraternize away from the mound then. Gibson explained in the radio interview that he kept his distance from opponents so they could not take the measure of his mind nor gain any edge at the plate.

"I felt that hitters just loved to get comfortable with you," he said. "And the more you consorted with them, the more you talked with them, the more comfortable they get with you. And I felt if I just stayed away from them and they didn't have any idea what I was all about, it would work in my favor. I still believe in that."

We never compared notes as Cy Young Award-quality 20-game winners. We may have nodded to one another as we passed on the field during batting practice, but there was no fraternization, as when we both returned as pitching coaches. We had somewhat contrasting personalities and pitching styles.

"I didn't really care what he was thinking," Gibson said of not picking my brain back in the day. "I knew I was going to have to be on my best game in order to beat him. I wasn't concerned about how he did it. He did it differently than me. I was a high-fastball pitcher and he was a sinker-ball (specialist). We both had a pretty good slider. But he was in and out a little more than me, and I tried to kind of overpower the guy most of the time."

In 1969, Gibson was so good any pitcher would have killed for his best game to eke out a victory, let alone win two consecutive outings against No. 45.

That's what pitching was like overall in the first season of division play. You regularly pitched for your life. Despite the lowering of the mound to promote more offense, the best pitchers still strutted their stuff as before in an era when complete games were the norm, and closers – such as they were – went two or three innings. They had few alternatives. Pitching staffs were comprised of 9 or at most 10 pitchers in 1969, contrasted to today's regular complement of 12 or 13.

Nine 20-game winners populated the National League in 1969. You'd run into an ace-quality pitcher with almost every team, even the tail-enders. You sloughed off your game only at your own risk.

Decades later, I'd be joined by Gibson, along with Tom Seaver, Phil Niekro, Juan Marichal, Gaylord Perry, Don Sutton, Steve Carlton, Don Drysdale, and Jim Bunning as prominent 1969 NL rotation members to make the Hall of Fame. Hardly any other of these worthy opponents approached the playoff intensity of my battles with Gibson.

Hardly any other worthy opponents approached the playoff intensity of my battles with Gibson.

The underlying Cubs-Cardinals rivalry ensured the entire atmosphere would be ratcheted up in intensity. I was a relative newcomer as a team ace in 1969. Gibson already had been a two-time World Series Most Valuable Player. He spun an astounding 13 shutouts with 28 complete games in 34 starts in his unforgettable 1968 NL MVP season. His microscopic ERA was a major spur to the Lords of Baseball to ensure we'd never have another "Year of the Pitcher."

I had extra motivation before I threw the opening pitch in the first of my matchups with Gibson on Sunday, June 29, 1969. The doubleheader at Wrigley Field was yet another test for us against the defending NL champions. At that point, the Cardinals, not the improving Mets, were still perceived as our chief obstacle to winning the new National League East division. Your goal was to win the game at hand, first.

Pomp added to circumstances on this Sunday afternoon. Williams – my friend, fishing buddy and carpool mate going to Wrigley Field – would break Stan Musial's NL consecutive games-played streak in the twin bill. He had not missed a game since the end of the 1963 season. A big between-games ceremony awaited. Between the attractions of the Cardinals and "Billy Williams Day," the largest paid crowd of the season showed up.

The huge crowd and Williams – often labeled as the Cubs' "quiet man" – getting his long-deserved due could not help but pump me up.

On this day, I simply could not allow a run. Gibson was at his sharpest starting out, striking out 7 of the first 10 Cubs he faced. After the game, I summed up my feelings as I watched Gibson mow down my teammates early on: "I just told myself I couldn't make a mistake early in the game. You don't have to give up for Mr. Gibson. He was really bringing it today, especially in the early innings. You could tell he really wanted this one."

I did not have my own strikeout pitch going to match Gibson's, but that wasn't an issue if I had good control. I tried to stay within my strength, throwing strikes, getting ahead in the count, making the hitter do part of the work. I had to be as stingy as possible with my performance. I had a game plan and catcher Randy Hundley and I would talk about the first three hitters in an inning. Lou Brock was the type of guy who wanted to hit a fastball and did not like breaking pitches down. Curt Flood was going to try to hit behind the runner. I knew the hitters as well as Hundley did. The game plan was to give up fewer hits than innings and do not let rallies start. Don't walk people.

Williams touched off his own day of personal heroics by gunning down Brock trying to stretch a one-out single into a double in the sixth as Flood steamed to third when the Cards tried to rally. That was a key out. I got out of that jam by getting the dangerous Joe Torre to pop up. Possessing a good slider that day really helped.

Then Williams really went to work, leading off the eighth with a double to thrill the crowd. Banks, at whom Gibson threw in the past, was undaunted, singling up the middle to break the scoreless deadlock. Smith then sent the overflow crowd into ecstasy with a two-run homer. I smelled the victory and allowed only a Vada Pinson homer in the ninth.

Gibson was vanquished, we had a win and I'm glad I'd helped set up good feelings for the big moment of the day, the between-games ceremonies. I wouldn't have missed them for the world, even after 9 innings of labor. Williams was showered with gifts. I presented him a Weimaraner hunting-dog puppy.

Then I sat back in amazement to watch Williams come through like few others on a day on which he was being honored. Getting 5 consecutive hits stretching back to Game 1, he collected 2 triples, a double, and a single, as we battered the Cards, 12-1, behind Dick Selma.

"This was a beautiful day, wasn't it? This was my day," Williams said afterward. "I've never had a day like this. I even shed a tear and I've never done that."

Typically working on three days' rest though in that era, I had the luxury of an extra day off as Leo Durocher held me back for a rematch with Gibson on July 4, with a series at Jarry Park in Montreal taking place in the intervening days.

I did not have the benefit of a night game on a Friday to get a break from the heat. Like all other teams, the Cardinals played a holiday game during the day. In person and on TV back in Chicago, you no doubt noticed my road uniform remained its original gray while my teammates' uniforms grew darker by the inning with copious perspiration. One of Gibson's nicknames was "Bullet," and he was sweating them that afternoon in his home white and red uniform.

I was prepared. Pitchers could not afford to bow out due to the heat in those days. Remember, you felt your job was on the line constantly. I ran every day of the intention of having my body in good condition. We ran line to line under the command of pitching coach Joe Becker. The nice thing about it was the conditioning I put my body through. I did not perspire. I always wore a long-sleeved shirt. I might change that, but not the outer flannel shirt. An ice bucket in the tunnel was very helpful. Overall, though, you blocked out the temperature and blocked out the heat. I might lose 2 pounds. Later, I pitched in Texas a lot, and it would be 100-degrees-plus for night games in Arlington. If you condition your body prior to a pitching assignment, heat won't bother you. My body just stayed loose.

A lot of times it is mind over matter, so you're on a mission to win a game. I had to be conditioned to beat the best, and this game went into the 10th. Durocher was the kind of manager who'd walk in front of you in the dugout while we were hitting and say, "Hey, big fella, you still OK?" Almost always I answered in the affirmative. Always stay positive. He wanted to question your psyche. If he didn't have the bullpen up, it was still your game.

I may have battled Gibson to a 1-1 draw through 9. But Kessinger – despite swimming in his own sweat – was the dominant factor. He scored the game's first run on Glenn Beckert's sacrifice fly. Then he saved me trouble with two "boarding-house reach" plays in the hole, prompting me to tell reporters later, "He's the all-star of all-stars. He's my shortstop in any league." Fifty years later, Kessinger has got to be rated in the top three shortstops in Cubs history in my opinion.

Playing deep and not really able to turn a double play, Ron Santo also cut down the potential lead run by nailing Flood at home plate. Even though I have the Cubs season strikeout record, I could have never gone as far as I did in my career without spectacular defense.

Then, professing to be near the end of his physical rope due to the heat, Kessinger led off the 10th against Gibson with a single. On weary legs he somehow stole second. He went to third on Beckert's bunt single and broke the deadlock to score on Williams' double. Beckert then came home with an insurance run on Santo's single. Gibson was then pulled, the first time in 57 games dating back to 1967 he was knocked out in the middle of an inning.

I made the lead stand up for a 3-1 victory, finishing with 10 strikeouts. You might say in humid Busch Stadium that I served the Cardinals a big dose of "dry heat."

I'd go on to three more head-to-head duels with Gibson. We both went in prepared to go 9 innings, or more, and battle to the final pitch. There was no mindset of seeking relief from the bullpen. Remember, Gibson completed 28 of his 34 starts in his unparalleled 1.12 ERA season in 1968. With 22 victories, Gibson had 6 complete-game losses, matching my total when I had 30 route-going starts with 24 victories in my Cy Young season in 1971.

"It's really sad they blame pitchers (for not going the distance anymore)," Gibson said in 1996. "It's the way the game is played today."

Ace pitchers were under the microscope if we did not go the distance in our primes.

"The press would criticize you when you didn't finish ballgames," Gibson said.

Now, the old derisive criticism of pitchers departing way too early – "five and fly" or "five and dive" – is almost the standard for starting in the 21st century. Forgotten is the concept of finely conditioned pitchers accustomed to endurance since the days of Gibson and I.

Gibson was long retired by the time I came back for my second stint with the Cubs in 1982. Later, we connected – and talked – in Old-Timers Games and Hundley's Fantasy Camps. All my head-to-head matchups against Gibson were teaching moments for any pitcher. Concentrate and focus and get in the finest shape possible. Those are the edges needed to not let the most fearsome opposing ace nor the extremes of climate get the best of you.

Kel Kissamis / Kelcub Studio

The Two Sides Of Mr. Cub

The way Ernie Banks sang for his supper in 1969, you'd think he was auditioning for yet another of his many careers.

Few people can walk in Mr. Cubs' shoes. I grew up as an only child in a middle-class family in Chatham, Ontario, 60 miles from the urban grittiness of Detroit. My doting mother Deloris made sure I was well-dressed and well-mannered. Our Baptist church was a big part of our life. I lacked for few things. Although my life was not prejudice-free, there was more color-blindness in my youth than in Banks' childhood in Depression-era, Jim Crow Dallas. Banks grew up dirt poor, the second of 12 children of Eddie and Essie Banks. He had little coming up except his natural athletic ability. He truly was a self-made man, all the way through his early Cubs seasons, and certainly as he was found in 1969.

Already well-established in his role as Mr. Cub, still an accomplished No. 5 hitter and spreading his wings in broadcasting and business, my road roommate would sing for a big TV audience, a society wedding, or his 24 teammates and coaches (although not necessarily for manager Leo Durocher).

Such was the case around 7:00 P.M. Sunday, June 29, 1969, as homebound fans tuned into professional singers at that moment on Ed Sullivan's CBS-TV variety show, America's communal weekly prime-time get-together that birthed the Beatles' international reach. An unlikely source of entertainment was available to the intimate gathering at the ballpark. A surprised beat writer, George Langford of the Chicago Tribune, trying to get home for part of the evening before starting a road trip to Montreal the next day, noticed a familiar face and voice filter out of the Cubs clubhouse in the leftfield corner.

Banks may have been the last player out of the clubhouse after the marathon Billy Williams Day sweep of the St. Louis Cardinals that. Langford described Banks swinging a package as he walked in via the leftfield line, then made a left turn to stand atop the empty pitcher's mound. He had a lot to celebrate. His eighth-inning single off Bob Gibson drove in the go-ahead run in the 3-1 victory in Game 1. Then, backing up his almost daily "let's play two" advocacy, Banks slugged a 3-run homer, his 13th of the season, off Jim "Mudcat" Grant in the first inning of the nightcap to set the tone for a smashing 12-1 triumph. He thus advanced the dual countdowns to his 500th homer, his career 512th, and his hoped-for first World Series appearance in a stellar 16-year career.

"I could have danced all night," Banks sang, his familiar voice echoing toward the far corners of the Friendly Confines. Banks then walked the 60-feet, 6-inches from the pitcher's mound toward home plate, still in full song: "I only know we took a doubleheader from the Cardinals. I could have played all day and still played some more."

Then the greatest home-run hitter and one of the most popular players in Cubs history, walked into the grandstand and down a ramp, timing the walk to his car after the dispersal of the typical mob of autograph seekers, who were already long gone. In a voice Langford described as "flat, cheerful," Banks' impromptu serenade faded with: "...and done a thousand things I've never done before."

After the dramatic 11-inning, Opening Day win over the Phillies, powered by Willie Smith's walk-off pinch homer, Banks crooned, "Those Were the Days, My Friend," amid the riotous post-game celebration, a song popularized by folk-singer Mary Hopkin.

On June 19, he broke out in "Get Me to the Church On Time" while attending Manager Leo Durocher's wedding at the Ambassador West Hotel. Two weeks after the empty-ballpark concerto, while gathering fellow Million Dollar Infield members, Ron Santo, Don Kessinger, and Glenn Beckert around the batting cage, he belted out "Chicago, That Toddlin' Town" for "Cubs Fever," the WGN-TV mid-season Cubs special which aired July 21 and is still preserved today on YouTube. In a reprise to 1969, Banks sang, "Hey Hey Holy Mackerel, No Doubt About It," at Scottsdale Stadium during the next year's spring training for WGN's, "A Look at the Cubs, 1970."

Banks' teammates pick up that "Cubs Fever" Melody!

Banks' celebrity-hood increased in the Cubs' golden Sixties by leaps and bounds. Wrigley had made him a player-coach in 1967, the added designation likely just ceremonial, but also an acknowledgement of his long and meritorious service.

He then flashed a hint of his old-time power in 1968, a Jekyll-Hyde season for us. A cold finish was a stated motivating factor for Banks going into 1969, when he would hit his landmark 500th homer.

He truly became a media star in 1969 while likely ranking as one of the first African-American celebrities in Chicago to enjoy massive crossover appeal, in my opinion. In addition to his Tribune column, which often was in close proximity to an ad for his Ford dealership, WGN hired him in a dual role. Banks anchored the sports report when the Cubs were home on the 10 p.m. Sunday night TV newscast. He added the video duties to an ongoing WGN-Radio role. On July 8, 1968, Banks debuted a regular series of recorded interviews at 7:50 p.m. on weeknights. He'd also file radio reports from St. Louis and Detroit during the 1968 World Series.

Despite being a rock-ribbed Republican, Brickhouse – also running WGN's sports department -- was militantly color-blind. He was a member of the Urban League. Five years previously, he hired black sportswriter Wendell Smith, who had close ties to and had covered Jackie Robinson in 1947. By 1967, Smith began anchoring the 10 p.m. sports segment with its coveted Cubs taped highlights. With Banks aboard, the conservative Tribune-owned WGN fielded a black sportscaster on its newscast seven nights a week in '69.

Banks also taped a 5-minute radio interview show that ran at 7:50 p.m. weeknights when not pre-empted by a road game. Singing, chanting slogans and happy conversation was not the same as the diction required for sportscasts. In 1997, Brickhouse recalled the challenges of tutoring Banks for his broadcast gigs:

"I took Ernie aside one day. I want you to pronounce the 'g' on that 'ing' at the end of the word – inning, nothing, it's one to nothing in the fifth inning. Say it for me. He'd say it 10 times. Now we get on the air, it'd be 500 times, I couldn't get him to pronounce that 'g' all the time. My story is I'm supposed to influence his delivery, but he was such an overwhelming personality that he handled me. I found myself saying, 'He get it.'"

Indeed, the Banks' Sunday night sports became must-viewing for fans as Banks narrated his own highlights. "In the fifth innin,' I came to the plate," he'd say. New pronunciations were concocted: "Orlander Cerpeder came to bat in the sixth," was how he unfortunately pronounced Hall-of-Famer Orlando Cepeda's name.

But armed with his tape recorder, Banks roamed around the field collaring players and managers for interviews for the radio segment. He turned the tables on Tribune columnist Robert Markus one day, literally putting him up against the wall.

Banks had no room to conduct the interview in the cramped Wrigley Field clubhouse. So he took Markus into the stygian stairway that led up from the locker room to a ballpark concourse. Markus compared the tight quarters to a tomb for an Egyptian pharaoh.

"Ernie cranked up his tape recorder and shoved his microphone right under my nose," Markus wrote on May 29, 1969. "I stepped back to avoid swallowing it and he pressed closer and finally I had my back up against the wall and my head back as far as it would go and that's the way we did the interview. I thought any minute he was going to ask me to say, 'aaah.'"

Markus then professed he did not quite understand Ernie's question about the new NL East and West divisions. But he then concluded how he comprehended the nerves many athletes endured on the other side of the microphone.

The pre-season positive prognostications for the Cubs – by far the best in Banks' career – along with the inspiring Opening Day and fast start – no doubt energized Mr. Cub like nothing else.

He did not possess the 40-home run power of a decade previously or the ability to hit .300. But those fingers playing the bat like a piano as he waited for the pitch could still flick the bat expertly in RBI situations.

When he ranked just behind Santo in RBI in the National League in the first half of 1969 – he had 67 to Santo's 69 at the end of the June 29 doubleheader – his popularity broke through the roof as the first man to break the color line on the Cubs roster. That's something to sing about.

As much as singing, Banks loved his connections to St. Louis, having slugged his first career homer off Gerry Staley at old Busch Stadium in 1953 and his record-setting fifth grand slam of the 1955 season there against Lindy McDaniel in 1955. Banks added that his idol, Cardinals' Hall-of-Famer Stan Musial, taught him to play the harmonica.

We heard Banks all the time as a lounge singer on our team planes and buses, and in the clubhouse. Later in life, Mr. Cub even hung out with professional singers like Chicago's Corky Siegel.

The singing was the sunniest side of Banks' baseball life, and he thoroughly mastered it from 1955 through his eventual 500th homer on May 12, 1970. Yet, Banks survived a determined early effort by Durocher to force him off his first-base post. 'Leo The Lip' eventually had to give up pushing Phil Wrigley-favorite Banks aside until the latter's knees and the ravages of his age finally caught up with his franchise-icon status when the 1970s began.

Almost everyone has two sides and Banks was not an exception. I was fortunate to be able to witness about one-third of it all – his entire public and baseball side and just a smidgeon of his private life, although I did have not a wide-open window at all to Banks away from baseball, even though we shared a room on the road and occasional dinners with our wives. Banks' hotel chatter – and he was a talker on and off the field – always centered around baseball.

And so Banks rarely delved into his personal life. Eloyce revealed in the spring of 1969 to Chicago Tribune columnist David Condon that the Banks' twin sons, Jerry and Joey, attended boarding school: St. Joseph's Military Academy, run by Catholic nuns, in southwest suburban LaGrange Park. Banks never mentioned his sons' educational status to me, nor made a peep about his relationship with his then-wife, Eloyce. He never mentioned his frustrations with Durocher. In his Tribune newspaper column and other public comments, he always praised the manager.

Santo eventually passed Banks as the highest-paid Cub at $85,000 in 1968, even though the team captain started his big-league career in Banks' seventh full season, but I never heard anything one-on-one about his salary status. I often car-pooled to Wrigley Field and O'Hare Airport with Williams from our South Shore neighborhood residences. In contrast, Banks almost always drove alone from his 81st Street brownstone in an adjoining neighborhood.

The happy-go-lucky Banks remained for public consumption well past his career, through his Hall-of-Fame induction in his first year of eligibility in 1977. He'd quietly go off the active roster without fanfare, with no farewell ceremony at Wrigley Field, his final game batting cleanup against the Philadelphia Phillies at home on September 26, 1971.

The happy-go-lucky Banks remained for public consumption well past his career.

Garnering publicity as the first black Ford dealer and only the second black car dealer with any brand in the country in the summer of 1967, Banks dropped out of his partnership with World War II Air Force flyer, Bob Nelson at the 7600 S. Stony Island dealership in Chicago less than three years later. Phil Wrigley's attorneys assisted in extricating Banks from the deal.

The further Banks got away from baseball, the more his other side began showing through the cracks. He logically could have coasted the rest of his life as an elder statesman in Chicago as Mr. Cub – but that status escaped him. His marriage to Eloyce ended in 1981. In the settlement, Eloyce wound up with his 500th home-run ball and other valuable artifacts of his career, then proceeded to sell many of them. Banks spent years trying to buy back these valuables. He spent years going through relationships, jobs, and moves, eventually living on the West Coast for a long time, somewhat displaced for someone so closely identified with and having benefitted so much from Chicago. As it turned out, he always believed the 1969 cubs were going to the big game, a fact he revealed in a 1998 interview.

"I never felt we weren't going to win," said Banks. "I always enjoyed that moment. I guess I lived with the attitude of the precious present. What I'm doing now in the present is precious, and I got to enjoy that. Not thinking about something else, or somebody else, or tomorrow, or last week, or last year. That's where I've always centered my life. It was just this day, and it really helped me a lot."

When the Chicago Tribune announced on June 10, 1969, that Banks would write a regular column, "The Wonderful World of Ernie Banks," in its sports section, he summed up his public philosophy loud and clear, "It doesn't cost you anything to be happy. That's the way I'm going to write – through rose-colored glasses. There's enough trouble in the world without baseball, or sports, getting into hassles. When I come to the ballpark, I leave the world's troubles and mine behind. I enjoy baseball so much, and the enthusiasm of the fans, that I'd be happy to spend my nights at Wrigley Field if they'd roll out a cot for me near first base. Am I ever grouchy? Well, I'm not going to say I jump out of bed every morning and start putting on my Cub uniform while humming a tune. Sometimes, I give myself a pep talk when I look into the mirror in the bathroom. I tell myself I'm the luckiest guy alive. I look at Wrigley Field as my castle and I'd like to stay there."

Using the rose-colored glasses angle, Banks stretched his career on. Leo The Lip consistently made comments analyzing that Banks was past his time on the Cubs, but other first-base candidates were found wanting and Banks kept his job.

Banks also could play dodge ball as well as anyone in sports when it came to the media. Tribune columnist Robert Markus would eventually write about Banks' verbal style on May 29, 1969:

"While Ernie will talk, incessantly at times, he does not talk about what you want him to talk about. Ask him a question, for instance, and he might burst into a few bars of , "It's A Good Life," or maybe he'll say something like: 'Don't worry about a thing, 'cause pretty soon you're going to have to push a wheelbarrow of money into the supermarket to buy a loaf of bread.' It's always fun to interview Ernie Banks because you never know what he's going to say."

WGN's Jack Brickhouse said Banks knew exactly what he was trying to get out of him in TV interviews. He displayed more range than he ever did at first base. A 1997 Brickhouse recollection recalled the dodge-ball talent:

"One of the big fun things about Ernie (was) he knows you're putting him on and trying to get him to say something critical about somebody, and he won't do that. I'd say, 'He sure didn't do that one very well,' and Ernie would make an alibi for him. It was a fun game between the two of us."

Jack Rosenberg, Brickhouse's off-the-air sidekick in the booth and longtime WGN sports editor, seconded the Banks' style of shifting the focus away from himself and bestowing praise – and never blame – on others. "He would give everyone else credit," Rosenberg said. "He would see me and say, 'Jack Rosenberg, thanks for making me famous.' I can certainly confirm what many others discovered: Banks often talked at you, not with you."

Stunningly, in a 1998 interview, he revealed another, deeper side that went far beyond the sunnyside-up Mr. Cub. He actually stated his existence would still be complete, even if the Cubs did not win the World Series in his lifetime. Banks, of course, sadly came up almost two years short of witnessing the end of the unparalleled championship drought in 2016, "I think we will (win)…If we don't, it's OK," he said in 1998, a season which produced a last-ditch, wild-card playoff berth. "I think some things, it doesn't matter. We're still breathing, we still have our life, we still have things to do."

He was definitely an effervescent, life-of-the-party type who dominated so much of 1969 and beyond.

Banks finally did get his batting stance-image statue by Wrigley Field's main gate on Opening Day 2008, in recognition of his contributions. Hank Aaron himself noted the delayed action, stating in a speech the Banks statue was a decade late during dedication ceremonies in which Banks demonstrated his old stance live. Within three years, statues of 1969 heroes Williams and Santo also were erected by the ballpark's southeast entrance. Banks continued to make appearances into his 80s and was awarded the Presidential Medal of Freedom by President Barack Obama in 2013.

Mr. Cub died on January 23, 2015, eight days short of his 84th birthday.

A Rip-Roaring Start

The best measuring stick of how deep the hunger Cubs fans felt was for winning, pennant-contending baseball was never better displayed than at Wrigley Field on the late afternoon of Sunday, April 13, 1969.

They witnessed a 7-6 win over the expansion Montreal Expos that mimicked what broadcaster Jack Brickhouse always called "the married men versus the single men at the company picnic" to describe a zany game. The Cubs and Expos apparently did not get all the spring training baseball out of their system, combining to yield 11 unearned runs between them. Three misplays in the field and a bases-loaded walk allowed us to wipe out a 2-run deficit. We had brain cramps, too. Adolfo Phillips, heading home with the tying run on the walk, made a right turn for the dugout before reaching home plate. Ernie Banks made sure Phillips completed his trek on the base paths. Moments later, Banks blooped the walk-off single to the outfield.

Bedlam then ensued. That's what a 5-1 start will provoke after so many decades of second-division finishes and 1-8 or 1-9 beginnings. "

Swirling, swarming like a locust plague they came, pouring out of Wrigley Field's stands, almost blotting out the infield," the Chicago Tribune's George Langford wrote. The Cubs had caused a good portion of the tens of thousands in attendance to go "berserk," Langford added. "Most Wrigley Field veterans said they had never seen such a wild postgame melee by the fans on the field."

To have any number of fans swarm onto the field not for a miracle rally or game-ending homer, but a Keystone Kops ending was still inspiring. The Cubs rooters celebrated on the field on July 2, 1967, after I pitched the Cubs into a first-place tie with St. Louis. Once more, I needed a cordon of Andy Frain ushers to get to the clubhouse. Some fans ran into the field nearly three weeks later after a ninth-inning rally against the Giants. But this time, the dam had really burst. They wanted a Cubs winner badly and just could not hold back.

Reliever Phil Regan was awestruck by the fans' riotous celebration.

"I remember sitting with Randy Hundley," Regan said of the Cubs' catcher. "He came in and one shin guard was off and his clothes were almost all ripped. He couldn't get from home plate down to the leftfield corner to get into the clubhouse. The fans swarmed onto the field. That was really unusual.

"We were down 2 runs in the ninth inning – so quick it turned around."

The afterglow from what I believe was the most dramatic Opening Day in Cubs history on April 8, 1969, still shines brightly. Our fantastic start would keep on going, all the way to 11-1, best team record out of the gate since the 1935 Cubs. That set the tone for the season I, along with Cubs fans of the day, will never forget it.

We'd continue flying high, all the way to the coveted 20-over .500 level early on at 36-16 on June 6 and 40-18 on June 14 as chants of "Cub Power" began to reverberate around Wrigley. The guys handled it well, and were buoyed by big crowds, home and away, and even more gatherings of fans in hotel lobbies and welcoming us coming off our flights home. Along the way, we'd acquire one of our most colorful players of that season, get a preview of our most motivated opponent, and set up further controversies in centerfield with the banishment of what management projected as a key player going into the season.

Brickhouse's and Vince Lloyd's from-the-gut calls of Willie Smith's walk-off homer on that Memorable Opener were still ringing throughout countless ears when we hammered the Phillies 11-3 in our second game. Before we really established ourselves as the National League team to be reckoned with 10 days later, my longtime buddy Billy Williams got some overdue recognition. Often taking second-fiddle status to Banks and Ron Santo, and certainly possessing a lower-key personality than either, Williams was the center of attention, with 4 doubles in the victory, tying the major-league record for one game. Cubs radio analyst Lou Boudreau was one of the fellow record-holders, achieving that back in 1946. Williams proved he was Cooperstown-bound by not changing his sweet stroke despite the wind howling out on an uncommonly nice April day.

"A lot of hitters, when they come in here on a day like this, start trying to hit the ball up in the air," he told reporters afterward. "Me, I just enjoy hitting line drives. I try not to worry about the wind, whether it is blowing in or out. I just try to keep my same stance and not mess it up."

A few feet away, Banks called Williams "the most underestimated player in the game." In two of the next three seasons after 1969, he'd enjoy MVP-caliber seasons, beaten out only by should-have-been Cubs draftee Johnny Bench. When the Hall of Fame came calling 18 years later, the quiet, under-the-radar tag vanished forever. In 1969, though, Williams was irked by being branded the quiet man.

"I'm a label man," he said. "They always label a player when he first comes up to the majors and I was labeled quiet. You say I haven't gotten the publicity I deserved over the years and that I'm an underrated ballplayer. Well, that's up to you guys. I can't write about myself."

They did not write great things about me when I got racked up by the eventual 110-loss Expos for the Cubs' first defeat on Saturday, April 12. Fortunately, we got back on track quickly to win the final three games of our home stand to go 7-1. Then we endured our first test – two road games against the NL defending champion Cardinals, who had blown a 3-games-to-1 lead over the Tigers in the 1968 World Series. We did not soon forget how we were shut out in three consecutive games at Busch Stadium the previous June, the center of our record 48 scoreless innings in a lineup keyed by Williams, Santo and Banks. This time, we returned much of the favor when first I, and then Bill Hands blanked the Cardinals.

My 1-0 victory, first of the season, over Steve Carlton on April 16 was marred by our first injury. Cards third baseman Mike Shannon, a longtime Cubs killer, bowled over Glenn Beckert at second amid a complicated infield sequence.

A seventh-inning Shannon liner hit rookie umpire Dave 'Satch' Davidson – who'd be crucial in our season's fate in September – just past Santo. The ball ricocheted back to Santo, who threw to Banks at first as Shannon continued to second. Banks' throw to Beckert apparently was in time. Shannon and Beckert butted heads in the collision, Beckert's head was jerked back and he was dazed. Shannon had a bruise on his head and got up to a mixture of cheers and boos. As he arose, I handed him his batting helmet, which he proceeded to angrily spike into short-center field. Beckert was sent to what is now Barnes Jewish Hospital, where X-rays were negative, but doctors said he suffered from a "little amnesia," a vintage term for what now would be termed concussion symptoms.

Shannon was booed at Wrigley Field in subsequent visits as a result of the knockout play. Beckert cleared his head – faster than he would have in 21st century concussion protocols – and returned to the lineup. We derived a huge boost by stifling the Cards. My next start, another win against the Expos in cozy Jarry Park in Montreal on April 20, brought our record to 11-1. Meanwhile, the Cubs purchased infielder Nate Oliver, a veteran of some Dodgers winners earlier in the decade, from the Yankees. We were thin in reserve infielders when Beckert was hurt in St. Louis. Rookie outfielder Jimmy Qualls was pressed into service to finish out the game at second, then started the next game.

We came back down to earth a bit in the next week with two losses in spacious Forbes Field in Pittsburgh. The Pirates gave a preview of how they'd be a real pain to us – especially me – over the next few years. Then the Mets gave a hint of their coming spirit when, after we won three in a row at Shea Stadium in New York, April 25 to 27, Cleon Jones broke up a scoreless game with a 3-run, walk-off homer in the bottom of the ninth off lefty Rich Nye to salvage the second game of a Sunday doubleheader.

By the time of our first visit to Shea, we had Dick Selma returning to familiar territory. One of a cadre of hard-throwing, homegrown young Mets pitchers emerging since 1966, Selma had always pitched well against us, including one of my five 1-0 losses in 1968. Both expansion teams had veterans to deal, and the Padres had Selma to peel off in exchange for Joe Niekro on April 25.

"I was still young," Niekro said in 1987. "I didn't know I was being dealt away. It was Yosh Kawano (clubhouse manager) who told me I was traded, not the general manager (John Holland). I came into the clubhouse and found my bags were packed."

Niekro had worn out his welcome with Manager Leo Durocher, who did not like idiosyncrasies in the right-hander.

"He always fiddled with his cap, after every pitch," recalled Hundley. "It drove Leo berserk; it was irritating to him. Leo kept hounding him. He finally said, "Get him out of here,' and Joe was traded."

Niekro's stuff was proving a little short. Even with his sketchy pitching and Durocher's irritation with him, we did not understand the trade, as nobody expected Niekro to be dealt. To be sure, Selma was a different kind of individual, almost a lefty in a right-hander's body. He richly deserved the nickname "Loony Tunes." Often spurred by Durocher, Holland proved to be a relatively impatient general manager, well into the era where our contending team was established.

Selma quickly won us over soon after the impact of the trade wore off. He pitched well as soon as he became a Cub, eventually getting off to a 10-2 record with us through mid-summer. And he kept the entire ballpark loose with his cheerleading duties for the Bleacher Bums. Durocher wanted Dick to continue waving the towel to provoke noise from the Bums after his maestro action apparently worked in a second-inning rally. And Selma was smart, always using his left arm to wave the towel or gesture to the Bums.

Selma also greeted his former New York teammates in their first visit to Wrigley Field on May 2. For the Sunday, May 4, doubleheader, first of the season at home, 40,484 packed every corner of the ballpark. Some 20,000 more were turned away. Some had personally sampled our brand of baseball already and wanted a lot more. Others were making their first pilgrimage to see for themselves what they had witnessed on TV all over the Midwest. Fans' tastes were still tilted to taking advantage of the two-for-the-price-of-one "bargain bill" as it was called at the time, of a Sunday doubleheader. No doubt a few people not knowing the necessity of getting in line early for the 22,000 unreserved seats traveled a long way, only to arrive close to noon, to be disappointed the turnstiles were shuttered.

Those who got in were let down in another way. We dropped a pair of 3-2 decisions, after winning the first two games of the series, and may have welcomed the Mets into the pennant race via an old-fashioned beanball war.

Santo had driven in 10 runs against the Mets in the previous six games in 1969. New York ace Tom Seaver took matters into his own hands. In the second inning of the opener, he knocked down Santo on a pitch far inside on an 0-2 count. Seaver knew there would be quick payback, since our starter was Bill Hands, also our top enforcer. Hands drilled 'Tom Terrific' on his left forearm on his second pitch to Seaver in the third. If the Mets were a sleeping dog up to that point, expected to maybe flirt with .500 in 1969 after seven previous seasons of frequently comic expansion baseball, they now proclaimed to be wide awake.

"I think that when Hands hit me, it helped our whole ball club," Seaver said afterward while admitting he threw at Santo. "The whole dugout suddenly came alive. It gave us a lift. (Santo) hits me hard. I wanted him to know I was protecting myself."

Seaver was not done. The first pitch to Hands in the bottom of the third knicked him in the left leg. Umpire Frank Secory unofficially warned Seaver. Having pitched for 18 seasons, I can attest the retaliation factor does motivate a team. And the Mets had long lingered in or near last place, considered by popular culture a doormat and the butt of jokes in baseball and on TV. They looked at us and others as teams have long thought they would do to the Mets - carpetbag us – but not anymore.

Hurting more than the imprint of the baseball on Hands' leg were complete-game victories by both Seaver and lefty Tug McGraw, normally a starter, as they stymied our attempts to rally. Each Mets starter yielded 9 hits. McGraw would go on to be a decade-long antagonist to the Cubs and our fans, once giving the "choke" sign to fans in the bleachers while working in the outfield before a game.

Winning two low-scoring, 1-run games in one day on the road proved good training for the Mets. In September, they'd gain renown by sweeping a doubleheader against the hard-hitting Pirates by 1-0 scores.

We took note of the Mets' minor surge, figuring their pitching was coming on. Most of us assumed their lineup was underpowered. Even when the Mets acquired the slugging Donn Clendenon from the Expos, their batting order did not seem contender-worthy. The Cardinals' talent and experience was still a first priority in our projections ahead. We had a merry month of May with a 16-9 record and impressive individual and team feats.

Bill Hands and I had trouble keeping up with Ken Holtzman's sizzling start. The lefty, searching for consistency after ups (1967's 9-0 record) and downs (11-14 in 1968), fired off three consecutive shutouts against the San Francisco Giants on May 11, the Houston Astros on May 16, and Los Angeles Dodgers on May 20. Holtzman proved human in earning wins in slugfests against the Giants on May 28 and the Cincinnati Reds on June 6.

After a 3-1 win in Atlanta on June 10, Holtzman was 10-1. If he wasn't the next Sandy Koufax, a projection some had for him back in his 1966 rookie season, he was at the next level as a solid-to-star-level. Hands and I helped Holtzman during starts by signaling whether he was using proper mechanics, but leaving the pitch-calling to Hundley. Such collaboration always helps. Cy Young Award winner Greg Maddux confirms this; he went further than either of us by calling pitches from the bench for fellow starters Mike Morgan and Frank Castillo – two pitchers I coached – in 1992.

The hapless expansion San Diego Padres would become our punching bag while history was made. On May 13, we roughed up the Padres 19-0 at Wrigley Field, with Selma completing the shutout and newly-acquired utility infielder Nate Oliver, nicknamed "Pee Wee," collecting a homer and 4 RBI. Oliver got his day in the sun and worthy publicity, but still could not match Banks' 2 homers and 7 RBIs in the same game. Banks loved the playing against the Padres in 1969. On May 24 in San Diego, Banks slugged his 12th and final career grand-slam homer in the fifth off Jack Baldschun.

After his emotional two homers in his first two at-bats on Opening Day, Mr. Cub was a run-production machine early, despite just a .264 average on May 24. The grand slam brought his RBI total to 38 in our 42nd game. Santo had 32 at that point. Our race out of the gate was partially credited to these hot run-scoring machines. Banks had 62 RBI through our 67th game, June 22, still ahead of Santo before the team captain pulled ahead in July.

On the same West Coast road trip as Banks' grand slam, Hundley provided a double-barreled cause for celebration. On May 28 in San Francisco, the Rebel, as he was known, slugged his own bases-loaded blast off Ray Sadecki to highlight a 7-run third in a 9-8 victory. The day before, wife Betty gave birth to son Todd, their third child, back in Chicago. Hundley celebrated in absentia. "In those days, you never thought of going home for a birth of a child," he said recently, noting players in the 21st century are typically given a short paternity leave if they're on the road.

Meanwhile, a festering sub-plot that began in previous seasons and reached a crescendo in May 1969 led to the unsettling of the key position of center field and became an issue the remainder of the season. Adolfo Phillips, deemed on Opening Day by Holland as a crucial player who could settle down the Cubs by his very presence, never got untracked after breaking his right hand in spring training. Although the cast was removed April 4, Phillips did not appear in center until April 19, coming in for defensive purposes in the 11th inning of the game. Durocher had awarded the centerfield job in Phillips' place to Don Young, a very unlikely candidate coming into the season after washing out of the organization a few years earlier.

Durocher had long been hard on Phillips, who was a sensation in the first half of 1967 – including a 4-homer performance in a June 11 Wrigley Field doubleheader, also against the Mets. Having come over in the trade with me from the Phillies in early 1966, Phillips was seen by many as the cornerstone of the trade. Almost immediately, he flashed some good power along with prodigious strikeout totals in the whiff-prone 1966 Cubs lineup. Phillips stole 32 bases in that rookie season and no one else, not even a young Lou Brock, swiped more in a single year as a Cub in the 1960s. Nearly another decade passed before Jose Cardenal passed up that theft total with 34 in 1975.

Since the final two months in 1967, Phillips had flashed his five-tool talents only occasionally with increasingly shaky play in centerfield. He became what many in baseball called a "head case." Thus, a Durocher-Phillips tangle was the ultimate clash between a demanding old-school manager and a sensitive player from another culture who reacted poorly to big-league stresses.

He went into a shell after Mets pitchers threw at him and Gary Gentry finally hit him. He became gun-shy and the close pitches took the fire away, in my opinion. Before that, he just loved to play. He put too much pressure on himself, believing he was not carrying his share of the load. We had played together at Chattanooga and Little Rock in the Phillies system. I roomed with him.

He always worried, "Do I look okay?"

He developed an ulcer and felt Durocher did not back him up, especially when he was thrown at. Durocher had built him up, even comparing him with Willie Mays as he did with other young, fast outfielders of color. Off the field, we went to the track a lot in New York and Los Angeles, but I'm sure being the Cubs' only Latin player, the majority of his time here left him on a kind of island. With his 1967 heroics, the bleacher fans chanted

"Ole!" repeatedly in his honor. Interestingly, they don't have bullfights in Panama, but the rooters seemingly had no other way to relate to a Latin player.

Whatever goodwill had been built up by Phillips in 1967 disintegrated during our bad, season-busting slump in June 1968. After a June 28 game, Durocher fined Phillips $200 for not hustling on the base paths in running out a potential double, and then not sliding at second. Durocher said it was only the second time he ever fined a player that much in such a situation.

And when Phillips did not seize his job back in recovering from his broken hand in 1969, Durocher did not give him the benefit of the doubt. He still verbally lashed out at him like no other Cub.

"I'm tired of seeing him sitting around," Durocher said on April 16 in St. Louis. "He better get back in there and in a hurry."

Phillips' comeback pace was still pokey though, I thought, as Durocher finally put him back in center on May 6 against the Dodgers at Wrigley Field – albeit after another tongue-lashing, a day after he told a packed B'nai B'rith Sports Lodge event that Phillips "lacked desire." He implied Phillips was enduring his last chance to make good as a Cub.

"All Dolf has to do is show me he wants to play," Durocher said. "That's all. I don't expect him to make spectacular catches, or bat .300, or knock in 95 runs, or hit home runs. Just give me 100 percent."

Phillips didn't go with Durocher's expected flow. He struck out twice in his return and dropped a fly ball for a three-base error. Phillips went four more hitless starts before he collected a pair of singles in a 19-0 spree against the Padres. When we went on the road soon after that, he was riding the bench again while Young returned to center. Then, while on a West Coast swing, Phillips made seven more starts, but made no real headway in his offensive numbers before his final benching. His 28-game, 66 plate-appearances Cubs line in 1969 was 1 RBI and a .224 average before he was traded June 11. Phillips never got his career untracked as a part-time outfielder with the Expos in the next 1-½ seasons. He was last seen in the majors in 1972 playing center in old Comiskey Park for the Cleveland Indians, flanking a long blond-haired right fielder named Buddy Bell. Phillips's career ended at age 30.

Phillips' final failure created an absolute revolving door in center. The '69 Cubs employed a total of nine men in that position, including Young, Qualls, rookie Rick Bladt, veteran Jimmie Hall, Jim Hickman, and Al Spangler moving over from their accustomed homes in right field. The constant shuffling swept in 19-year-old rookie, Oscar Gamble, in a premature promotion that proved disastrous for Gamble's future as a Cub. Also used out of his normal position was Popovich in the late innings via a double switch by coach Reiser, filling in for an AWOL Durocher. I don't know though if Phillips would have caught the two misplayed fly balls by Young in an infamous July game I lost.

Centerfield became such a huge hole for us, you could drive four semi-trailers side-by-side through it untouched. The position would remain unstabilized until Rick Monday's arrival in the 1972 season.

No North-type of player was ready to seize the center-field job in 1969. The Cubs' farm system was still feeling the effects of under-spending, under-evaluating, racial quotas, and the long-term effects low recruiting in the early Sixties.

Phillips' flameout ensured our challenges would only increase as the summer of 1969 heated up.

Everybody wanted their company name next to the Cubs logo!

An Appreciation Of
"Whistler" Billy Williams

C all them the pre-meeting meetings.
    Rather than a crowded cubbyhole locker room with Leo Durocher presiding and the conversation going one way, from Durocher to us, my daily gabfests with Billy Williams in 1969 were full of friendly give-and-takes.

Comparing baseball notes, pitcher to hitter and back again, was the best way to spend our 45-minute morning commutes to Wrigley Field, up South Shore Drive, then onto Lake Shore Drive, through downtown, and getting off at Belmont, snaking to the Cubs players' parking lot next to the firehouse on Waveland Avenue. We'd split the wheels we'd use, my purple-and-white T-Bird or Williams' Buick Wildcat. He derived one of his many nicknames from his car, including the one year he had a gold Wildcat.

In 1969, though, the old saying went: "Home-run hitters drive Cadillacs" and our Ron Santo was well-known for his Caddy – reports of the third baseman's luxury wheels tooling through your Chicago neighborhood would spread like wildfire. Symbolically, with his next-step-down General Motors product, Williams was not a home-run hitter, per se, just a simple pure hitter for whom homers were a byproduct of a picture-perfect swing.

Wildcat and Whistler, the latter for his Alabama hometown, became our nicknames for Williams. If we wanted to save a syllable, it'd be "Whis." For media and fans, "The Sweet Swinger" and "The Classic Hitter" certainly sufficed.

Banks said of Williams: "He loves the game as much as any of us. He just has a different way of expressing it. Some guys like me go around hollering, but he quietly does it all," and, "It's too bad that a lot of things Billy does are overlooked. He is a tremendous asset to the team. He gets so many big hits, makes so many great plays and yet he is the most underestimated player in the game."

After winning the NL Rookie of the Year award though in 1961, a huge feat amid the chaos of the College of Coaches debacle, Williams subsequently batted third in front of Santo and Banks, starting in 1962. He faithfully got on base to provide the grist for much of the production of both of their 100-RBI seasons. But as we developed into contenders going into 1969, his speaking-event invitations and other off-field moneymakers paled in comparison to the Nos. 4 and 5 hitters. Three times he had reached 30 or more homers and twice he had more than 200 hits going into 1969. He had a mounting consecutive-games-played streak since September 22, 1963, when he sat out against southpaw Hall-of-Famer Warren Spahn at Wrigley Field. As the streak kept going, Williams cautioned he was tired, but would not take off a day until it reached 1,117 consecutive games, which put him into fourth place overall at the time and first in the NL with a slight cushion. It was ended by mutual agreement of Williams and Durocher on September 3, 1970, at Wrigley Field. Cleo James took his place in left field, in the only game he missed in '70.

"I remember sitting on the bench and thinking when I get back in there they're goin' to have a hell of a time getting me out," he said in 1969 of his last game missed.

Maybe the finest reliability in baseball just got taken too much for granted. Williams was just so consistent and dependable. Cleanup-hitter Santo could be moved down to No. 5 and even No. 6 in the order, if need be. Banks could occasionally replace Santo at cleanup, but also be dropped down from his usual No.

> *The finest reliability in baseball just got too much taken for granted.*

5 or even taken out of the order all together in Durocher's occasional attempts to find a replacement. Williams, however, simply stayed at No. 3, year-in and year-out, even up to two seasons beyond Durocher's tenure as manager.

Finally, in 1969, Williams began to receive long-overdue recognition – in a season where he had his second-lowest home-run total (21) of his Cubs' career up until his final season in 1974. He tied a National League record with four doubles in 1969's second game. His streak was considered so inviolate that when he fouled a pitch off his instep in Cincinnati in mid-June, Durocher went to great lengths to get him a pinch-hit at-bat to keep the streak going. Durocher even said he'd push Williams up to the plate in a wheelbarrow if necessary. Even though, from time to time, he'd profess to writers he was tired, Williams kept pushing on in his streak. He simply expected to play every day.

On our drives to the ballpark, the subject of the streak never came up. Williams did his talking about it by staying in shape for his years-long grind. He went to bed at 10:00 P.M. at home. He consumed wheat germ and honey as a diet supplement. He kept his weight in check. Like shortstop Don Kessinger, Williams did not have an ounce to lose over the long seasons. He'd enjoy a steak, for sure, on the road and he'd have a glass of wine before meals, but his only unhealthy habit was smoking – although many players lit up back then, before we knew how bad it was. Williams would sneak a cigarette at the end of the dugout, whenever he could be blocked from view of Durocher or the umpire, or he'd take a quick smoke in the tunnel behind the dugout.

No matter though, we had a special player on our hands, befitting of high honors. So the grand ceremony of the season took place on June 29, 1969 at Wrigley Field. We honored Williams for breaking Stan Musial's consecutive games-played streak of 895 with a between-games ceremony in which he got a Chrysler Imperial and a boat, among other big-ticket items.

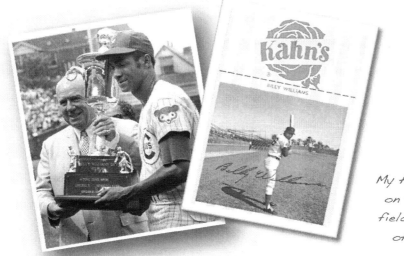

My friend on the field and off.

The Weimaraner dog from me was a fairly practical gift. We hunted together quite a bit. We tracked pheasants and ducks around south-suburban Kankakee. He had been a deer hunter back in Alabama and also loved to fish. Off the field, he was my friend and these two brothers of America's pastime enjoyed these simpler pastimes.

In the ceremony, emceed by WGN's Jack Brickhouse and televised live, I have always felt we should have also announced Williams' batting feats, which were just as impressive as his record-breaking endurance. He gave a textbook example on his great day, going 5-for-9 in the doubleheader – 2 doubles, 2 triples and a single. How many players so honored came through as magnificently on their special day? Usually they're too nervous or too distracted with emotion. For Williams, on either side of the ceremony, it was just another day at the park.

Williams was a thinking man's hitter. Williams often said, in the complete-game era, he'd simply wait and watch through the first three at-bats against a starter – like a patient predator stalking his prey. By the fourth time up, batting against a diminished fastball of a tiring pitcher, Williams would lower the boom. You could not easily make Williams swing and miss three times in an at-bat. He only once struck out as many as 80 times in a season – 84 in 1964.

"Billy is probably the best hitter I saw in baseball," said fellow Hall-of-Famer Brock. "I never saw Billy take a half-swing at a ball, which is hard to do. The consistency which Billy had is the only thing you ask for in a hitter...He is the symbol of success."

Williams said he knew he was a good hitter after his 25-homer, .286 rookie season, but he also made 11 errors in left field. Always a hard worker on any deficiency, he spent as much if not more time in spring training 1962 working on his defense. In addition to developing reliability in the outfield, he knew how to play Wrigley Field's often-capricious elements. Knowing the wind was blowing in, he would not give up on the ball, catching Hank Aaron's would-be homer while backing into the vines in left in the seventh inning of Ken Holtzman's no-hitter on August 19, 1969.

The patience he displayed at the plate and the equanimity with which he handled his consecutive games streak finally got Williams his recognition in everything but an MVP award and a World Series ring. After the 1969 season was consigned to the record book, he finally became noted for being a premier siege gun at the plate rather than an endurance freak. Few have channeled natural hitting talent with such hard work and mental preparation as my fishing buddy.

Desire, ability, and a battle plan. That's why Williams never missed a game and spent 57 seasons drawing a check from the Cubs. He worked as a minor-league and big-league player, minor-league roving instructor, big-league hitting coach and bench coach, special assistant in the front office, and speaker's bureau coordinator. I'm glad that Williams never strayed far from the Cubs' embrace – even after he retired in 1976 ending a few years in Oakland as a player and coach.

Williams did not have to wait long to get voted into the Hall of Fame, in 1987. I'm glad he was there to greet me for my induction speech in Cooperstown four years later. Who'd have projected that scene on hot days when we commuted up Lake Shore Drive together (or talked sometimes better than we fished) wherever we found water?

Patience, as exemplified in Billy Leo Williams, has its rewards.

Come Get These Memories

A Cubs fan writing to Ernie Banks' column on September 7, 1969, complained that all the attention on Wrigley Field attendees focused on the Bleacher Bums – some 1,000 of the 40,000 in a full house by her estimate.

The fan protested she already had attended 25 games of the season. What about some attention on the intensity of loyalty from fans in the $3.50 box seats or $1.75 grandstands.

At the time, Cubs management and players did address those fans' needs. Mothers had written the team complaining all players did not sign autographs for their children. So, to serve the hordes patronizing the non-bleacher sections, an autograph booth opened in the main concourse behind the dugout on July 11, 1969. Relievers Ted Abernathy and Hank Aguirre were the first signers. The longtime heart of the lineup – Billy Williams, Ron Santo and Ernie Banks – did triple duty one day, signing before the 12:30 p.m., July 13 doubleheader. Almost all players participated in this pre-game reach-out to our loyal supporters.

As the commentary to Banks' column stated, the other Wrigley Field inhabitants deserved their due. We will give them their own words in a chapter in which we travel back in time and allow them to recollect their happy and sometimes sad times in Wrigley Field and beyond.

Jan Poledziewski, Munster, Indiana

Jan epitomizes the love of the Cubs passed along from generation to generation. Her memories of 1969 with her father reflect that torch-passing. One key player from that season would also touch her life and that of husband Wayne in a special way, exactly 40 years later.

I grew up a Cubs fan in the far south suburb of Calumet Park, blatantly disregarding the geography that mandated I should root for the White Sox. The person responsible for my life-long allegiance to the Cubbies was my dad, John Juby, who was a World War II veteran (8th Army Air Force) who served in England.

He and my mom, Eleanor, were pen pals during the war. My mom worked at International Harvester with my grandfather. My grandfather asked my mom if she would like to write to one of his sons in the service, a practice very common during the war years to keep up morale. When the war ended, my dad returned to his family home in south-suburban Blue Island, met my mom in person, and he married her in 1947. They would go one to build a modest brick bungalow in Calumet Park and, a few years later, I arrived as part of the Baby Boomer Generation.

I grew up an only child in a neighborhood full of kids. Though I had no siblings, there was always an abundance of playmates. Since my block was overrun with boys, it was common for us to get together for an impromptu baseball game on almost any day in nice weather. The games were crudely constructed with cardboard bases, an infinite number of outfielders, good faith ball-and-strike calls and little regard for three outs to end an inning.

As I grew up, my outside love of playing America's pastime transitioned to my indoor love of watching the Cubs on WGN-TV with Jack Brickhouse on the call, or listening to Vince Lloyd and Lou "Good Kid" Boudreau on my transistor radio. Brickhouse was a staple in our living room. To this day, I can still close my eyes and hear Brickhouse's voice, yelling his famous, "Hey Hey!" which I knew meant good news for the Cubs.

After the war, my dad worked as a photographer for Root Studio in the Loop. He worked most weekends, but the upside was that he usually had a couple of days off during the week – perfect for catching a Cubs game. My mom did not share our love of baseball, so our outings to Wrigley Field were father-daughter and sometimes included my best friend, Debbie.

On Game Day, we always left early. My dad either drove us or we rode the Illinois Central commuter train from Blue Island to Randolph Street and then took a bus to the park. Often, we went on Ladies Day (the discounted price was just right), and occasionally we lucked out with a doubleheader. Game 1 was followed by just enough time to eat a hot dog, then Game 2. We loved it.

In those lean Cubs years, we had our pick of the "good seats." Before the games, we routinely went down to the brick wall by the third base dugout to catch glimpses of our heroes as they returned from pre-game practice. Occasionally, my dad brought his Brownie Instamatic movie camera. One of my dad's greatest days as a Cubs fan was capturing an Ernie Banks home run on 8 mm film, as Banks was his favorite Cub.

"He plays the game the way it should be played," Dad said of Mr. Cub.

My dad loved everything about baseball, every nuance – the pace, the strategy, the mechanics, the stats, the history – everything. He loved Wrigley Field, the players, and the 1969 Cubs most of all.

In the summer of 1969, I was getting ready to start my senior year in high school. It was a tumultuous time in history. The news was full of civil unrest and a raging war in Vietnam. Baseball was an escape from what was wrong with the world. As the baseball season progressed, Cubs fans were getting cautiously excited. Dare we think it? Was it possible that the 1969 Cubs could win the National League pennant? After all, Neil Armstrong had just walked on the moon, so anything was possible.

For us, 1969 was the Dream Team. We rooted for the players who would become icons in Cubs Nation – Banks, Santo, Williams, Fergie Jenkins, Glenn Beckert, Don Kessinger, Randy Hundley, Rich Nye, Dick Selma – these were the guys destined to end the North Side drought. As my dad would say in later years, "On paper, they couldn't miss."

That emotional connection from 1969 reached out over future decades. Many years later, in 2009, my husband Wayne and I (along with my childhood friend, Debbie, and her husband) had the privilege of personally meeting Santo at Wrigley Field before a game. Six weeks earlier, my husband's right leg had been amputated after a severe infection, and Santo, a double amputee due to his Type 1 diabetes, offered words of encouragement and advice: "Listen to your doctors and do what they say. Look at me, I can do everything I did before, and you will, too."

Back in 1969, I never dreamed that 40 years later, Santo would become more than a baseball player to me. To this day, my husband Wayne credits Santo's words as his catalyst for a successful recovery. When Santo passed away late in 2010, we drove in a snowstorm to attend his wake. It was as if we lost a member of our family. And the following year, 2011, Wayne stood on his new prosthesis for an hour without stress or strain waiting for the start of the ceremony dedicating Santo's statue at Wrigley Field.

19s each week passed in the Summer of '69, my expectations grew. I was 17, full of baseball fever, and absolutely giddy at the prospect of having my team head into the World Series for the first time in, well, forever in my eyes. It seemed everyone was talking about the Cubs, and, for once, the conversation was exciting and optimistic. I lived in a land of White Sox fans (including much of my family) and had endured more than my fair share of teasing when it came to baseball. Now it was my turn to hold my head up high. It seemed everyone had a renewed interest in reading the sports columns and catching the sports news on TV. The stats didn't lie, and the Cubs' won-loss record put them atop the NL East by 8 1/2 games in mid-August. When they played, we expected them to win. They were on fire.

But as the 1969 season started to wind down toward September, I noticed my dad was somewhat reluctant to share my enthusiasm. September was a nightmare and the Mets would become a hated four-letter word. The season of 1969 has been sliced and diced over the years in an attempt to understand what happened.

My dad was furious with the Cubs' manager known for his tirades, big personality and blurts like, "Nice guys finish last," although that is generally attributed to his days working for the Brooklyn Dodgers. Well, that philosophy got *the Cubs nowhere either. Yes, to the day he died, my dad blamed "The Lip" for breaking the hearts of Cubs' fans in 1969. (I do know, however, that he would have loved 2016 World Series-winning Manager Joe Maddon.)*

I lost my dad suddenly in 2002. He was a young 79. Although he lived to enjoy the Cubs playoff teams of '84, '89 and '98, those seasons ultimately ended like 1969, with the familiar mantra of, "Wait 'til next year."

I'm sad that he never experienced the euphoria of a World Series championship. When the Cubs were in the World Series in 2016, I thought of him often during each game. I can't quite explain it, but during the playoffs, I truly felt his presence.

I think he heard me screaming when they won.

Dr. David J. Fletcher, Monticello, Ill.

"Doc" Fletcher lived and breathed baseball even as he roamed the world as a physician, first as a U.S. Army doctor, then in private occupational-medicine practice. He thought nothing of making that boring 2½-hour drive through the cornfields from his central Illinois home to Chicago's ballparks. As he explains here, in the 2000s, Fletcher sought to build a Chicago Baseball Museum, partially based on the memories of long travels to an ivy-encrusted ballpark in another century – in 1969.

As a west suburban kid growing up in the late 1960s, baseball was virtually my whole world. Looking back a half century later at the Cubs magical yet tragic 1969 season, I just remember profound sadness in my 14-year-old mind after closely following the Cubs rise and fall. I can recall crying in my sophomore Latin Class at Glenbard West High School in Glen Ellyn as the Cubs endured another heartbreaking loss to the Mets during that infamous September swoon.

My eyes matched the redness on the eyes of Ernie Banks, who in the twilight of his Cubs career, knocking on the door of 500 career home runs and his possible first trip to the postseason, worked the Sunday night WGN-TV sportscasts.

On air, I recall Banks' eyes were bloodshot during the collapse. His perpetual smile and sunshine personality – the "Cubs Will Shine in '69" – was muted those final five weeks of the season. It was a struggle to watch him read the script on Channel 9 that last month. Cubs fans could personally feel the pain he was experiencing as his playoff chances slipped away. He tried to put a positive spin on the waning Cubs highlights as they blew a 10-game, August 13 lead on the Miracle Mets.

Watching Banks doing the Sunday night sports was always an experience. The other WGN-TV and radio broadcasters - Jack Brickhouse, Vince Lloyd, Lou Boudreau and Lloyd Pettit - all seemed like family and helped comfort me through those difficult teenage years. We were fortunate in Chicago in the late Sixties to have virtually every Cubs game on TV thanks to WGN, unlike some other cities that rationed the number of televised games. Watching the White Sox games in 1969 was more challenging. The images on the UHF stations were ghost-like and required constant tinkering with your antenna.

In person, I saw around 25 games at Wrigley Field, thanks in part to the pass I was given as a baseball player for Glenbard West. Getting to Wrigley Field proved to be another story. Glen Ellyn was 26 miles west of Wrigley Field and I was not old enough to drive myself to the ballpark.

Today, a 14-year-old would not likely be allowed to roam that distance, making multiple public transportation transfers, especially without an older escort. Yet, 1969 was a different time. Believe it or not, my liberal-minded parents allowed me to take three trains to get to Wrigley Field, even though the journey was an adventure.

There was no sleeping late for me on summer vacation. I had my own morning rush hour, and then some. My goal was to arrive before 10:00 A.M. at Wrigley to claim the best seat when the ballpark opened, and the 22,000 day-of-game seats were up for grabs.

On a few occasions, I even brought my 12-year-old sister Sally and 6-year-old brother Tom to join me on these two-hour journeys to get to the ballpark. My parents seemingly were not concerned that their young children ventured onto Chicago's subways, unaccompanied by an adult at a time of tremendous change in Chicago and in the country.

I had virtually no money those days, but looking back, it did not seem to matter. The joy of the ballpark and seeing the Cubs play with a largely consistent eight-man lineup was all I needed. If had I a few spare nickels, I would even pop for a Ron Santo Pros' Pizza. My only certain purchase was getting a scorecard for that day's game. I still have several 1969 scorecards in my archives that bring back a warm memory. After games at Wrigley, I would scoop up scorecards left by fans to add to my collection and to give extras to friends.

The Tribune headlines from the September swoon still ruminate in the dark recesses of my brain – "Cubs Reach Depths of Despair" and, "It's Like Old Days for Cubs; Empty Seats and Struggling." The final headline "Somewhere The Sun Is Shining," from the September 25 Tribune, when the Cubs got officially eliminated from the NL East, still brings me misery.

What I learned from that '69 season is that life is not fair. I could not count on my Cubs reaching the World Series after believing in postseason heaven for five months. I had seemingly lost my innocence when the Cubs collapsed.

My love for baseball has faded a lot since that summer of 1969. There are so many other distractions that get jammed into life, plus, the game has changed so much due to the business of baseball, as have fan tastes.

Seeing the Cubs win the World Series finally in 2016 was nice. But for fans of my generation, the 1969 Cubs – even though they ended up in second place in the East – will be forever my favorite Cubs team.

Scott Nelson, Skokie, Illinois

Scott was one of several avid 1969 Cubs fans who ended up working in the Cubs front office in the 1980s and 1990s. Nelson was hired in 1983 by respected player development chief, Gordon Goldsberry, a Cubs area scout in 1969. Nelson worked for the Cubs, rising to director of baseball operations, through the early Theo Epstein front-office regime.

1969 was the year I fell in love with the Cubs at age 13, and it changed my life forever.

I've always thought of the 1969 Cubs as not just a sports story, but also a sociological phenomenon, an escape from the turbulent summer of 1968, revolving around the Democratic Convention and the assassinations of Dr. Martin Luther King Jr. and Robert F. Kennedy.

Starting on Opening Day, when Willie Smith hit that unforgettable game-winning home run, the entire city caught Cubs Fever. My brother Jeff and I were in the car with my mom heading back from a trip to the dentist when Smith won the game with that blast. Jeff and I were jumping all over inside the car when we heard Vince Lloyd call the shot that started it all!

I lived in Naperville that year and my friends and I lived each day to watch or listen to the Cubs games as they marched to the National League pennant – or so we thought.

Our local Phillips 66 gas station had a sign posted each day with their Magic Number to clinch the division while the local Jewel grocery store gave away Cubs' photos and sold Cubs' mugs and phonograph records, of which we couldn't get enough. We made daily trips to Bart's Hobby Shop as well, buying packs of Topps baseball cards – just wanting to find Cubs players as we shuffled through each pack.

My friends and I memorized and copied the batting stances of Don Kessinger, Glenn Beckert, Billy Williams, Ernie Banks, Ron Santo, Jim Hickman, and Randy Hundley, and the pitching motions of Ferguson Jenkins, Bill Hands, and especially the submarine delivery of Ted Abernathy while we played ball at the local ball field.

A trip to Wrigley Field was a special occasion, which we made a few times that year. I can always remember how excited I would get as I sat in the car, staring out the window, as we approached Clark and Addison Streets, anticipating my first glimpse of the ballpark. We entered the park, purchased a pencil and scorecard, and took that walk up the steps while Wrigley Field unfolded in front of us in all its glory, including: blue sky; scoreboard; bleachers; ivy; the outfield grass; and the infield -- straining my neck to see which players were on the field; and who might be signing autographs near the wall.

One big visit to Wrigley I missed out on that summer was a Naperville Park District field trip on Tuesday, August 19. I was staying with my aunt in Michigan at the time, but Jeff got to go. That day, Kenny Holtzman threw his no-hitter, beating the Braves, 3-0, with Santo hitting a 3-run home run in the first inning. When I spoke to my parents on the phone about listening to the game that day, they were hesitant to tell me that my brother had been there. My heart fell as I was happy that Jeff got to see the game but angry I had missed it, not knowing that was the day of the Park District's field trip.

Sadly, we didn't realize that game was to be the last great highlight of the season, as the Cubs went on to go 15-25 and our 10-game lead over the New York Mets steadily faded away. I can remember watching the last telecast from Wrigley Field that season, on October 2, as Jack Brickhouse recounted what was a wonderful summer but heartbreaking ending. The Bleacher Bums all jumped over the wall from leftfield and sat sulking around the pitcher's mound.

For me, the biggest takeaway from the 1969 season was watching and falling in love with Santo. I couldn't wait to watch his every at-bat and defense at third. His passion, his style and his charisma inspired me in a way that drove me to want to become a Chicago Cub with the same intensity and dedication he exhibited.

How I ended up working as a batboy and in the Wrigley Field home clubhouse and then on to a 30-year career in the Cubs front office, finishing as director of baseball operations, is another story. That inside-out view of the Cubs happened thanks, in part, to Yosh Kawano, but also the inspiration of Santo.

I consider myself so fortunate to have been able to become friends and work with Santo in his later role as Cubs radio analyst while I was a team official. Many times we traveled together on road trips. We'd get together after the game and talk baseball. I would tell him from time to time, that if not for him, I wouldn't have fallen in love with baseball and the Cubs and he would just listen. I don't know if he believed what I was telling him, but it is true – and it really started in that magic summer of 1969.

That fall, it was a sad time for us as the reality of the Mets winning the pennant set in. School had started again, the Magic Number sign at Phillips 66 was quietly taken down, football cards replaced the baseball cards at Bart's Hobby Shop and there were a lot of leftover Cubs records and mugs at the Jewel. Disbelief, but without a doubt, hope for next year.

Mike Klis, Greater Denver

Although his sports-beat assignment covering the Denver Broncos for KUSA-TV in the Mile High City took him far away from home, Klis is still true to his childhood roots in Oswego, just southwest of suburban Aurora. That was his vantage point for rooting for the Cubs in 1969, and a day trip to Wrigley Field was a treat.

Like every other longtime fan of the Chicago Cubs, I was both exuberant and relieved when they won the 2016 World Series. World Champions, yes ... but second-best to the 1969 Cubs in my lifelong fandom. It was the 1969 Cubs who made me a skeptic for life.

Age was a factor in my profound affinity for the 1969 Cubs. I was 10-years old – too young to care about the societal upheaval caused by the protests of the Vietnam War, but the perfect age to idolize Cubs players.

The year started with the most wonderfully, surprising piece of mail I've ever received – an 8-by-10 glossy, black-and-white portrait of Ernie Banks.

"To Mike, Lots of Luck, Ernie Banks, "Shine 1969."

A four-figure refund from the IRS would not bring me greater joy. As I remember it, my uncle, Joe Plaskas, had run into Banks somewhere and arranged for the autographed picture. I was hooked. At that point, I wrote letters seeking autographed pictures from Bill Hands, Randy Hundley, Billy Williams, Fergie Jenkins, Jim Hickman, Glenn Beckert, and other greats.

I made the decision then I wanted to become a sports announcer, specifically Jack Brickhouse's job, for one reason: I could get all the autographs I wanted. Ironically, when I later become a member of the sports media, I became one of the last people in the human race who could get an autograph, as it states on the bottom of all sports credentials that autographs are not allowed. Fortunately, I have long outgrown my athletic worshipping stage.

In 1969, I got home from East View Elementary in time to watch Banks hit one of his 2 homers on Opening Day, and then for Willie Smith to win it with a pinch-hit homer in extra innings.

I attended one game at Wrigley Field that season, on Saturday, May 31. I went with a whole group, including my dad, brother, neighbors, and friends. We parked for free on a Chicago street six blocks away and walked to the park. (You can't park anywhere on many Chicago streets for free nowadays, let alone near the ball park). Before the game, I got an autograph along the Braves' bullpen from knuckleballer Ken Johnson, who signed my scorecard.

We brought brown-sack lunches, but our dads bought us hot dogs and frosty malts, anyway.

Although I attended just the one game at Wrigley – it was a major undertaking in 1969 to ride in from Oswego to Chicago – I swear I watched almost every game on Channel 9 in Grandpa Joe Klis Sr. (JaJa) and Grandma Stella's apartment on the downstairs level of our tri-level home.

Many evenings after dinner, grandpa and I would sit on the back porch and talk about the Cubs game we had watched. During one exhilarating evening, Cubs' starting pitcher and Bleacher Bums cheerleader Dick Selma came to our little town of Oswego to sign autographs from a shack-like business structure. I remember the line as a couple of town blocks long. I remember one of my school mates, Dick Cain, excitedly yelling as we got near him, "Hey, Dick!"

East View was buzzing the next day. Dick Selma!

I never liked Santo's heel-clicking antics down the left-field line either after a victory. Brickhouse always went nuts for it, but even at 10-years old, I was afraid Santo would jinx things. And as the Cubs swooned and blew their big lead in the NL East – they were 75-44 and 9 games up on August 16, but 84-59 and only 1 game down on September 10 – I developed a strong hatred for the New York Mets.

My grandpa, on the back porch, often said during the Cubs' slump – "They're not choking, they're just having some rotten luck!" – adding that Leo Durocher should let Kessinger take off for a couple days of fishing. Grandpa also said Durocher should go fishing, although I think for reasons other than fatigue.

Sometimes, I think you had to be 10 in 1969 to really share in true Cubs heartache.

Funny, but the most vivid memory I have of the 1969 Cubs was Jimmy Qualls leaping over Cincinnati Reds catcher Pat Corrales to score. When the Cubs beat the Los Angeles Dodgers to win the 2016 National League pennant for the first time since 1945, I jumped up and down like a kid, leaped into my son Blake's arms and then shouted into the cellphone my son Johnny was using as a video camera: "This one's for you JIMMY QUALLS!"

Carol Haddon, Glencoe, Illinois

At Wrigley Field, seniority must be served, and that means Carol Haddon is No. 1. She is the single-ranking season-ticket holder with seats in her own name, having first bought the boxes in 1971, just in time for my Cy Young Award season. Carol was just as loyal to the Cubs two years earlier, acquiring her seats each day.

You'll still find Carol close to the action and as loyal as ever. The televised close-up sight of her eyes watering, standing in her front-row seat as the Cubs were zeroing in on the World Series victory in 2016, is a classic.

In 1969, I was a recently retired special education teacher living in north suburban Morton Grove with my two children and my husband. My students learned a lot about life and about the Cubs under my direction!

I hopped aboard the Skokie Swift train and headed down to Wrigley Field almost daily. All games were played during the day, so I was able to return home before dinnertime. By 1969, the fine gentlemen in the ticket office knew me to be a regular. I was sold awesome seats along the first base line, which were often in the front row, as early-season weekday crowds only averaged 10,000 or less per game at that time..

I was even welcomed into the ticket office for a 'hot toddy' on those cold days in April or a "cold one" during the hot days of summer. Who could resist an invitation like that? I often sat down the baseline near the visitor's bullpen and learned a lot about the art of pitching. Players spoke easily to me in exchange for the fried chicken I brought them during the game.

I met Jack Brickhouse, Vince Lloyd, and Lou Boudreau, the Cubs broadcasters during this time. Their interviews were often conducted near the on-deck circle where I also sat on many occasions. And, I had a hilarious experience the year before on my first baseball road trip with my girlfriend Judy, around the Cincinnati Netherland Hilton Hotel swimming pool. As Lloyd and Boudreau and others looked on, Brickhouse made an elaborate dive into the pool and almost lost his bathing trunks in the process. That led to a lot of laughs and good will. As a result, I could occasionally venture up to the booth and quietly watch and listen to the broadcasts in progress. I became an official season-ticket holder in 1971 and Section 26, by the visiting on-deck circle, became my seat on a daily basis.

During this time, I learned much about what went on behind the scenes at Wrigley, but the real action was happening ON the Field. On June 29, Billy Williams broke Stan Musial's then "Iron Man" National League record by playing in his 896th consecutive game. On August 19, I saw my first no-hitter, when Ken Holtzman beat the Atlanta Braves.

Earlier in the season, it was apparent that Adolfo Phillips would not be the hoped-for superstar, but it was that trade that brought Ferguson Jenkins to the Cubs. Jenkins treated us to his third consecutive 20-win season, throwing more than 300 innings and leading the NL in strikeouts in 1969. The fans were ecstatic. Even Morganna, the famed "Kissing Bandit," would make an occasional on-field appearance to smooch a targeted Cubs' ballplayer. The Andy Frain ushers never stopped her.

Although the Mets took the smiles off Cubs' fan faces that October, the 1969 players remain forever in our lives. Hundley, Banks, Beckert, and Kessinger are all part of our memories. Jenkins and Billy Williams participated in team PR events and Santo became the "voice" of the Cubs. Jenkins continues to devote generously of his time raising funds for charity throughout the year. Cubs' fans saw excellent baseball that year.

Little did anyone then realize we were watching four future Hall-of-Famers all on one team!

When the team celebrated Wrigley Field's 100th anniversary, the Cubs asked me to participate in several TV interviews. One station introduced me as the longest-standing season ticket-holder, as told to them by the Cubs. This surprised me, but the Cubs made that a seeming fact. Perhaps there are families that have changed the names on their accounts as they were then able to pass the seats on to another family member. I know of several longstanding accounts now in the name of the children. My two seats have always been in my name. So, I am surely one of the most senior season-ticket holders. I know of no one else at this level, but this is what I do know … I have likely attended more games than anyone else. Most people have had to work or share their seats with partners. Lucky me! I have successfully combined family and my love of baseball. Wrigley Field has been a second home for me.

I've said it before and I'll say it, again. The 1969 Cubs roster was bigger than those of us in the dugout. It was the fans, the ones who stool in lines waiting for the day-of-game tickets, the ones gathering their friends and neighbors for time in the sun at Wrigley, the ones who made their lives attached to the team that broke their hearts, and the ones who cried happy tears when dreams came true after waiting half a century.

I'm happy to give them their due in these pages.

They certainly gave us ours.

Toast Of The Bleacher Bums

Close, but no cigar, for Ron Grousl.

Maybe I should have offered the former spiritual leader of the Left Field Bleacher Bums a big, fat stogie and advertised the dirigible-sized smoke as being of Caribbean origin – hint, 90 miles from Key West – to break all embargoes. That might have lured the now-senior citizen the final 50 miles from Woodstock, Illinois, to a mini-reunion of the Bums, in which I participated, at Bernie's Tap & Grill, across from, Wrigley Field, near the start of the 2018 season. I'd like to have seen if Ron would have again been the life of the party.

Grousl was Chicago's most publicized street performer . . . and adlibber . . . of 1969. Hardly a week passed when Grousl was not featured in a newspaper.

Yet, within a few years – about 1973 – Grousl was gone. Poof! Just like that.

Eventually, Grousl was tracked down back in Chicagoland, although he shied away from a reunion meeting with me.

I had good reason for desiring to see Grousl. More than any other Cub, I believe I had a special connection with the Bums and I think the feeling was mutual. After a rude 1966 introduction to Mike Haley, Grousl's right-hand man in directing the fun and frolic in left field, I ended up getting a toast to my good luck at Ray's Bleachers before every home start. Although the Left Field Bleacher bums may have only had a half-decade run as a semi-formal group, in the process, they earned notoriety as one of the most distinctive groups of fans in Chicago sports history. And they made the cheap-seat bleachers, just $1 in 1969, the *most* coveted place to sit in Wrigley Field.

In any WGN telecast in 1969, the Bums cheering en masse for us was a staple shot several times a game for producer-director Arne Harris. After a Cubs homer, the center-field camera often swung right to show the Bums' reactions. An accompanying TV shot featured pitcher Dick Selma performing several towel-waving gyrations while standing in the bullpen to direct the Bums' cheers, at the impetus of Manager Leo Durocher.

The Bums-Cubs connection benefited from a time, place, and relationship that probably could not be duplicated before or after our era. They fed off us and we fed off them.

Bleacher Bums bugler Mike Murphy, like Grousl, patrolled the top of the wall in that last pre-basket season in 1969. The group's origin is traced as just a small collection of diehards coming together informally during the dark days of 1965 and 1966.

When we suddenly surged to first place on July 2, 1967, the Bums began an organized "club" of sorts, symbolized by Grousl sticking his head in the hole of a huge bedsheet that was labeled, "Hit the Bleacher Bum," when a Cubs slugger came to bat. The Bums began traveling to St. Louis and other road destinations within reasonable driving distance.

By 1969, even after having driven opposition outfielders nuts with their guerilla-theater tactics, the Cubs themselves endorsed the Bums. This fan recognition . . . something today known as the extra man in many professional sports, was a new concept at that time. And it wasn't just recognition that they received; owner Phil Wrigley paid up to $10,000 to send 65 Bums to Atlanta for a 3-game series, August 29 to 31, 1969. He recognized that the fans really were part of the team.

Eventually, too many mass incursions of fans onto the field, and the harassing of visiting players, led to management distancing itself from the Bums. "Kind of the best and the worst things happened," said Chuck Shriver, the Cubs' media relations director in 1969. "At first we encouraged it (with the paid-for trip to Atlanta). Unfortunately, as the season went along, it kind of got to be a problem."

Meanwhile, it got to the point where a request to allow several Bums onto the team charter to Atlanta was turned down by the team. "We never make arrangements like that," General Manager John Holland said at the time. The basket was installed following the first home stand in 1970, after an anti-Vietnam War group stormed the field and nearly assaulted several players at the conclusion of the home opener.

Soon though, with our successes mounting, a tradition began where I got that good-luck toast the day before every start. I'd stop into Ray's other times for a beer after a game. Through these personal traditions, I got to know many of the Bums.

Meanwhile, other fans were ready to be mobilized by any upsurge. For years, Howard and Doris Herbon of suburban Morton Grove, home of Cubs lefty Dick Ellsworth and ex-Cub and author, Jim Brosnan, took their sons Jack and Kim to the left-field bleachers most weekends and holidays. Sometimes Howard could get out on Thursdays via his split off days as a postal worker, while Doris worked the switchboard at Baxter International. Howard Herbon though, turned out to be a talented amateur sign-maker with bedsheets. That impromptu talent would be put to good use starting in 1967.

The Bums came into their own in recognition during the Cubs' 33-14 mid-summer surge in 1968, especially during the mid-August series against the NL-pacing St. Louis Cardinals that attracted huge weekday crowds. The separation of bleacher fans by age and style – youthful Bums in left, older stalwarts in right – was chronicled in a front-page Chicago Tribune story by Bill Granger, later a prominent Chicago Sun-Times columnist. And that's how the bleaTchers would be divided long past the Bums' heyday. Right field already had been staked out, allegedly, by a longtime group of gamblers in direct line-of-sight of the pitcher-batter-catcher, better for more accurate betting on every pitch.

"When the gates opened, the kids went to [the] left field benches with their trumpets and banners and baseball gloves," wrote Granger. "They cheered batting practice, blew their bugles (obviously a reference to then-17-year-old Mike Murphy), and drank soft drinks.

"The veterans, who remembered Hack Wilson and Hank Sauer, went to right field with their beer, their paunches and their memories."

Veteran "Bum" Eddie Augustyn complained, "All they got is kids in left. We sit here because of the kids and their noise" while Paul Lindholm proclaimed, "This is where the real Cubs fans are. We're even here when they lose 100 games in a season."

In the end, the Bums were a predominantly male, testosterone-based, dominant bunch of characters. Lindvig estimated perhaps 20 to 25 percent were female, usually wives or girlfriends of the male Bums.

Lindvig, meanwhile, had just a $3 allowance to last the week. On non-school days, she'd sometimes walk the four miles each way to the ballpark, mimicking the 1940s foot journeys from the Milwaukee Avenue home of avowed Cubs fan Mike Royko, sainted columnist of the Chicago Daily News.

"I was there to have a good time. Every game I went to back in 1969, I'm lucky if I spent $1 or $2 total," Niles North's Anderson said. Many fans bought their own food. Hot dogs were 30 cents while Frosty Malts were a quarter. Some patronized Ray's Bleachers' grill, which opened to a window on Sheffield Avenue. "Greatest hot dogs in the world," said Anderson. "Just a great place."

So the Bums created a community of all classes, from all walks of life, city and suburban. The bleachers and the corner tavern across the street, was their common meeting ground, their own clubhouse.

"The magical thing is most of us came by ourselves, or with a friend, like my friend Nancy," said Lindvig. "We came together in the bleachers."

Wandering the outfield in 1969 as the oldest son of Ron Santo, Ron Santo, Jr. remembered the sight of scorecards dangling from string and ropes from the top of the left-field wall, as fans hunted for our autographs.

Another time, female fans gathered their foundations for a "Bras for Brock" day. In the earliest days of women's liberation, shedding the confines of a bra was a big issue. The tossing of bras at the misplaced Cub on the Cardinals was not original. On September 5, 1969, WCFL-Radio deejay Clark Weber, new to the station, concocted a promotion where women would turn in their bras downtown at State Street and Wacker Drive. Thousands of men and some women gathered during the lunch hour on the streets, with hundreds more watching from the vantage points up to the seventh floor of the Marina City parking garage across the Chicago River. The promotion proved much ado about nothing though, with fewer than a dozen bras turned in, none in an on-site strip job. The Chicago Sun-Times appropriately headlined "Bra protest falls flat." Fortunately, we players had no excuse to watch since we were about to play a 1:30 p.m. game against the Pirates at Wrigley Field.

A Bum named "Smokey" concocted a rubber hot dog with a bun on the crutches tossed toward Pete Rose in center during that Reds' first trip into town, but Rose threw the crutches back into the bleachers.

Two incidents backfired on us and the Bums. The Grousl-led chanting of "Ruthie! Ruthie!" to the Dodgers' Willie Davis may have cost us a victory in May. And, responding to thrown objects from the fringe fans, Jim "Mudcat" Grant of the Cardinals whipped a series of fastballs at the feet of Murphy's Bleacher's own Mike Murphy before a late-June game . . . one of the balls hit a young fan.

The street-theater package was made complete by Selma's debut as the Bums' bullpen-based cheerleader in late May 1969. Seeing the crowd unnaturally quiet late in the game, Selma began gesturing the Bums to make noise. They complied and we staged a game-winning rally. Always superstitious, Durocher encouraged Selma to continue, just as he did with Ron Santo's heel-clicking. The act was was unprecedented for 1969 baseball decorum. Langford called it "totally unorthodox behavior." But Selma vowed to continue cheering.

When you hear them cheering, cheering, cheering, it makes you want to do just a little bit better.

"When you hear them cheering, cheering, cheering, it makes you want to do just a little bit better," he said at the time. "Other teams think it's bush and maybe it is to a certain extent. But I do it for a purpose. I'm sitting here in the bullpen one day and I think we've got 15,000 and 20,000 fans out here just itching to let loose for the Cubs." Later in the season, when we thought we'd be celebrating a postseason run, Selma proposed a party for the Bums in which some players would appear.

But the Bums could not contain themselves to Wrigley Field as we got rolling, so they took their act on the road, everything, it seemed, except how to pay for travel and lodging. The Bums were Bums because they were tapped out.

"Ray Meyer Sr. rented three buses to go to Cincinnati, St. Louis and Pittsburgh," Lindvig recalled. "One bus was for other fans, another was for the middle group like Grousl and Haley, and the third was for the teeny-boppers. Ray Sr. and my dad were friends, and Ray promised him he'd look after me on one trip. But Ray was drunk much of the time!"

But the Bums pooled their pennies and Vershbo remembered staying seven to a room.

I ended up a safety valve for cash-strapped Bums at the Chase Park Plaza in St. Louis. The likes of Haley and Ray Meyer Jr. would ask if they could crash in my hotel room. I had a couch, and roommate Ernie Banks often wasn't around, stating a lot of times he was visiting with cousins. I'd order room service and the boys would eat. Haley and "Little Ray" would stay, then leave about 3:30 A.M. St. Louis was not a late-night town like New

York or even Chicago with the 4:00 A.M. bar closings, so I have no idea where they went. The next morning, I'd see them again and they'd come over again for room service.

For my July 4, 1969 start in St. Louis, the Bums must have had a middle-of-the-night departure in Chicago to be first at Busch Stadium. Some 200 Bums in the left-field stands were described as singing and chanting in the still-empty park at 11:20 a.m., almost two hours before game time. The height of the Bums' reign came when the Cubs funded a trip to Atlanta. Grousl claimed he had proposed a junket to San Diego. He obviously had his eye on beach time even then.

Near-empty Jack Murphy Stadium offered plenty of seats, but the cost was prohibitive for the Cubs' tastes for cross-country travel. Airline-hub Atlanta was deemed more suitable. Reports had the Cubs kicking in between $8,000 and $10,000 for the trip. Grousl was given the option of choosing 65 trip-goers. In addition to Bums loyalists, Grousl tapped several Burns Security guards with whom he had been friends. Anderson was invited, but since he was still just 17, his parents forbade him from making the trip. Chicago newspaper writers accompanied the Bums on their Delta Flight and tagged along at the hotel and Atlanta Stadium.

As if on cue, Morganna the Kissing Bandit, still just a teenager and not part of the Bums' stunt, lumbered on the field on August 31 to kiss the Braves' Clete Boyer while he was batting. Hundley, a close-up witness, praised Morganna's appearance.

But more than a month later, the bloom began to fade from the Bums' rose. After the Mets had done their stretch run, the Bums decided to celebrate a still-memorable season during the final game of the 1969 season on October 3 at Wrigley Field. Just under 10,000 fans showed up. A smoke bomb thrown onto the field stopped action in mid-game. A conga line of fans snaked out of the bleachers with participants dancing atop both dugouts. Finally, another wave of fans stormed the field after the final out of the Cubs' 5-3 victory. Tribune baseball writer Ed Prell wrote a scathing denunciation of the Bums for what he called "making a mockery of the game."

Anderson joined the on-field swarm. He shook hands with new-found friend Oscar Gamble in center field, then went to the pitcher's mound.

The Bums still stayed together, but in a lower-profile manner. Yellow helmets were still worn, yet not as visible without the street-theater antics and Selma's cheerleading. The fans still made road trips as groups and Anderson recalled rubbing shoulders with a Cubs icon during a St. Louis trip in 1971.

"We're at the Chase Park Plaza, and Jack Brickhouse walks in with (new TV partner) Jim West," he said. "He sees our group of Bums, maybe 15 or 17. He said, 'I love you guys, I'll buy you breakfast.' All of sudden, Jack gets up, and tells West, 'I'll see you at ballpark.' Jim had to pick up the check!"

"The Bums, the way I looked at it, came from one of three groups," Hershbo said in analysis. He asserted that one group was the older fans who always came in bad years. The second were their early and mid-20s, leaders like Grousl and Haley and Rebel Peterson. They were the *cool* group of Bums. At same time, Randy, me, and Ray Meyer Jr., were teenagers. As we moved along in the Seventies, the young group was still there. Hershbo eventually moved to Boston with the 1980-vintage transfer of the sports statistical service for which he toiled. Anderson still lived in Skokie, working maintenance at a nearby high school. Mike Murphy also stayed on in Chicago, worked in sales, and began hosting a "fans talking to fans" radio talk show in 1989. "Murph" would work for three different radio stations – WLS, and all-sports outlets WSCR-The Score and WMVP, now ESPN 1000.

Lindvig has been a minister for 34 years. Still a Cubs fan despite moving to Seattle, she is senior clergyperson at Seattle Unity Church. "The community we had in the bleachers kind of inspired the way I have tried to create a community at our church," she said.

A "junior" Bum, who was 15 in 1969 and did not get any publicity in that era, was Ned Colletti. He commuted to Wrigley Field via two buses and two trains from northwest suburban Franklin Park. Ned eventually became a sportswriter before working in the Cubs media relations department when Dallas Green first came in. He was the Public Relations (PR) chief for the first night game on August 8, 1988, and President Ronald Reagan's visit a month-and-a-half later. Soon thereafter, Ned moved into the Cubs baseball operations department where he stayed until the reign of General Manager Larry Himes. He then hooked onto the San Francisco Giants as assistant general manager and eventually acquired many of the Los Angeles Dodgers' present impact players as their general manager.

The remnants of the Bums transferred their allegiance from Ray's Bleachers when it was sold to Jim Murphy, to Bernie's, one-and-a-half blocks west on Waveland. By the 21st century, Anderson had moved his hoisting and Cubs toasting further away from the ballpark to the Nil Tap on the Northwest Side of the city. That's where he and the gang celebrated the 2016 World Series title. More than a year later, I had a surprise 75th birthday party thrown at the Nil Tap with Cubs chairman Tom Ricketts, ex-teammates Hundley and Rich Nye, and former Cub Sean Marshall in attendance.

Sadly, Haley died of complications from diabetes at age 67 on December 31, 2016. He lived long enough to see a Cubs World Series title and finish his last year as a fan of a winning team. Ma Barker – Doris Herbon – lived a long, long life, passing away at age 92 on December 2, 2014.

Grousl, though, dodged the Grim Reaper. He survived several surgeries for stomach cancer. I'd still like to see the old Bum again. We're not in the 9th inning of life just yet. We need to meet again before the last out.

The Imperial Leo The Lip

Sometime on July 27, 1969, while I notched a forgettable loss against the Dodgers at Wrigley Field, a livid Philip K. Wrigley placed a call from his Lake Geneva, Wisconsin, estate to Herman Franks' home in Utah.

Wrigley was white-hot with anger upon learning Manager Leo Durocher had sneaked off in the third inning on July 26 to his stepson's Parent Day visitation at Camp Ojibwa near Eagle River, Wisconsin, some 400 miles north of Chicago. The gum mogul's reflexive action was to fire the man who had brought the Cubs from last place in 1966 to a 5-game, first-place lead on July 27.

Durocher already had missed the June 18, 3-2, 10-inning loss in Pittsburgh, slipping away unexcused that morning to return to Chicago for his bachelor party, a day prior to his June 19 wedding to Lynn Walker Goldblatt. And on July 2, Durocher was absent for another close loss in Montreal after allegedly lighting up the lively town till past 3:30 a.m. that day on a double date with Ken Holtzman and two early 20-something Jarry Park usherettes. Reflexively a playboy and a player, allegedly as soon as two weeks after his wedding, the 62-year-old Durocher was described as nauseous from his strenuous wee-hours activity and was sequestered in his hotel room. The Montreal Star did not take at face value the Cubs' explanation of more gastro-intestinal problems for Durocher. Two reporters were dispatched to knock on his room door while another called the phone. No answer either way.

Durocher again used the cover of illness to excuse himself from the July 26 game, turning over acting manager duties to third-base coach Pete Reiser. When team physician Jacob Suker called Durocher at his apartment to check on him, no one answered – not even his new bride. Then, as parents at Camp Ojibwa gathered for the celebratory evening, one Cubs-savvy man noticed Durocher's presence.

A 25-year veteran of the beat, reporter Enright soon called Wrigley to report his finding. Further investigation found Durocher went directly to the downtown Meigs Field airport from the ballpark. Despite a stomachache, he and a pilot flew to Camp Ojibwa.

Although back in town just in time for the July 27 game, Durocher opted not to return to Wrigley Field that afternoon.

Normally even-tempered amid all his eccentricity, Wrigley was enraged. He called Franks, who had retired from baseball after managing the Giants to four consecutive second-place finishes from 1965 to 1968. Wrigley only looked at Franks' recent accomplishments and did not consider his longtime close relationship with Durocher. He had been one of The Lip's trusted coaches for the Giants in New York in the early 1950s, and the pair had remained close ever since. In 1969, the financially savvy Franks was handling Durocher's off-the-field business affairs and investments.

Yet, when Franks picked up the phone, Wrigley offered him Durocher's job.

"I told him, 'You can't fire him, that would disrupt the team too much. I'm not going to replace him,'" Franks recalled telling Wrigley. That remembrance took place in mid-season 2004, during the then-90-year-old Franks' final visit to Wrigley Field.

Franks' continuing closeness to Durocher was confirmed a year later. Halfway through the 1970 season, pitching coach Joe Becker had to depart due to heart problems. With a coaching vacancy, a pitching staff to run and a clubhouse fire or two to keep under control, Durocher brought on Franks for the remainder of the season.

Had Franks accepted the offer, the firing of Durocher would have burst onto the front pages to compete with Ted Kennedy's ill-fated, late-night ride at Chappaquiddick for appointment reading. He was baseball's highest-profile manager in 1969, certainly a "different kettle of fish" in the words of my rotation-mate, Bill Hands. And had Franks taken over the helm at Wrigley Field, our fates as Cubs players might have changed forever.

Upon urging from wife Helen, Wrigley quickly calmed down and opted to keep Durocher after Franks got off the line. He kept a relative cool as Durocher's summer holiday story leaked out and reporters called him. At first, he felt Durocher needed a mea culpa. Later, he suggested Durocher had simply needed to inform him he was zipping up to Camp Ojibwa. Wrigley didn't even issue a slap on the wrist for his manager, who seemed to have a kind of Svengali-like spell over the owner. Durocher was back on the job for a memorable comeback win over Juan Marichal and the Giants on Monday, July 28. He would later simply meet Wrigley at his apartment, not for an originally projected summit-like meeting, but for a mere five minutes prior to the Tuesday, July 29, game. All was forgiven.

That's how prominent Durocher was at the height of summer, 1969. He was almost bigger than the Cubs he was charged with trying to earn a World Series berth. And Wrigley obviously thought of how far, how fast he had brought the Cubs from annual hopelessness earlier in the Sixties. He overlooked Durocher's faults with this rationale, expressed on September 30, 1975: Wrigley had just retired John Holland for general manager duty at age 65 after 19 years in favor of park Operations Chief Salty Saltwell, and the owner's analysis came up of how strict a manager should be:

"The closest we came to winning was under Durocher in 1969. The players hated him," Wrigley said.

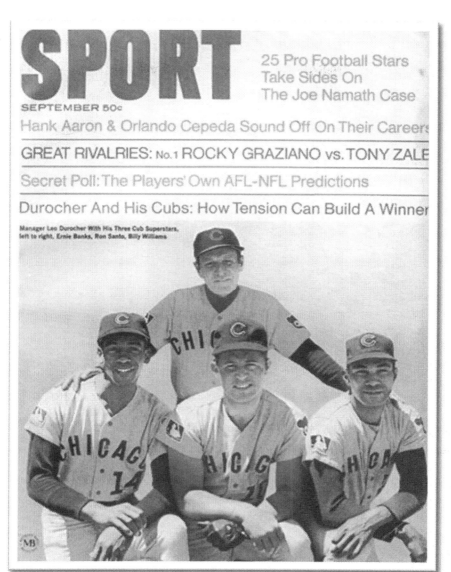

SPORT

Manager Leo Durocher With His Three Cub Superstars.
Left to right, Ernie Banks, Ron Santo, Billy Williams

Leo Durocher with his 3-4-5 hitters:
Ernie Banks, Ron Santo, and Billy Williams.

The story of how Durocher did not manage his personnel correctly down the stretch has been told umpteen times. The likes of Don Kessinger and Ron Santo played too much with slick-fielding, not using switch-hitting Paul Popovich to give them a breather, despite Popovich having his best offensive season ever, hitting .300 or better while he was with the Cubs. Meanwhile, Catcher Randy Hundley was encouraged to go straight from a hospital bed to the starting lineup. And Durocher grossly overused Phil Regan out of the bullpen, in my opinion, while almost completely forgetting the submarine delivery-motion of Ted Abernathy, not to mention lefty Hank Aguirre. Both Dick Selma and I started on two days' rest in situations far from the desperation of a prospective September pennant-clinching situations.

As if he snapped out of a trance, Durocher made the lineup changes only after it was too late, when we had ceded first place to the rampaging Mets in mid-September. In the off-season, Durocher suggested he would have played nine pitchers if he knew his regulars were tired. Many years later, Durocher admitted he cost us a potential pennant with his actions in a mea culpa at Hundley's Fantasy Camp. And while hindsight is always 20-20, the answers weren't always that simple.

What Durocher did is well-established. Yet, Durocher should not have 100 percent of the 1969 blame bestowed on him. We as players needed to perform better and needed to be smarter about our ability to play 'tired' as the dog days of August yielded to the September pennant stretch. Not having the conditioning and sports-medicine knowledge of the 21st century was no excuse, in my opinion. Durocher posted our lineup, mostly unchanged, every day in the clubhouse. It was on the players to let Durocher know if they could not go, as I did when I declined to start an August 26 game on one-day's rest against the Reds at Wrigley Field.

We have to look at several storylines to understand Durocher, the complicated person, along with Durocher the imperious celebrity and of course Durocher the manager.

When telling the story of the 1969 Cubs, we have to trace how Durocher, the first-year Cubs manager in 1966, was willing to experiment with me in the starting rotation and with Kessinger as a switch-hitter, let alone dabble with other young pitchers in major roles, as he devolved, in my opinion, into a rigidly unadaptable leader who used only two-thirds of his 25-man roster. Here was a man regarded, despite all his faults and volubility, as a daring chess-piece mover with the Dodgers and Giants back in his 30s and 40s.

Jack Brickhouse may have summed up the contrast best, if not most appropriately. He called the Big Apple version of Durocher a "son of a bitch, but he was a sharp son of a bitch. But by the time he was finished in Chicago, he was just an old son of a bitch," the voice of the Cubs was quoted as saying in Paul Dickson's biography of the manager.

But in 1969, even as we were flying high and nothing but positives were coming out of Wrigley Field, the knives were out. Durocher increasingly had conflicts with writers, while a feud with Brickhouse that began in 1966 was ongoing. He nearly got into a fight with Chicago Sun-Times writer Jerome Holtzman, backing down when the pugnacious scribe would not give an inch. And I believe Durocher mistreated radio announcers Vince Lloyd and Lou Boudreau. Sun-Times feature writer Tom Fitzpatrick, later a Pulitzer Prize winner, was commissioned to write a long piece for the tabloid's Sunday magazine edition, September 7, 1969, which was scheduled well before our pratfall, which began in earnest that weekend. Descriptions of clubhouse dissension to which I never witnessed were included in Fitzpatrick's narrative while The Sun-Times posted billboards around Wrigley Field to plug what I considered a hit job. Meanwhile, Durocher's unexcused absences added fuel to an already simmering fire.

Interestingly, if the media wanted to find out the hows and whys of the Cubs, Durocher was the ultimate misdirection play. Writers were upset at Durocher's periodical non-cooperation on daily ballclub news -- such as identities of forthcoming starting pitchers -- and began asking in late August if we were tired. There was almost no focus on the understaffed, under-evaluating Holland-led organization. But baseball coverage in the era was narrowly focused on the games, the players and the managers.

No writer seemed to critically look at why Don Young, consigned to Class A in 1968, opened as our center fielder. Or that few really talented minor-league reinforcements were called up. Or why the Cubs had little speed, while the likes of Maury Wills of the Dodgers, Lou Brock of the Cardinals and other base thieves had transformed the game, just in time for artificial turf-covered ballparks. Or why the Cubs in August carried four catchers, only one of whom, Hundley, played. Or why ineffective reliever Don Nottebart (7.00 ERA) took up a roster spot all year. Or why Oscar Gamble was called up at just 19, a year out of high school in a small Southern city, to start in center for a first-place team and was turned loose on the distractions of a big metropolis.

Before his 1969 moves are analyzed, Durocher, the brassy, often profane personality that he was must also be categorized. Coming up from hardscrabble roots in Massachusetts, He was a hustler on and off the field, a kid shortstop on the Yankees of Babe Ruth and Lou Gehrig, once accused of stealing The Babe's watch. But he also could be appealing enough that on his second team, the Cincinnati Reds, Durocher developed a patron in owner Sidney Weil. He was a centerpiece on the famous Gashouse Gang world-champion St. Louis Cardinals in 1934, a character among characters. He earned the nickname "The Lip" for his 'bleep-highlighted' argumentative style on the field, in which he gave no quarter to umpires and sometimes a sore shin, kicking up dirt in disputes.

Durocher turned out to be just the man as a player-manager to kick-start the Brooklyn Dodgers in 1939, his budding show-biz personality serving as an interview subject for legendary announcer Red Barber on the first-ever game telecast. He often clashed with allegedly hard-drinking Dodgers boss Larry MacPhail, who impulsively fired him multiple times, but almost immediately hired him back. That set a pattern for Durocher's entire career – you love him, then you hate him; you want to boot him out, but you just can't live without him.

Durocher led the Dodgers to their first pennant in 21 years in 1941. He soon survived the transition of Brooklyn leadership from the near-wild MacPhail to the pious, pontificating Branch Rickey. The concept of opposites attracting applied to the religious Rickey and the fast-living Durocher. They had a workable alliance for nearly five years as the Dodgers were beaten out for the NL flag by the powerful Cardinals in a 3-game playoff in 1946.

Durocher endured the biggest setback of his career in 1947, just as he was designated by Rickey to oversee Jackie Robinson's break-in season in the majors. Ostensibly because of questionable associations with shady characters, Commissioner Happy Chandler suspended Durocher for the season. A former roommate of actor George Raft, who crafted a film career playing gangsters and other heavies, Durocher never attracted any rebukes from prior Commissioner Kennesaw Mountain Landis, who always had a key eye out for evidence of gambling and sordid connections to baseball after he had banned for life the famed 1919 Chicago Black Sox players two years later, who were accused of throwing that World Series. But Durocher plucked Day right out from under the relationship with her previous husband. That kind of "theft" was tolerated in Hollywood, but not in the ultra-conservative environs of baseball, where Rickey had to navigate a storm of opposition to integrate the sport with Robinson.

When Durocher was reinstated for the 1948 season, his relationship with Rickey began fraying. Instead of outright firing Durocher, the Mahatma, as he was known for engineering Robinson into baseball, engaged New York Giants owner Horace Stoneham in a kind of gentleman's agreement to allow The Lip to take over the Giants' managing job from Mel Ott, meaning Durocher did not have to leave the New York market. And so he had the best of all worlds – celebrity status in the Big Apple and off-seasons still rubbing shoulders with the Hollywood crowd, now including Frank Sinatra. His stewardship of the miracle Giants of 1951, pulling off the most famous stretch run in history this side of the 1969 Mets, dramatically added to his public resume. The Giants had started out the 1951 season 3-12, then trailed the Dodgers by 13 games on August 11. Out of nowhere, they went on a wild 37-7 toot to tie Brooklyn for the NL pennant and force a 3-game playoff, culminated by Bobby Thomson's walk-off "Shot Heard 'Round The World."

But beyond Chandler and umpires with whom he quarreled, few people outside baseball said "no" to Durocher, even though he did readily accept "no" for an answer. He admitted to straying on Day in comments to writer Roger Kahn in 1954. Describing picking up a woman for the evening, Durocher told Kahn his first action was to place his hand on her genitals. Some would immediately knock his hand away. No problem, reasoned Durocher, there was plenty of time to find another date. He told Kahn he would be surprised how many famous females did not refuse such a direct advance.

After finally winning the World Series with the Giants, riding the back of MVP Willie Mays in 1954, he and owner Horace Stoneham grew apart. Durocher was forced out of his Giants job as the 1955 season closed. He would not manage again for 11 seasons. He was no dignified or lovable skipper of consistent winners like John McGraw, Miller Huggins, Joe McCarthy, Casey Stengel, or even Walter Alston.

With his voluble personality and bully-pulpit standing in the New York market, he got tremendous mileage and a celebrity reputation out of three pennants and just that sole one world championship with two teams in 16 seasons managing. He had some standout failures, too. His 1942 Dodgers gave up a 10-game lead on August 5 in just five weeks to the archrival Cardinals, benefiting from Stan Musial's first full big-league season. In 1946, Brooklyn led the Cardinals by 7 games on July 4. But the two teams tied at season's end, with the Dodgers losing 2 straight in a best-of-3 playoff. And so, several rumors surfaced about Durocher's managing not being aboveboard in 1946, but the allegations were never proven.

Durocher hardly ever needed to pound the pavement looking for work away from managing. To maintain a high-living style, he soaked up the offers as employers came to him. When he left the Giants in 1955, a friend at NBC-TV had a $50,000-a-year gig waiting for him, with the job description being to line up talent for the network's variety shows and work as a sports announcer. He was even pressed into service hosting two episodes of the network's Sunday night "Comedy Hour," going head-to-head against the ultimately popular Ed Sullivan Variety Show. Durocher was out of his league, though, in that venue, and drew bad reviews. He did manage to call in a favor from buddy Frank Sinatra to guest at an under-market rate on Dinah Shore's variety show. But Durocher was in his element as color commentator on weekend network baseball telecasts alongside play-by-play man Lindsey Nelson. A fan of all sports, Durocher even handled college football on-air analysis.

But by 1960, Durocher was itching to get back into baseball after a lack of job offers over the previous half-decade. As luck would have it, he snared the Dodgers' third-base coaching job, so he did not have to move from Los Angeles and could still hang out with the elite Hollywood crowd he coveted and almost immediately, he comported himself to the public as if he, not the strong, silent Walter Alston, was the Dodgers' manager. Inevitably, speculation abounded that he tried to undercut Alston, but he still dodged firing by Dodgers General Manager Buzzie Bavasi.

But before Durocher coached even one game at the Los Angeles Coliseum in 1961, he led a delegation of Dodgers players as guests on Shore's Chevy-sponsored program. Durocher also was major domo guest on a famed 1963 "Mr. Ed" sitcom episode, when the talking horse tried out for the Dodgers, with special effects showing the equine athlete sliding into home at Dodger Stadium. Helping out was another part-time actor of sorts – Sandy Koufax. And after the conclusion of his four-year coaching stint, in which he picked up a World Series ring in 1963, he guested in civvies on "The Munsters" sitcom, providing an evaluation of Herman Munster's baseball skills.

While coaching in LA, the only discernible contact for a managing job came from the Cardinals, near the end of August, 1964. Upset after his Cardinals fell a season-low 11 games behind the Phillies a few days earlier, owner/bon vivant Gussie Busch recruited top Cardinals announcer Harry Caray to drive Durocher to his Grant Farm estate during the Dodgers' final visit to St. Louis. Busch was close to dumping manager Johnny Keane after firing much-admired General Manager Bing Devine a few weeks earlier. But Durocher-Busch relationship did not click, the Cardinals did rally to win the World Series under Keane and then Keane turned the tables on Busch by jumping to the Yankees. Interestingly, with the job officially open, Busch did not look again to Durocher, instead promoting the much-admired Red Schoendienst from within.

Durocher left the Dodgers after 1964, but did not stay far from baseball the following year. He returned to the broadcast booth as color analyst during ABC-TV's one season airing the Saturday afternoon "Game of the Week," and Durocher's first-guesting analysis was informative and spot-on. He also hosted a 90-minute daily sports-talk show on KABC-Radio, an experience that would resurface amid controversy five years later in Chicago.

Having totally scrapped his College of Coaches scheme and with attendance plummeting toward the 600,000 annual mark after another second-division finish,

Wrigley concocted a radical shakeup of his Cubs during the 1965 World Series. Like Rickey, he'd pair himself with a polar opposite, offering Durocher the position instead of again recycling a familiar name from within the Cubs organization. Only this time, Wrigley was even more reticent in the public eye and not as baseball savvy as Rickey.

Holland, meanwhile, contacted Durocher during the 1965 World Series and the pair shook hands on a three-year contract. Introduced at the September 25, 1965 press conference, sans Wrigley, in the Pink Poodle lunchroom, Durocher made a famed remark about the Cubs "not being an eighth-place team" as he evaluated them. More interestingly, he claimed he'd have equal say with Holland on trades. Brashly, Durocher predicted he'd get the best of the deals – and he was proved right to an extent in the trades that brought me, Hundley, Hands, Regan and Hickman to the Cubs, the very best in Holland's checkered general manager career here.

"I think he overwhelmed Mr. Wrigley. He had that kind of charisma," said second baseman Beckert, who was one of five lineup holdovers from 1965.

Durocher did tread a little lightly at first in 1966, knowing he had a rebuilding job from the partial blank slate he was given. He had to take the gauge of the market. Yet, pundits needled Durocher for finishing 10th and dead last with 103 losses after proclaiming the Cubs were not eighth-place material.

However, behind the scenes, he already displayed characteristics of a man who continually was given many things – or simply took what he wanted. For 1966, Durocher was tendered $22,500 from WGN for his five-minute "Durocher in the Dugout" pre-game radio show and frequent in-season appearances on a new "Sports Open Line" live audience-participation TV show at the WGN studios at 9:30 p.m. Mondays. However, Durocher reportedly wanted his entire pay up front before he ever did one program. That stance angered Brickhouse, who supervised the WGN sports department in addition to his ubiquitous on-air work. Thus the roots of an off-air feud began, with Durocher later claiming Brickhouse was upset because he was not invited to the manager's 1969 wedding.

The tension between Durocher and Brickhouse broke out in the open on a June 12, 1967, "Sports Open Line," as WGN producers showed tape of the 8 Cubs homers, including four by Adolfo Phillips, in the previous day's doubleheader sweep of the Mets at Wrigley Field. After the highlights concluded, show-host Brickhouse sent a little gibe Durocher's way

"Do you realize the Cubs in that ballgame yesterday hit probably as many homers as you did in your whole career?" he nervously asked as the studio audience laughed.

"So?" Durocher replied.

"I supposed you were going to say next, 'Well, how many did you hit?' I was going to answer, 'None, and that makes us pretty even.'"

Durocher had the last word, noting sarcastically: "You're very funny tonight."

Brickhouse, however, really could have used some editorial legwork at that moment, because Durocher actually slugged 24 career homers.

Meanwhile, off the field, Durocher put a monetary value on his name and personality. When famed author Roger Kahn arrived in 1966 to research a Saturday Evening Post magazine feature on Durocher, the writer hung out during the manager's beat-writer interview sessions. The Post had once paid Durocher $25,000 to write his baseball memoirs with Kahn. Spotting Kahn, Durocher asked if he'd be paid for the magazine article. When the answer was negative, he responded with a gesture of 'zipping his lip" and keeping overtly quiet around Kahn. After the writer spent the better part of the week taking in Durocher interviews, The Lip finally emoted, repeating twice, "You're stealing money right out of my mouth! You're stealing it right out of my mouth."

Another time, WCFL-Radio's Red Mottlow, allegedly the first Chicago reporter to take a tape recorder into a locker room, asked Durocher for an interview. "Sorry, kid, I have my own show," he replied to Mottlow, then in his early 40s.

And so within a month of the "Sports Open Line" bad-humor exchange, Durocher was truly the toast of the town. We surged into first place and tied the Cardinals for the top of the NL on three occasions in July, 1967. Even after the Cardinals pulled away in August and September, our third-place finish was still considered nothing short of a sensation and Wrigley was truly in Durocher's thrall. He earned a new two-year contract at $50,000 per year while several key Cubs got handsome raises. The Lip was now viewed as the colorful ringmaster of our climb into contender status.

But even our record 48-inning scoreless streak in June 1968, which knocked us out of the pennant race, did nothing to diminish Durocher's appeal, which continued to grow when we got hot for 1 ½ months in mid-summer. However, when Durocher claimed he did not feel well after a Friday, July 26, 1968 game and went home, team physician Jacob Suker insisted Durocher join him for dinner downtown. The ruse lured him to a surprise 63rd birthday party. Arriving at Sage's East, players, team officials and media toasted a man drawing admiration the likes of which he had not even received in New York.

Similar honors for Durocher continued well into the next season. On June 3, 1969, Durocher enjoyed the first of two bachelor parties in advance of his wedding. Some 150 attended, including almost every player and Cubs officials at a roast co-hosted by Robert Walker, Durocher bride-to-be Lynne Walker Goldblatt's brother, at Sandberg Village on the Near North Side. Gag gifts included a nose guard for Durocher's in-your-face jousts with umpires, a dum-dum bullet to use on himself if the Cubs did not win the pennant (it was not deployed) and a wig from celebrated bald actor Yul Brynner.

All along, Durocher ensured his new-found constituency he was Hollywood-in-Chicago. He enlisted Sinatra to "manage" an inning during a spring training game in Palm Springs. Another time, the Chicago Tribune's George Langford recalled Durocher inviting the beat writers to Jilly's, a swanky Palm Springs restaurant he described as the local "mob hangout."

"What Leo enjoyed doing is playing the big shot," Langford said. "He told us, 'My friend Frank' is coming. We had a table in back. There's no Sinatra. Suddenly, there's a rush at the door. All these people came in, these guys were in Sinatra's entourage. Leo says, 'Hi, Frank,' but Sinatra rushes right past him. He thought it was an advantage to him."

Durocher always had a love-hate relationship with reporters. In New York, he knew how to manipulate the press. Kahn recalled for the Sporting News in 1954 how the Giants writers were under Durocher's thumb:

"He had lined up all of the writers and worked out all their weaknesses and calculated how he could work on their weaknesses to get positive press. One writer was a serious alcoholic and so Leo kept him in booze. Another was impecunious, so Durocher lent him some money and said that if the writer ever knocked the club, he would go to his paper with the notes that the reporter had been required to sign."

From the get-go in Chicago though, Durocher could not similarly corral the four traveling beat writers and columnists. And while Durocher made the Cubs beat competitive, the Tribune's Langford, still in his late 20s when he began covering Durocher, remembers reporting and writing for his life going up against the Chicago Sun-Times' Jerome Holtzman. The first era of quotes had arrived with writers cultivating player sources. Langford hit it off with Ernie Banks, while Tribune colleague Richard Dozer, a veteran going back to the mid-1950s, always had go-to guys in the Cubs' clubhouse. None had Durocher as an anonymous source.

"Let 'em gut me up. They aren't getting any novice," Durocher told Tribune lead columnist David Condon before his first Cubs home opener on April 19, 1966.

But Durocher's real feelings toward the beat writers came out in a gag, a "Durocher in the Dugout" tape that somehow got copied a number of times. One version found its way into the syndicated Diamond Gems radio show, copious 'bleeps' notwithstanding. On the tape, Durocher accused Chicago Today's Enright of being a sneaky politician around the clubhouse and not asking questions of Durocher directly. He roasted the Chicago Sun-Times' Edgar Munzel for supposedly being a barfly. Calling the kettle black, Durocher described Dozer as a hyperactive road Romeo. He exempted Cubs beat newcomer Ray Sons of the Chicago Daily News as "a nice boy," but then implored Daily News top editor Roy Fisher to "go (f---) himself."

"The broadcasters, thought Leo was a jerk," Langford said though. Boudreau was bedeviled with Durocher's profanities, sometimes uttered on purpose, that scotched "Durocher in the Dugout" tapings. On at least one occasion, Boudreau was forced to go live with the show, his nimble former shortstop's hands the only defense at the ready to yank the microphone away if Durocher went blue in his language. Sure enough, one day in Los Angeles, Durocher swore live, Boudreau yanked the microphone just in time and callers to WGN-Radio asked what The Lip had said. Another time, Boudreau simply gave up and told Lloyd to handle the taping. But Good Kid Boudreau, then absent due to his son's wedding, did not escape Durocher's profane barbs on the gag "Durocher in the Dugout" tape.

Early in the 1969 season, the Sun-Times' Holtzman and Durocher got into it during an interview session, with threats of fisticuffs. Ex-World War II Marine Holtzman would not back down and Durocher did not escalate the session to hand-to-hand combat. "Leo said, 'Go ahead and hit me. I'll sue,'" witness Sons said. The Lip did intrude on one writer's work space on the team plane, grabbing the first page of his story out of his typewriter and crumpling it into a ball. "I don't like it. Write me a new one," he commanded.

Durocher did not instigate all the conflict though. One blatantly unethical interview was pulled on The Lip. WMAQ-TV sportscaster Johnny Erp arranged an off-the-cuff talk with Durocher by the Cubs bullpen. But Durocher did not realize Erp had a hidden microphone to record the conversation. Meanwhile, a WMAQ-TV camera close to the dugout filmed the pair. Durocher, of course, had the right to explode through the ceiling when the interview was aired.

Whether by design or simply by coincidence, Durocher taking the media spotlight onto himself did the players a favor while allowing executives more culpable for the team's faults to slip under the radar.

"What Leo did was keep the press in a major city off the players," said Beckert. "He would tease guys like Jerome Holtzman and Rick Talley (a major Durocher antagonist with Chicago Today). I didn't realize it until I was out of the game. It was planned by Leo. It was fun watching Leo tease the press. When the team was going bad, Leo took the pressure off us."

Amazingly, Durocher rallied around those who curried his favor or whom he genuinely liked. But he never cultivated his softer, even loving persona, except perhaps behind closed doors with Lynne Walker Goldblatt and her three children, or briefly with a favorite coach.

"I spent a lot of time with Leo privately before and after games (in 1969) when the media wasn't around," recalled first-base coach Joey Amalfitano, who had first played under Durocher as a New York Giants "bonus baby" in 1954-55. "There were two different Leos – the tough, hard guy the public saw and the other person I got to know. I felt sorry for him (during the 1969 pennant stretch) because I know how heartbroken he was."

The ability to present a kinder, gentler Durocher might have seriously cut down the sharp edge offered to his players and keep those who wanted to probe into his life at bay. But some of his actions, verbal and otherwise, showed that he had a redeemable side that could have served him a lot better as he moved through his 60s.

Meanwhile, the cold war between Durocher and Brickhouse continued through 1969 and beyond. And yet, Rosenberg, for whom Brickhouse stood up at his wedding to beloved wife Mayora, got through to Durocher in a way his boss never could. "Rosey" was in charge of booking guests for the "Leadoff Man" and "Tenth Inning" shows and gathering other information for the broadcast. He had to cross paths with Durocher on an almost daily basis. "Rosey" was the ultimate people person with whom all got along, but Durocher was the acid test.

"I was in Durocher's office before every game," Rosey recalled. "'Your man Brickhouse can't carry Vin Scully's shoes,' Leo said. He told a story that if he was (out of luck and on the street), he'd need $50 to pay back later, Brickhouse would just keep on walking while ignoring Leo. 'Now, I walk a little further, and I see you. And I don't even know if you have $50. If you got it, you reach into your pocket with no question...You can have any (f-----') thing in this clubhouse you want.' And he turned around and walked out. That's when Pete Reiser said, 'You just got praise from Caesar.'"

Beckert, however, appeared to be Durocher's favorite everyday player. He constantly praised Beckert. Perhaps the star second baseman's batting style most approximated the vintage Durocher's, although Beckert was a far better hitter. He absolutely left Billy Williams alone – the only regular whose lineup position (No. 3) never changed during Leo's 6 ½ years at the Cubs' helm. And yet, the player with whom Durocher connected the most, and had the longest association, was Gentleman Jim Hickman. Durocher saw something in Hickman to finally give him the right-field job on August 3, 1969. Gentleman Jim came through in a manner resembling the legends of Durocher's past. The reward system was paid back, with compound interest, and neither man ever forgot.

"I have to give Leo credit for my career, so to speak," Gentleman Jim recalled decades later. "He got to the point where he had confidence in me. Leo saved me. I was just a part-time player. He gave me the chance to play. I started the (1968) season in the (Pacific) Coast League. At that time, I thought I was just about through. Then I got over there with the Cubs farm team (Tacoma), got hot, got a few hits, next thing I know I got called back to the big leagues.

"Leo just took care of me. He gave me a real good chance to play. After I had a little success, I felt he had a little confidence in me, and that helped me."

And Durocher's long memory extended into 1987, when the debt-burdened Hickman, amid an agricultural depression, lost his Henning, Tennessee, farm. Although allowed to stay on the property as tenants, the Hickman family was so cash-strapped that $700 from making an appearance at Hundley's Fantasy Camp had to tide them over one winter. But as the Hickman financial disaster reached a crescendo, Durocher contacted him with an offer of $25,000 to bail him out, according to Hickman family friend Jim Peyton. Appreciative of the gesture, the proud Hickman declined the offer. The cash amount was not enough to pay off the debts anyway. Gentleman Jim genuinely liked Durocher and did not want to feel indebted to him.

Durocher did not go out of his way to publicize the positives he extended to others. He almost relished his bad-boy, edgy image and never tried to reform as he aged. He would not be a statesman-manager when we approached the 1969 season. Durocher still got the lion's share of the credit for the quick Cubs rebuilding program. Most of the players lauded his managing and strategy, even though the world was achangin' outside baseball while Durocher was channeling the bygone behavior and player-handling of the 1934 St. Louis Gashouse Gang era. The mass praise no doubt made him into almost a colossus of Chicago, by far the straw that stirred the Cubs' drink. No owner or executive was around to curb his excesses nor correct his faults. He had a grateful Phil Wrigley at his side while General Manager Holland was slavishly loyal to Wrigley and went along with the program, although likely cringing at some of Durocher's actions.

Durocher was The Law with the Cubs. He was the imperial manager and a dictator who was not exactly benevolent to those outside the core lineup and rotation.

"Durocher is king," wrote D.J.R. Bruckner of the Los Angeles Times in early September, 1969. "He may be only one step from becoming a goat, but right now he is still king. This may be the biggest news of the decade. For years, everybody has known that Richard J. Daley, the mayor, owns this town. Now Durocher owns it, and everybody in it. When he walks down a street, people stop to stare at him, applaud, shout, give advice, argue. When he is in a restaurant, knots gather outside to wait for him to come out. His recent wedding, to yet another beautiful woman, was the social event of the past few years."

From on up high, in any of his managerial incarnations, Durocher was famous for two phrases: "Nice guys finish last" and "Back up the truck," or the implication that any kind of dogging or desire for motivation from without had immediate consequences.

He certainly never coddled younger players at all. However, Durocher had given a whole host of us a chance to break in as regulars in 1966-1967.

"He realized pretty quickly we were not a contender his first year," said Kessinger. "To build, he had to play the young guys. He was willing to do that and take his lumps to make us better. Early on in (his Cubs) career, Leo always seemed to be an inning ahead of the game, what pinch hitter he might have ready. He had a real knack for that. As we all got to play more, and he felt more comfortable with us, he preferred a set lineup. We thought that was the right thing. When we got to the ballpark, we knew we were going to play."

But once Durocher felt confident with his core lineup, with his Big Three - Jenkins, Holtzman, and Hands - in the rotation and the closer Regan in 1968, he seemed to get especially tough with younger players and their mistakes or indecision.

"We were like puppies who were being whipped," 1969 rookie pitcher Jim Colborn said.

None of this still-acerbic Durocher handling of players ever filtered back to Wrigley. He was still in thrall of the manager who had revived his franchise after all other attempts, albeit misguided or inept, had failed since 1945.

"Leo's improved tremendously because he's mellowed with age, as we all have," Wrigley told Sports Illustrated in a June 30, 1969 Cubs cover story. He's mellow enough now. I don't want him to get too nice!"

Having cast a spell on Wrigley, having been lionized by fans. and believing he was even more exalted by our 40-18 start in 1969, Durocher apparently believed he could do what he wanted, whenever he wanted and to whom he wanted. Afflicted with what he later called a hiatal hernia, a painful stomach condition, he had easy cover for missing a number of games in the first half of 1969.

"Some guys would just love to write his obituary," Santo told Dozer in a Tribune article published August 19, 1969. "They can't wait to see him fail. But I'll tell you this. He won't fail. Because for him to fail, we have to fail. And we won't as long as he's our manager.

"He says what he thinks, and he does things his own way. Some newspaper men don't get along with him. They write about his private life because it's news, I suppose. Well, they can write all they want. All I know is we are up there because of Leo Durocher, period."

The King of the Cubs was hardly out of the woods in the big city he had conquered and claimed as his own. For four months he had felt the mounting pressure to win. Just one world championship, and with MVP Willie Mays leading the way, seemed inadequate for lionization of Durocher as an all-time manager. He never forgot that he was the proverbial good-field, no-hit shortstop back in his playing days, always battling for respect among the stars on the dynastic Yankees and Cardinals.

Now, a Cubs World Series title would be his crowning achievement, having built the Cubs from perennial losers to the masters of baseball in just three years. And he'd reward Phil Wrigley, the baseball-befuddled benefactor who rescued him from managerial exile and did not second-guess him like past bosses.

But in baseball, you cannot try too hard. Few positives come from trying to force the issue as a player or manager. I could not try to throw at Nolan Ryan-Kerry Wood speed of 99 mph, nor could Williams try to hit the ball to the other side of Sheffield Avenue. So with relatively few calling him on his tactics just yet, Durocher's desire to win in the worst way would haunt the Cubs for many decades to come.

Leo Durocher in 1969.

Chapter 12

Cub Power Off The Field

I went back to my reliever roots–"pitching" two days in a row–on July 15 and 16, 1969. On a sultry early July 15 evening, Ernie Banks and I showed up at a cancer benefit softball game at the venerable Thillens Stadium, six miles northwest of Wrigley Field, where baseball's trademark center-field camera had been pioneered 18 years before. I was asked to throw a couple of innings, and why not? A good cause benefited with a packed house of several thousand. And the game was the Chicago-centric version of softball with the melon-like, 16-inch Clincher. You pitched underhanded, the natural throwing motion, and my opponents did not touch me.

Then the next afternoon, wouldn't you know it, I gave up 4 runs on 5 hits to the New York Mets in the first inning at Clark and Addison before more than 36,000 watching in steamy 91-degree heat. When I served up a Tommie Agee homer leading off the second, Leo Durocher gave me the hook. At least little Al Weis, who slugged his only 2 homers of the season on back-to-back days in the series, did not reach the seats off me. My buddy Rich Nye had the honors, grooving a pitch to the Punch-and-Judy Weis in the fifth inning as the Mets won 9-5.

"I wasn't around long enough today to find out what kind of stuff I had," was my succinct post-game analysis.

I know what you're thinking; "Fergie" should not have heaved that Clincher at Thillens, it took away from his stuff the next day. Both then and now, from the hindsight of a half-century later, the two events were not linked. The near-effortless underhanded delivery in Chicago-style, 16-inch, gloveless softball – so many of its greatest pitchers work frequently – did not take away from my big-league stuff at all.

The difference between 1969 and the present day is perception. Players back then thought nothing of helping a good cause after-hours with a short demonstration of athletic skill. Now, though, they would never try, due to risk of injury or an effect on game performance, given all the handlers from their team, agents and the wildfire spread of information via social media. An ace pitcher working two softball innings, then getting racked up the next day would get roasted alive from all quarters.

But being asked to pitch in a softball game with a mob of grateful fans waiting for autographs afterwards was part of life as a 1969 Cub. Our team was in such demand after hours that a fan had to really try hard not to rub shoulders with a Cub outside Wrigley Field or not notice our presence in endorsements, advertisements, record albums, ghost-written newspaper columns and regular broadcast appearances. We gave the public what it wanted, as the term "Cub Power" permeated the marketplace.

While Banks and I were at Thillens, on the border of Chicago's West Rogers Park neighborhood and suburban Lincolnwood, some 23 miles south, more than 12,000 fans showed up to cheer a score of our teammates in the shadow of old Comiskey Park. At 47th Street and Damen Avenue, the "We Love the Chicago Cubs Night" highlighted the Back of the Yards Neighborhood Council's 1969 Fun Fair. The majority of attendees were South Siders who you'd expect to cheer for the White Sox, so we truly appealed to fans who were outside the Cubs' traditional fan base.

The huge crowds showing up on both the South and North Sides was just one night's example of how 1969 Cubs Mania swept through Chicago and well beyond in a manner not duplicated until the 1985 Super Bowl XX Bears. The latter is a high bar. A Bear had to be hibernating to not have a busy personal appearance schedule or a broadcast gig. Some of the thousands who showed up to welcome quarterback Jim McMahon to a Northwest Side mall autographing appearance rocked the Punky QB's limo as he arrived.

The dual three-peat champion Bulls also lifted the city, led by an all-universe Michael Jordan, who had to arrive late and leave early from movies to avoid being mobbed. Backup center Bill Wennington drew a bigger crowd than me – then Cubs pitching coach -- and three starting pitchers when he made a personal appearance at the same business at which we appeared in the northwest suburbs. The 2016 Cubs, of course, scratched sports' longest-running itch, but the typical player earning a multi-million-dollar salary did not have to be out and about as we did.

But the frenzy at increasingly packed Wrigley Field, on the streets, at appearances, in living rooms watching WGN or in cars or on the beach or in the park listening to WGN Radio has scarcely been duplicated through the decades. It was simply a special time and place, and the change of culture and consumer attitudes cannot recreate it.

"The whole city is a bit insane," wrote D.J.R. Bruckner of the Los Angeles Times in early September, 1969, when a pennant seemed oh-so-close. "Old ladies sit in the parks holding transistors, with earplugs stuck into their ears, like teenagers. The effect can be wild: you walk along and suddenly see three or four old people with plugs in their ears jump off their park benches, cheering. You do not know what has happened, but you can guess. A judge in criminal court ejected a spectator from the courtroom when he noticed that the man was frowning and smiling secretly to himself, and that there was a telltale wire running from his ear down under his shirt collar."

In the post-mortems about 1969, many claimed the players were too distracted – and thus drained – from numerous appearances, commercials and other spare-time activities. Unless every one of us was present at closing time at Rush Street hotspots many times a week, then that does not hold water. Once we were done with our day jobs around 4:30

p.m., it was hardly a strain to sign autographs at car dealers or other businesses for 90 minutes to two hours a couple of times per home stand, at most, after games.

Unless, of course, your promoter did not provide enough autograph material. One time the Cubs asked me to help open a McDonald's in north suburban Skokie. I was given 150 photos of myself to sign. But I ran out of the photos in about half-an-hour and signed for the remainder of my time on hamburger boxes and napkins, any kind of flat surface fans could conjure up. The pleasure of our company was desired everywhere, including when we boarded and deplaned our flights at O'Hare Airport, drawing mobs of autograph seekers. Even after we returned from our disastrous September 8-16 road trip, a welcoming crowd of hundreds engulfed us at the gate.

Taking a lot of the heat after the '69 season was agent Jack Childers, who coordinated many of the appearances with player rep Phil Regan. A pool comprising the appearance fees was set up and was to be distributed evenly, like World Series shares, after the season. But the fact Childers was in our cramped cubbyhole clubhouse daily before games did not sit well with some critics, one of whom described our locker room as a "hustler's paradise" in the following off-season.

"I remember one time they gave Ernie Banks $500, and all he had to do is tell what his favorite peanut butter-and-jelly sandwich was," recalled Regan years later when asked about the Childers-coordinated system. "A lot of people say one of the reasons we lost was all the endorsements and extras. It really wasn't. Childers did a great job. He went out and got a lot of things for the players. But he brought them in and (we) just signed them. The players did not spend a lot of time going out and doing the things that a lot of people said they did."

When players typically made $20,000 or $30,000 a year as five-year veterans and worked in the off-season, an appearance fee of $100 or even $200 meant you'd dive head-first on the offer. Even the top stars were not swimming in endorsement gold, compared to the payouts decades later.

"It wasn't why we did what we did," said Nye. "Money wasn't a factor. If you were asked to do a bar mitzvah for $25, it was, 'Oh, thanks!'"

Added the front-office's Chuck Shriver: "Then, $50 was a standard speaking fee."

Surprisingly, we were easy to get – and my cameo appearance on the mound at Thillens proved it.

The benefit game was the brainchild of Les Grobstein, then a 17-year-old fresh graduate of Von Steuben High School, maniacal Cubs fan and aspiring sportscaster, taking a tape recorder to the ballpark to perform mock play-by-play. Back in 1964, seventh-grader Grobstein was suspicious of the Lou Brock trade. Forty years later, he still charged the Cardinals knowingly traded an injured pitcher in Ernie Broglio, a charge vehemently denied from the same historical vantage point by '64 Cardinals General Manager Bing Devine.

In 1969, 'The Grobber' attended around 60 games, usually in grandstand seats which he was sometimes able to upgrade to boxes. Always a hustler, he got to know Shriver, our media relations director, and thus garner game notes before he was granted his first press credential. Grobstein used his rapport with Shriver to his advantage when he desired a couple of Cubs to appear at a cancer benefit softball game at Thillens Stadium on July 15, after our game with the Mets. Elaine Grobstein, Les' mother, had set up an organization in memory of Bea Goldstein, the Grobber's grandmother, who had died of cancer in 1968. Grobstein aimed high with his player requests: Banks and me. But when we were informed of the charity nature of the game, we both agreed to appear. I don't recall the size of our fee. Grobstein does, but in his often close-to-the-vest style won't reveal the dollar amounts even to this day.

"A lot of my Von Steuben classmates were stunned when we got Ernie and Fergie," the Grobber said.

When we arrived, Grobstein claimed I told him I'd like to pitch in the game. I don't remember – but I also don't doubt his recall. "Are you serious? You've got to be kidding?" he claimed he replied to me, knowing I had a date with the Mets the next day. But when I saw that 16-inch Clincher, I did not see any strain. Although it felt awkward in the first-ever time I pitched it, like handling a small basketball or volleyball, I soon figured it out and went two innings. Grobstein said I pitched well, and again I don't doubt him. Left unsaid was the fact many participants injure fingers fielding the Clincher in the gloveless Chicago game, but fate was not tempted by my brief outing. After I retired from the mound, I joined Banks in signing autographs for the big crowd, then made the 25-mile drive home from Devon and Kedzie to South Shore.

Rubbing shoulders with Banks, the Grobber and me on the platform behind home plate was 13-year-old Bob Pollack, who lived a block away on the 6400 block of North Troy Avenue. Pollack was an all-around Thillens utilityman. "I spent my summers there," he said. Pollack tended to the field and worked concessions. When we showed up, "Thillens (management) told me to throw on a uniform, and I couldn't have been happier," said Pollack, who handled the lights and the ball and strike switches. The lights were right next to the PA announcer's microphone, which the Grobber handled. All of us were publicized together in a much-published photo.

But Pollack's brush with us wasn't his only contact with Cubs stars, and an example how even the team's biggest names easily intermingled with the general public, not worried about stalking or security, as with 21st-century baseball descendants. Pollack recalled how Thillens owner Mel Thillens Jr. and stadium manager Frank Mariani were friends with Ron Santo.

"They worked it out where Ron would pick up me and my cousin, Richard Reisman, at Dunkin' Donuts on the corner of Devon and Troy on his way to the ballpark," said Pollack, most recently a Chicago-based camera operator for CNBC. "Before, we'd take the No. 155 Devon bus from the end of the line at Thillens to the Howard 'L' to get to Wrigley Field. But Ron picked us up about a half-dozen times in his white Lincoln Continental four-door. The door handles were in the center and opened out. He had a license plate, 'RS10.'"

To this day, I don't know if Pollack's or my memory was flawed. Santo typically drove a big Cadillac by my recall. After all, "home-run hitters drive Cadillacs" was the slogan of the day to show how the big boppers were prosperous. People who lived within a mile or so of Thillens remembered reports spreading like wildfire if Santo's Caddy was seen in the neighborhood. Whichever the top-of-the-line model, from either GM or Ford, Santo spared no expense on wheels and filled the car with his sons and Wrigley-bound kids.

"Ron would take us early to games for batting practice," Pollack said. "It was the greatest thing ever. We often got free tickets. After the game, if you grabbed one row of seats and put them up (to enable cleaning), you'd get seats to the next game."

Pollack cannot recall if Santo had started his trip from his previous longtime home in Park Ridge or his well-publicized new home in the Valley Lo subdivision of Glenview. Inbound, "It was mostly small talk," Pollack said, riding with Santo, known for his backstreet alternate ways.

But Santo was famous for abhorring the worst of traffic-clogged streets main streets and the jammed Kennedy Expressway. As a radio announcer later in life, he hinted of a semi-secret escape route going home. One problem – Santo would still have to switch to a busy arterial street to cross the north branch of the Chicago River.

But small talk generally dominated the inbound trip. Outbound was different if the Cubs lost, and you know how Santo took such setbacks. Son Jeff Santo, 5 ½ in 1969, recalled looking for a different ride home after losses. "I guess it was quiet," Pollack recalled. "It wasn't an uplifting trip."

However, a score of kids would have gladly traded places with Pollack and Reisman. "We'd wait by the fire station and we'd chase players (for autographs) for 45 minutes to an hour before Ron came out," he said. "It was just a dirt parking lot. The kids were jealous when they saw we got in the car with Ron. We just got lucky."

And Santo did not mind giving kids a lift 1,600 miles away. Jay Vershbo, a teenage Bleacher Bum, was allowed to travel to spring training by himself in 1970. "I had only $12 to last the whole week," he recalled. "At baggage claim, Ron was picking up his family. I introduced myself, and hitched a ride with him to Scottsdale. I'm kind of awestruck and was struck by his everyday conversation with (then-wife) Judy: 'Did you throw out the milk, did you stop the mail?'"

In that entire era, rubbing shoulders with the Cubs in and outside Wrigley Field was just so much easier. On the same night we were at Thillens, Ron and Judy Santo, along with Jeff and older brother Ron Jr. headed south from Wrigley Field to the Back of the Yards Council's Fun Fair. Regulars could not believe how the Cubs had turned the allegiances of South Siders.

Cubs players' families were invited. Drawing the loudest applause was Billy Williams, who, along with wife Shirley, stopped on their way to their South Shore home. Daughter Valarie, then 8, loved her Mickey Mouse balloon. A St. Michael's parish nun took care of 14-month-old Sandra while the parents took a dinner break. Regan and wife Carol with their four kids, Don and Carolyn Kessinger, Rich and Lynda Nye, Gene and Marilyn Oliver, Jim and Jennie Colborn, Kenny Holtzman and his date and Willie Smith all basked in the attention of the ballpark-sized turnout.

A more typical appearance compared to the South Side mob scene and participatory Thillens game was Tom Edwards' auto dealership in Elmhurst corralling a Cub every night from September 18-21, pushing his brand-new 1970 models. Holtzman, Randy Hundley and Bill Hands appeared at the showroom along with Regan, misspelled as "Reagan" in a newspaper ad.

Cubs-themed souvenirs like mugs and buttons were well-stocked all over grocery stores and other retail outlets, with Banks' smiling face on an ad enticing customers to come to Jewel for the booty. Sears reportedly sold nearly 1 million 15-cent Cubs bumper stickers with your choice of photos of Banks, Williams, Santo, Kessinger, Beckert and Hundley. The grocery chain also peddled some 200,000 Cubs T-shirts in a two-week period. The shirts continued selling at a 100,000 weekly pace. Martin Oil, a Cubs radio sponsor, planned to offer 50,000 glasses with Banks' photo adorned on them in a period of two weeks. They sold out in two days.

Meanwhile, Seno Formalwear presented a savings bond to a Cub Player of the Month. In July, O'Connor and Goldberg vice president Philip Rauen was shown presenting the bond to Santo as the monthly winner. Hands joined in as a top-pitcher recipient of a bond as O'Connor and Goldberg was touted as, "Where Chicago's Athletes Buy Chicago's Finest Footwear." I recall going with Williams to get some top-of-the-line shoes at O'Connor and Goldberg.

Banks was rated by Childers as having a two-to-one advantage over all other Cubs in product sales. Next up were Santo, followed closely by Hundley and Kessinger.

TV spots and paid broadcast appearances were not as plentiful as, say, for the 1985 Bears. But the stars plucked some good ones. I did a Serta Perfect Sleeper Mattress spot and another commercial throwing a ball into a window pane. If I missed and had to do a mess of re-takes, I would not have heard the end of it. Hundley touted the advantages of banking at Uptown Federal Savings on TV. International Harvester came out with a new Cub tractor while certified country boy Jim Hickman and reliever Phil Regan got tractors for appearing in a commercial.

With decades of broadcast work to his credit, Manager Leo Durocher would never get shut out of such a land rush. He attained the high ground, starring in a Schlitz beer commercial on WGN-TV Cubs broadcasts. Durocher enthralled the assembled cast with the story of his 1961 dirt-and-shin-kicking episode with umpire Jocko Conlan. "He kicked me, and I kicked him" was Durocher's narrative. Writers had a field day with Durocher's commercial pitch: "Have another Schlitz, fellas."

Banks, of course, began a multi-year stint with his much-mimicked Sunday night sports-anchor gig on WGN-TV in 1969, to go along with a frequent 7:50 p.m. weeknight, taped segment on WGN-Radio. His "Wonderful World of Ernie Banks" ghostwritten column in the Chicago Tribune made a ballyhooed debut in June, 1969, but was cut back to a much-shorter, four-to-eight paragraph "Ernie Banks Says" later in July. Even Banks had limits on his time as everyone was pulling at him.

Not to be outdone, the Chicago Daily News afternoon newspaper signed up Santo for a modest-length ghostwritten column. Santo also landed radio work in mid-August with late-afternoon radio segments with an on-the-rise Brent Musburger on all-news WBBM-Radio. The scheduling permitted Santo to appear after home and road day games and before road night games. My own regular TV gig lay two years in the future around Bucket No. 6 on WGN's "Bozo's Circus."

Even though we might have been born a little bit too soon to take full advantage of side broadcast gigs, existing newscasts were still in an expansion motif. And if they hired athletes, they'd typically went after Chicago Bears like record-setting Johnny Morris and quarterback Rudy Bukich, who could work Monday through Friday, even during their seasons. Daily NFL practice wasn't as all-encompassing as it developed into during later decades and the Bears players were even more modestly paid than we were. So they grabbed the TV dough when offered. Sports-talk radio, which employs players, coaches and managers to appear regularly on key programs, was still a couple of decades off into the future. Likewise with cable TV staples like ESPN and regional sports networks. Other than Banks, the only other Cub in my first Chicago tenure who snared a regular TV deal was Milt Pappas, with WLS-TV, after his big 1972 season, which included a near-perfect game.

While broadcast outlets were a little slow on the trigger to employ platoons of Cubs, newspapers did try to jump on our bandwagon beyond the Banks and Santo columns. As early as July, the two tabloids, the morning Chicago Sun-Times and afternoon Chicago Today, started daily cartoon-like graphics counting down our "magic number" to clinch the National League East. The Today had the number at 62 near the end of July. The Sun-Times actually depicted Durocher wearing turban-like headgear, peering into a baseball-shaped crystal ball in which the decreasing magic number was depicted. Unfortunately, that number eventually stalled at 22.

Chicago Today sports columnist Rick "The Ripper" Talley even consulted Lee Wayne, "magician, para-psychologist and keeper of a Ouija Board." Wayne's prediction: "The Cubs should win but the big IF is Leo Durocher. I have the feeling Leo will leave the team again (after his unexcused departures before his wedding and for his stepson's summer camp Parent's Day in Wisconsin). For the Cubs to win, they should not change their routine. They shouldn't have any adverse thoughts...and they should continue to use their PMA (Positive Mental Attitude)." So how did Wayne come up with that narrative? "My mind is almost as good as a million-dollar computer. Those things just come to me," he replied.

"The Cubs should win, but the big IF is Leo Durocher."

Meanwhile, the Daily News ran a "Go-To-The-Series" contest in which readers would predict the date, hour and minute the Cubs would clinch the NL East. Winners would get two tickets to all World Series games, home and away, along with transportation and hotel and meal expenses for two. The first group of runners-up would tap into 49 pairs of box-seat tickets for all September weekend games at Wrigley Field. The final group of runners-up would be awarded Cubs-autographed baseballs. For nostalgia's sake, the newspaper interviewed prominent 1945 World Series-participant Cubs, like ace pitcher Hank Borowy and slugger Bill "Swish" Nicholson for their predictions. Borowy predicted a division-clincher for 3:45 p.m. September 19, while Swish forecast 3:50 p.m. September 21. "I know the pressure that's on them. And I know they'll come through," said Nicholson.

Cubs souvenirs intersected with the Apollo XI astronauts as they got a hero's welcome as an estimated 100,000 crammed the Civic Center Plaza by the Picasso Statue on August 13, 1969, after more than 1 million viewed their parade through downtown Chicago. The sons of Neal Armstrong and Buzz Aldrin, first men on the moon, all received Cubs hats and jackets.

Now though, the majority of the 1969 endorsements and promotions have been largely forgotten through the passage of time. But still replayed today, and best remembered, were our roles as part-time singers to join daily, unpaid crooner Banks. "Hey Hey, Holy Mackerel, No Doubt About It," named after the home-run calls of Brickhouse, Vince Lloyd and Lou Boudreau, became our informal anthem, and can still be heard around the Cubs Universe, along with "Go Cubs Go," and other songs penned through the decades. Almost all of the players took turns, some multiple times, trying to match Banks as a singer.

Left-Field Bleacher Bum alumnus Randy Anderson of Skokie, Illinois, still has unopened copies of "Cub Power," a decently produced record album for its time that enlisted the majority of players as participants. Consider the recorded entertainment choices of the day. With tape cassettes a new technology and home video recorders still more than a decade away from common use, the old-fashioned vinyl record was still the way to consume one's favorite entertainers away from movies, and TV and radio broadcasts.

"Cub Power," a $4.95 product, earned $12,000 for the player endorsement pool in its first day of sales on August 25, 1969. Prior to its consumer offering, area companies snapped up 25,000 copies, earning the player pool $12,500 at the 50 cents-an-album arrangement. "Cub Power" was slickly packaged. Team photographer Barney Sterling's hatless color head-shot photos of the majority of players – to avoid licensing issues – served as a border to giant baseball photos. Center fielder Don Young, little-used reliever Don Nottebart and reliever Hank Aguirre were notable absences in the collage of photos. On the back cover was a black-and-white photo of chief Bleacher Bum Ron Grousl, shirtless but adorned in his yellow helmet, leading cheers into a megaphone.

"Cub Power" fittingly had Jack Brickhouse voice the introduction, handing off to No. 5 hitter Banks as the album leadoff man. Stating, "Everything is wonderful here at Wrigley Field," as only Mr. Cub could, he handed off to Hundley. Next voice was Santo's, who dedicated the album to the fans. The Bleacher Bums then jumped in with their version of "Take Me Out to the Ballgame," with Mike Murphy's bugle the musical accompaniment.

Our player-cheerleader of the Bums, Dick Selma, then piped in with the Bums' "yells," providing him and his teammates "a little more incentive…These are true baseball fans." The Bums then got their own section of Side One with a signature cheer of theirs, "Here we go Cubbies, here we go," and a challenge to the home-plate umpire, swiping from 1968 Democratic Convention protestors, chanting, "The whole world is watching…the whole world is watching."

The Bums then joined in Jack Kearney's Lowry organ rendition of the National Anthem, with the chorus substituting "Al Spangler" for "Star Spangled Banner." The WGN-Radio opening-game broadcast theme of "It's a Beautiful Day for a Ballgame," was given the Bum's rush, and after a custom-produced version of "Glory Hallelujah," the Bums sang, "We Got the San Francisco Giants in Our Hands…We Got the National League Pennant in Our Hands," We Got the World Series in Our Hands…We got the best damn team in our hands." Such was the fan sentiment at the height of summer, 1969.

And even more Cubs sent their greetings after an introduction by radio color analyst Boudreau: Regan; Hickman; Beckert; Kessinger; Ted Abernathy; Williams; Aguirre; and Paul Popovich. I also got a short speaking part, although the recording has me with a higher-pitched voice than I expected. I was 26 at the time, and I swear I had long ago gone through puberty.

Side 2 featured the tenor-singing talents of Nate Oliver, the joyous baritone of Willie Smith and the small-town barbership-quartet style of Gene Oliver crooning, "Hey Hey Holy Mackerel, No Doubt About It." Nate Oliver also took lead-singer role in a takeoff on the Righteous Brothers' "You've Got That Lovin' Feeling," altered to "We Got That Pennant Feeling." The Cubs voices also did, "Baseball, The All-American Game."

"Gene was the guy who put it all together," recalled Nate Oliver, still singing second tenor at his church in 2018. "We got Willie to sing. We did that version of the Righteous Brothers. I was second tenor and first tenor. Willie went with base baritone."

Since Banks sang at the drop of a hat in '69, the mystery continues as to why he did not make the Oliver-Oliver-Smith trio into a quartet. But Nate Oliver theorized that Banks was so big and so busy, he simply was not asked.

However, Nate Oliver was no rookie in such productions.

"I made part of an album in New York in 1963," he said of his Dodgers days. "Before the 1963 World Series, we won the final game in Philly, so I went to NY and made a partial album."

Rounding out "Cub Power" was a gaggle of Chicago musicians, including longtime local producer Johnny Frigo performing instrumentals of "Hey Hey Holy Mackerel" and "Take Me Out to the Ballgame." Frigo arranged and conducted the album. Sports agent Childers, of course, had his hands squarely in the disc as producer, along with businessman of international renown, Peter H. Wright.

We also sang in the cradle of teen idols in Philadelphia. After our July 19, 1969 game, a frustrating loss in the stifling heat at Connie Mack Stadium, the two Olivers, Smith, Williams Santo, Kessinger and Hundley recorded "Pennant Fever" at a local studio. Packaged on the record was a black-and-white photo of the session with the headline, "The Chicago Cubs Sing 'Pennant Fever,'" derived from "Fever" by Little Willie John in 1956 and later covered and popularized by Peggy Lee. "They gave us fever, pennant fever. And the fans are feelin' fine" were the key lyrics."

Although reports circulated that the record sold 25,000 copies by the end of August, neither Hundley nor Williams recalled making any residuals off the production. Nothing ventured, nothing gained, you've got to say though.

Still, another Cubs-oriented record came out, this the "Go Go Go Chicago Cubs," sung by Marie Fuller.

And our high profile spilled over into future off-seasons. The early 1970s included the formation of a Cubs basketball team that played exhibition games against all comers, a lot of times in high school gyms. In the winters, I did not live in Chicago, but I'd fly into Chicago from Detroit for selected games. The boys needed my nearly 6-foot-5 height, my dunking skills and my Harlem Globetrotters experience. Kessinger was a welcome addition off of his college basketball experience. Santo, who played in high school, could have been a blocking guard with his physique. Williams joined in, too. Dr. David Fletcher, then a west suburban Glen Ellyn resident, recalled Williams was the only person of color in the packed local gym when we played, sans a center named Jenkins, who could dunk the ball. A little more than a decade later, Williams made Glen Ellyn his longtime home.

Childers planned yet another promotion: life-like face masks of the players. I don't know if he ever went through with the idea, scheduled for mid-September 1969 release. By then, Tom Seaver commercials were all the rage.

Still, the reaching of the Cubs into almost every emotional pore of the Second City was without precedent, and unforgettable. We had basically a 2 ½-hour daily, live and in-color promo for our talents via WGN-TV and a booming 50,000-watt audio PR conduit on WGN-Radio. But the public did not stop there. They watched or listened to our games, then met us in person or heard us sing. We were the complete Chicago Cubs, except in the final season result, but still unsurpassed in my opinion by most pro teams to follow in a toddlin' town.

WGN Continental
Chicago Cubs Networking

Phil Wrigley did not have to spend a dime on advertising to plug the Cubs in 1969. For all but 18 road games, we had at least a 2 ½-hour, live-and-in-color commercial called Cubs baseball on Good Ole Channel 9.

Play-by-play giant Jack Brickhouse was our No. 1 salesman, our leading preacher-man, in his 23rd season at the Cubs TV mic with thousands of games under his belt. Brickhouse interspersed his throat-busting "Hey Hey!" home-run call with reminders of "22,000 unreserved grandstand and bleacher tickets go on sale the day of each game." Lloyd Pettit, best known for his Blackhawks "Shot and a Goal" play-by-play calls, served as "Leadoff Man" pre-game show interviewer and Brickhouse's middle-inning relief man. We'd get to meet the pair briefly on the field before the game and afterward, when we'd clomp up the ramp in our spikes to the broadcast booth for Brickhouse's "Tenth Inning" show.

Orchestrating it all from a big truck under the far left-field stands was Emmy Award-winning producer/director Arne Harris. A maestro at the remote master control, Harris crafted a network-style production with just four big ole RCA TK-41 color cameras, each nearly 300-pound monsters requiring strength and dexterity by its operator. He had one videotape replay machine, which reran the live image. The all-seeing Harris eye covered nearly every square inch of Wrigley Field, from Leo Durocher's perch in the dugout to girls showing off a lot of skin in the far corners of the bleachers. Known for his "hat shots," Harris and his crew always drew on-air credit from Brickhouse. It all combined to personalize Cubs baseball.

If you weren't near a TV set in a 200-mile radius of Chicago, you could also follow our daily drama via the folksy-yet-objective narrative of WGN-Radio play-by-play men Vince Lloyd and Lou Boudreau. Lloyd's baritone could go even deeper in his diaphragm than Brickhouse's to proclaim, "Holy Mackerel," for one of our homers, while Boudreau, an ex-Cubs manager and the pride of south suburban Harvey, chimed in with a higher-pitched, "No Doubt About It."

Lloyd and Boudreau were the ultimate multi-taskers. In their fifth season on radio together in 1969, the pair was so beloved that fans would send home-cooked goodies up to their booth.

And any viewer or listener knew the broadcasters were "homers" who rooted for us. True to their Midwestern roots, Brickhouse grew up down the road in Peoria. TV sidekick Pettit was a Milwaukee native who attended Northwestern University. Native South Dakotan Lloyd cut much of his broadcasting teeth in Peoria. Boudreau was the pride of Chicago's south-suburban Harvey. WGN-TV sports editor Jack Rosenberg hailed from Pekin, near Peoria. And WGN director-producer Arne Harris, who called the shots of our riveting images in the remote truck, was a native Chicagoan.

Cubs' players and coaches, and even our manager, with his 5-minute *"Durocher in the Dugout"* pregame show, did their part before and after games to make the broadcasts even more entertaining. Booked by Rosenberg for our guest shots, we received $50 checks to appear live on the "Leadoff Man" and "Tenth Inning" shows. All the big names did their turns with Brickhouse for the latter. That required a trip through the grandstands and up the ramp to the broadcast booth, usually with one's spikes still on. We took it slow under those conditions walking on concrete. I recall having an Andy Frain usher in front and back of me to run interference since you could not stop to sign autographs because time was of the essence to get upstairs.

If we won Star of the Game honors, we'd get free shoes from [well-known, Chicago-area footwear retailers] O'Connor and Goldberg. Billy Williams and I won it a couple of times and they never failed to get the right size for us. Mine were size 12 or 13.

"Every Cubs player was tremendous when it came to helping us," said Rosey. "It was a cinch deal to do. And it wasn't only the Cubs. Years before, I asked Jackie Robinson (for a post-game interview). "He had a feeling who was prejudiced and who wasn't. Jackie said whatever you need."

We also helped out when Brickhouse had to fill time during rain delays. In 1969, WGN did not go to recorded programming during delays. Thus, Brickhouse used his interviewing and adlib skills to hold the audience until action resumed. Or Pettit would chat with us on the bench so we would not have to go back to the booth.

One time, Rosenberg snared Glenn Beckert in the dugout on the road to gab with Pettit during a delay. Beckert, of course, was a nervous smoker, always needing to light up when he came back into the dugout after an opposition at-bat was completed. So this time, Harris prematurely punched up the camera showing Beckert and Pettit waiting to go on. Both were smoking. Harris quickly switched to another shot – firing up on camera was not acceptable. By the time the interview began, both had put out their smokes.

Brickhouse, meanwhile, had been famed for getting the audience familiar with players of color, like Ernie Banks and the White Sox' Minnie Minoso in the 1950s. He was a great ad-libber and skilled interviewer. While I was in the booth with Jack, he'd always take care to mention I was from Canada. He also often talked about wrestling, so I was amazed when I heard that Brickhouse did play-by-play in the 1950s for Saturday doubleheaders, then raced over to Marigold Gardens to host a 2 ½-hour wrestling show, starting at 8:30 p.m.

on WGN-TV. He often said an 80-hour week was like a vacation for him, and his schedule certainly bears that out.

Doing Boudreau's pre-game interview show was a breeze, by comparison. Boudreau would typically tape the session outside the clubhouse. We gave him a break with our one-shot appearances after he sometimes required several takes to record Durocher's "Manager's Show," mostly because of the manager's profane language or other false starts.

And Rosenberg's rapport with us extended beyond the ballpark. In 1969, he invited Ken Holtzman to his Passover Seder at his north suburban Lincolnwood home.

"Kenny responded, 'Thanks, but you've got to line me up with a date,'" recalled 'Rosey.' "I said, 'Holtzman, you guys got girls coming out of your ears. But I think my neighbor's daughter is good for you.' And they eventually got married."

The three generations of gum-magnate owners proved that comprehensive broadcast exposure builds up fan loyalty from the first day a kid watches or listens to baseball and whets the appetite for ticket purchases once that young fan is old enough to travel to Wrigley Field. With interest bubbling up when we began our revival in the late spring of 1967, the Cubs' philosophy proved once and for all that televising all your home games did not wreck your live attendance. Rather, it did the exact opposite.

Even when the Cubs drew just 635,000 to Wrigley Field in my rookie season in 1966, the fans were no further away than their TV sets. The kids still ran home from 3:15 p.m. final school bells to catch the last couple of innings of games with Brickhouse and Pettit.

The fans were no further away than their TV sets.

The dramatic increase in home attendance the next three seasons coincided with even more WGN telecasts and a much wider distribution via the regional Midwest network stoking those bus group trips from downstate Illinois and Iowa.

And so we'll give you a history lesson in Cubs broadcasting unmatched elsewhere. But the instruction is necessary to show how a team, the fans and a loyal broadcast operation came together to help create the contending Cubs in 1969.

Always mindful of how creative, eye-catching advertising promoted his gum business, William Wrigley Jr., the first of three generations in his family to run the Cubs, permitted wall-to-wall radio coverage of his contending and glamorous team in the late 1920s. Most baseball owners believed if they gave away an audio description of games, they would be hurt at the gate.

But in tandem with dynamic Cubs President William L. Veeck Sr., father of Bill Veeck, the elder Wrigley proved his colleagues wrong. With a pennant-winning 1929 team that was a precursor of our own appeal, the Cubs set a big-league attendance record of 1,485,166. Team officials noticed that cars parked around Wrigley Field bore license plates from all the surrounding states — as far as the radio signals of Cubs broadcasts extended. By 1931, seven Chicago stations carried the team and Wrigley charged none of them a rights fee.

Fifteen years later, in 1946, Phil Wrigley first let in the camera lenses of WBKB-Channel 4, Chicago's first TV station. In 1947, after a misplaced season broadcasting the

New York Giants on radio, Brickhouse joined Whispering Joe Wilson as an announcer, earning $35 per game on the WBKB telecasts covering all home games. Jackie Robinson's Friendly Confines debut before a record 47,101 fans on May 18, 1947, thus was televised. When Brickhouse became the first voice heard on the brand-new WGN-TV in April 1948, he became an immediate natural to work the Cubs telecasts.

Amazingly, in 1949, Chicago's third TV station opted in for the Cubs. ABC-owned WENR-TV, the Channel 7 predecessor of WLS-TV, installed its equipment in Wrigley. Announcing was Hall-of-Famer Rogers Hornsby, a veteran of the '29 Cubs. Only WGN-TV also covered the crosstown White Sox. With all that bulky equipment from a trio of outlets now installed, Wrigley charged each station a $100,000 "construction" fee. But like his father, the owner did not assess a rights fee.

WENR did the games for only one season, then WBKB dropped out after 1951 with more CBS daytime network programming taking precedence, leaving WGN with a monopoly. By now, Wrigley did charge a rights fee, but it was under-market rate for the then-second biggest TV market in the country. Even with the Cubs wallowing in the second division, WGN-TV had an automatic profit center for its beer and gasoline ads. The animated Hamm's bear comically dashing about the woods to the tune of, "From the land of sky-blue waters," with a tom-tom in the background in a commercial became just as memorable as the on-field images of the time.

And no way was Brickhouse, sunny by nature, prompted to kill the station's golden goose with on-air criticism of the team or the owner. At the same time, his "Hey Hey!" call, originally yelled extemporaneously, was brought to Brickhouse's attention by his technical crew, so he made it a mainstay for all Cubs homers. "Hey Hey!" was the top soundtrack of the summer of '69, both celebrating homers and the leadoff words to the team's unofficial anthem.

"Every once in a while you fall in a love with a word or a phrase or an expression, and you don't realize you've fallen in love with it and you're using it too much," Brickhouse recalled in 1997, a year before his death at 82.

"One day at Wrigley Field (circa 1952), Hank Sauer popped one out of the ballpark over the left-field fence. On the monitor on my set in the booth, the crew flashed the life-size letters, 'Hey Hey!' The minute I saw that, I knew what they were telling me. I had fallen in love with the expression "Hey Hey!" and didn't realize I was doing it. We had a little conversation about it. It doesn't hurt to have an expression identified with a broadcaster such as Russ Hodges' 'Bye-Bye Baby,' Harry's Caray's 'Holy Cow!' and Milo Hamilton's 'Holy Toledo!' We decided to leave it in."

WGN also pioneered a technical development that would keep viewers' attention to this day. In 1951, with no room behind the plate at Chicago's famed Thillens softball Stadium to place its camera for a Little League game, station technicians found an alternate spot out in center field. Thus the "center-field" shot was born. The pitcher-batter view from behind was quickly adapted for big-league use on WGN well before the national networks and other stations employed what is now baseball's standard coverage shot.

Still though, the Cubs and Sox continued to share WGN-TV. But the North Siders still had an exposure advantage, airing all 77, then 81 (starting in 1962) home games. The Sox barred any home night games for telecast until about 1963. Even when up to 15 road Sox night games were added in the early 1960s, the Cubs still televised more games on WGN. Interestingly, the Sox collected more in broadcast rights fees in totality even with less WGN-TV exposure.

And then an underrated lead-in program to the Cubs made its debut in September, 1961. "Bozo's Circus" was on the air for a memorable generation-plus run for an hour each weekday at noon. Bozo might have been the top children's show of all time anywhere in the United States or Canada. I can attest to its popularity, since I had a role after my Cy Young Award season in 1971, supervising kids in the Grand Prize Game. I ensured that I, as the top control pitcher in the National League, with 37 walks in 325 innings, always hit Bucket No. 5. Otherwise, I would have never heard the end of it from my teammates.

Meanwhile, the waiting list for Bozo tickets was four or more years. Pregnant women would order tickets so they could take their child when they hit kindergarten age. Countless kids and their moms no doubt watched Bozo, gritted through the 15-minute, 1 p.m., WGN newscast by a deep-voiced staff announcer and then perked up when the "Leadoff Man" signed on at 1:15.

But in the broadcast world, power piled up on power in 1958 when 50,000-watt clear channel WGN-Radio acquired the Cubs' radio rights. Wrigley liked young play-by-play announcer Jack Quinlan, who nosed out Milo Hamilton for the job after both handled the broadcasts on 5,000-watt WIND-Radio. Brickhouse told WGN boss Ward Quaal he might lose money in the first season paying a $150,000 radio rights fee, but would then make money "forevermore." He was almost right, as WGN-Radio only ceded the rights to CBS-Radio in Chicago in 2014 amid the financial setbacks of the President of Baseball Operations Theo Epstein's rebuilding program on the North Side of town.

Back in 1958 though, fresh from managing the Kansas City Athletics, former American League MVP Boudreau was hired to team with north suburban Wilmette native Quinlan, with the pair proving an immediate hit with listeners. Quinlan, easily a network-quality voice headed for even greater things, was tragically killed at 38 in a 1965 spring training car accident. Lloyd subsequently slid over from partnering with Brickhouse to do radio and Boudreau punctuated that by telling WGN execs he'd only continue if paired with Lloyd. Meanwhile, Pettit, a longtime WGN-TV newscaster in addition to his Hawks duties, succeeded Lloyd in the video booth.

But the Sox also lost out in radio exposure to the Cubs. WGN's daytime signal on AM 720 radiated out further in all directions from its Schaumburg transmitter than the Sox's on what was then WCFL, AM 1000. The night-time differential was even worse. The only station on its frequency as a clear channel, WGN's sky-wave signal potentially reached 38 states and much of Canada. But WCFL had a directional signal beaming east from its west-suburban Downers Grove tower to protect other stations on AM 1000. WCFL could barely be heard 50 miles west in DeKalb, while Sox chairman Jerry Reinsdorf recalled picking up the station clearly after dark while in college in Washington, D.C.

Soon after the arrivals of me, Durocher, and so many other contributors to the '69 Cubs, the Chicago baseball broadcast landscape changed radically and succeeding events tipped the town dramatically in favor of the Cubs. Sox owner Arthur Allyn desired a TV outlet to call his own. In 1964, for instance, WGN aired 86 Cubs games compared to 64 Sox telecasts. Allyn cut a deal with new UHF outlet, WFLD-TV, owned by Chicago Sun-Times parent Field Enterprises, in the mid-summer of 1966. The Sox would subsequently move to Channel 32 via a five-year, $1 million per year contract to air all home and the majority of road games, starting in 1968.

Brickhouse unsuccessfully tried to talk Allyn out of ceding the WGN high ground, even with fewer telecasts than the Cubs, but the WFLD contract was penny-wise, albeit pound-foolish. TV sets did not have mandatory UHF tuners installed until 1964. Only 30 percent of the Chicago market could receive UHF in 1966. Allyn overestimated his potential audience going forward, especially switching from a high-rated and well-established outlet like WGN.

In 1964, the Cubs aired just five road games, not even televising the season opener at Forbes Field in Pittsburgh since it conflicted with the White Sox home opener. WGN-TV instead aired the second Cubs game.

But in 1967, with the Sox departure for WFLD looming after the season, WGN-TV announced a schedule of 25 Cubs games for its new "WGN Continental-Chicago Cubs Baseball Network." Thirteen road night games, 10 Sunday home and road games and two holiday games were offered. The timing was perfect. One network game was my Sunday, July 2, 1967, 4-1 complete-game victory over the Cincinnati Reds before nearly 40,000 at Wrigley Field. The win enabled the Cubs to tie for first place for the first time that late in the season since 1945. Fans refused to leave Wrigley Field until the Cubs flag on the scoreboard was hoisted above all other teams. The color images had to be riveting down the network.

Ratings and share numbers in Chicago and outlying markets were stupendous for the July 24-26, 1967 series in old Busch Stadium. The viewership heartily supported the extra costs for WGN televising, for the first time, an entire 3-game Cubs road series, with the final game added to the original schedule.

The Cubs tied for first for the final time in '67 by winning the first game, 3-1, behind Ray Culp. For the Monday night, July 24 game, some 1.5 million viewers in the Chicago area tuned in with a 46 share (percentage of households watching TV at the time). About 100,000 more viewers in the originating market with an identical 46 share watched when WGN fed the Tuesday night, July 25, game to stations in Rockford, Peoria, Champaign, the Quad Cities, Milwaukee, Madison and Marion, Indiana. The regional audience was gauged at an astounding, for the time, 3.5 million. The groundwork for the Cubs as destination viewing in 1969 going forward had been firmly laid.

WGN-Radio also had an enormous reach, its signal radiating out about 200 miles during the daytime and much further via the ionosphere-bouncing "sky-waves" for night road games. However, in my first Cubs tenure, WGN-Radio did not set up a big network like its TV counterpart or the Harry Caray/Jack Buck Cardinals broadcasts on KMOX-

Radio in St. Louis, the latter totaling close to 100 stations in the Midwest and mid-South. The daytime reach was deemed good enough for the base of Cubs fans and those within a day's driving distance of Wrigley Field.

Only in the 1980s did Lloyd and Rosenberg, staying off their former road assignments, team to build up the Cubs radio network. So for those on the fringes of the afternoon radio signal, the new TV network – beaming into western Iowa and northern Wisconsin -- was a welcome sight for fans' eyes.

And developments in 1968 locked in the Cubs in Chicago as the prime baseball video attraction over the Sox. Having possessed a kind of gentleman's agreement with Allyn over sharing WGN, Wrigley was angry with the Sox owner bolting for WFLD. He told WGN executives they could not televise as many Cubs games as they pleased, without a significant rights-fee increase.

But Quaal and his ad salesmen were overjoyed. Now the Cubs would televise games from every NL outpost. The only exemptions were most weekday road games, weeknight West Coast games and the occasional Monday night games that conflicted with an NBC prime-time baseball telecast. Fans could now see such far-flung ballparks as Dodger Stadium and Candlestick Park. On the same night as the Democratic Convention riots on August 28, 1968, WGN aired a doubleheader from Los Angeles as a welcome diversion for some from the conflict. The Cubs' exclusivity on WGN was seen as a boon for the North Siders and a huge mistake for the Sox at the time.

"The White Sox made a drastic mistake when they left WGN-TV two years ago and signed a contract with WFLD," Chicago Tribune columnist Robert Markus wrote on April 16, 1969. "At the precise instant the Cubs were becoming a stronger gate attraction for the first time in years, the White Sox opened the door to head-to-head competition via telecasts of night Cub road games."

But yet another consumer factor pushing viewers to the Cubs was in play. WGN first aired Cubs and Sox home games in color in 1960, but the majority of households did not start buying their first color TV sets until the late 1960s. Even though these new sets had built-in UHF tuners, the purchasers often opted for Cubs telecasts. The day games at Wrigley Field were resplendent in all bright, sunshiny colors – the green grass and ivy-covered outfield walls, the blue Cubs uniforms, the otherwise red brick-perimeter walls, the outfield doors, the yellow Bleacher Bums helmets and always, always, the up-close-and-personal, multi-hued Arne Harris shots.

But after a major Wrigley Field renovation in 1967-68, three cameras were switched to the upper deck – one each behind third, home and first. Harris could focus face-on to the hitter with the proper camera, depending on from which side of the plate he batted. He could also switch from camera to camera more easily on a base hit to the outfield, showing the baserunner's progress and the fielder in sequence. The high-home camera could show homers' paths into the left-field bleachers or beyond.

Harris and his cameramen put on a great show, enhanced by improved lenses that permitted better close-ups or "tight shots" on players. The latter came in particularly handy when Holtzman was shown concentrating on Henry Aaron as the final batter in his August 19, 1969, no-hitter against the Braves.

WGN assertively promoted its Cubs highlights when we began taking off in 1967. The station zealously guarded the game tape's exclusivity on the 10 p.m. news, knowing viewers would change the channel from better-rated newscasts to watch the Cubs clips. Thwarted from using WGN tape, the three network-owned stations each sent film crews to Wrigley Field to record game highlights. That only increased our exposure thanks to the convenience of day games. The stations used motorcycle couriers to rush the unprocessed film to their downtown studios around 4 p.m. to be edited in time for the 6 p.m. news. Thus fans got a double-dose of their Cubs TV fix not possible with home night games. That was another reason the White Sox fell behind us in profile.

Big-name sponsors flocked to the WGN broadcasts for 1969. TV season buyers included Schlitz (replacing Hamms with a memorable spot starring Durocher), Allstate Insurance, Zenith, R.J. Reynolds Tobacco (cigarette ads were still permitted on TV until 1970), Pure Oil and Commonwealth Edison. Lloyd and Boudreau on radio were backed by Old Style ("fully krausened" from God's Country), Martin Oil Co. ("Purple Martin Ethyl"), Chicagoland Buick Dealers, retailer Montgomery Ward and Oak Park Federal Savings and Loan.

International House of Pancakes jumped aboard to sponsor "Cubs Fever," a half-hour WGN mid-season special at 9:30 p.m. Monday, July 21, during the All-Star Break. The timeslot formerly was used for the in-season "Sports Open Line" show, on which Leo Durocher made regular appearances in 1966-67. In the pre-VCR/DVR era, "Cubs Fever" gave fans a chance to relive video of some of the great moments of the first half. In another century, the special migrated to YouTube.

By this point in the '69 season, viewers were virtually spoiled by WGN-TV's heavy Cubs schedule. The Chicago Tribune had to run a story in its Tuesday, July 1 edition, confirming that afternoon's game from Montreal would not be televised, as it was not in prime time. An explanation from a WGN spokesman was required as some telecasts drew more than one-fifth of the total TV sets in the Chicago market.

Continuing to expand, the WGN Continental-Chicago Cubs Network covered all of northern and central Illinois, much of Iowa and Wisconsin and northern Indiana. At the height of summer, 1969, stations in Rockford, the Quad Cities, Peoria, Champaign, Milwaukee (where future Commissioner Bud Selig may very well have been a viewer), Madison, Lacrosse, Green Bay, Cedar Rapids, Des Moines, South Bend, Ft. Wayne and Terre Haute plugged into the network.

Still though, the "three-channel" universe that predominated from TV's early days still existed in most of those affiliates' cities and a Cubs telecast was a highlight of the week. Even in Chicago, ratings other than for the three network-owned stations and powerful independent WGN lagged far behind for public TV outlet WTTW, along with WFLD and ethnic programming-oriented WCIU on the UHF band. But where summer reruns predominated after June, the Cubs offered fresh, live programming with daily drama. And the home day games proved far more exciting than hokey game shows, stultifying soap operas and old movies. Kids still went out to play unorganized sandlot baseball from morning 'til after dark in the summer of 1969, with televised ballgames the only reason to stay inside during the day.

But the greatest-ever Cubs broadcast exposure in 1969 gave the widest possible audience for what is surely the Top 10 calls in team history. Brickhouse and Lloyd virtually broke the sound barrier with their calls of Willie Smith's walk-off, Opening Day homer. "Well-hit, deep to right, back, back, back…Hey Hey! It's all over! Willie Smith just homered…the Cubs win the game…And look at the reception at home plate for Willie Smith (gives out a war whoop)," was Brickhouse's rendition. Lloyd mustered his entire diaphragm for: "Willie hits one HIGH, DEEP RIGHT FIELD…IT IS A HOME RUN…A home run by Willie Smith! (Boudreau threw in a comical "Hey Hey!" in the background)" as each announcer pounded the table in pure joy.

Brickhouse's catch phrases came on prime display though and were mimicked forever. Following a 1969 Cubs home victory, before he'd sum up the "happy totals," he'd proclaim loudly, "The merry men of Wrigley Field roll on and on." On a particularly dramatic home run, Brickhouse would yell, "Weeee…" after his "Hey Hey!" often adding, "Atta boy!" ahead of the player's name. A dramatic play, good or bad, would elicit an, "Oh, brother!" And incidentally, Brickhouse adopted his "Hey Hey" for football on his Bears broadcasts with a variance of "Oh brother" as "Oh buddy!"

When a Cubs pitcher zeroed in on a no-hitter, getting to 2 strikes on a hitter with 2 outs in the ninth, or any similar dramatic situation, he'd set it up with, "Watch it…watch it now!" or, "You can cut the tension with a knife!" Meanwhile, "A Pier 6 donnybrook" was a baseball brawl. An "Alphonse and Gaston Act" was a mix-up between outfielders. A too-little, too-late rally came "after the horse was out of the barn" or, "a day late and a dollar short." A quick change of situation was, "For a hot minute there." A high-scoring, mistake-filled game would be, "The married men versus the single men at the company picnic."

The terrible ninth inning I experienced in New York on July 8, 1969, that drove me to smoking one of Beckert's cigarettes post-game was, "A disastrous turn of events here in Shea Stadium." Getting out of a tight jam evoked, "Somebody bring my stomach." Kessinger's fielding artistry in the hole to his right was a display of the shortstop's "boarding-house reach." Origin of "boarding house?" Brickhouse later explained at a boarding house, a resident was left hungry unless he had a long reach for food at the communal dining table.

Our relationship with TV was 180 degrees different than Dodgers and Cardinals fans at the time. Two decades into the TV era, fans of both franchises still followed their teams primarily on radio. Blessed with Vin Scully, perhaps the best announcer in history, Los Angeles rooters were limited to just a relative few road games on TV. But Dodgers' fans brought so many transistor radios to Dodger Stadium that you could follow the game via Scully's play-by-play all over the ballpark. Only 40 Cardinals games each year typically were televised, so Caray's voluble prime as a broadcaster was aural via KMOX and the Cardinals radio network, not visual, as in his Cubs days on WGN-TV 20 years later.

The predominance of Brickhouse as the almost daily face and voice of the Cubs had just one negative aspect. Lloyd's own talent as radio play-by-play man and a much-admired regular around Wrigley Field sometimes was somewhat obscured. In most baseball cities, Lloyd likely would have been regarded a standout No. 1 sportscaster. In my book, however, Lloyd has always been famed sports scribe Ford C. Frick-worthy as the annual inductee in the broadcasters' wing of the Hall of Fame.

WGN's broadcast crew, both announcers, camera operators and technical people in the booth and TV truck, had uncommon camaraderie. They worked backbreaking hours. Brickhouse often said an "80-hour-week is like a vacation to us." He and Rosenberg were particularly close.

"Why did we have such a bond?" Rosey asked. "It just evolved. It just happened where everybody had a comfort level working for WGN television and radio. Nobody worried about time. I impart to kids -- when you get a job, it's not always the money. If you're proud and somebody asks you where you work, and what you do, and you can tell them, it's worth everything. There's things that transcend (money).

"This was not just an ordinary job, where you get paid at the end of the week and go home. I know this sounds like a cliché. It was not just the money. It was the feeling we had of being part of history. How do you account for the seven-day weeks, flying around all the time?"

So no matter if it was TV or radio, the WGN announcers and technical crew were a huge factor in the staying power of the '69 Cubs. While WGN's original meaning was "World's Greatest Newspaper" for the parent Chicago Tribune, I'd have to simply say, "World's Greatest Network" and the even greater personalities who were so close to us.

"I personally don't think there will ever be a team quite like the '69 Cubs," said 'Rosey.' "It's the only time I've been in sports that I ever felt a team was destined to win it all. We felt the same in the booth every day. Whenever Fergie came out to pitch with Randy behind the plate, you felt they were going to win. When the Cubs tailed off in September, it was one of the most disappointing things I ever saw. These guys were part of the family."

The feeling was mutual.

The 1969 Chicago Cubs

A pocket-sized 1969 Cubs schedule. Soon to include televised road game designations

Enjoy these photos and memorabilia of the years surrounding and including The 1969 Chicago Cubs season. These memories have been provided through the generosity of friends, family, and MLB colleagues of Fergie Jenkins.

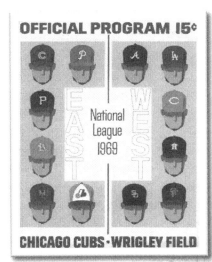

Dr. David J. Fletcher's pristine scorecard from Ken Holtzman's no-hitter on August 19, 1969. Dr. Fletcher, 14 when he went to the game, took three trains to attend the third-ever no-hitter without a strikeout.

From left. Outfielder Don Young from 1969, outfielder / first baseman Willie Smith from 1969, reliever Ted Abernathy and outfielder Al Spangler.

From left: Starting pitcher / Author Fergie Jenkins, outfielder Billy Williams, first baseman Ernie Banks and starting pitcher Dick Selma from his only season with the team.

From left: Reliever Phil Regan; shortstop Don Kessinger; starting pitcher Ken Holtzman; and third baseman Ron Santo.

From left: Catcher Randy Hundley; outfielder Jim Hickman; starting pitcher Bill Hands; and second baseman Glenn Beckert.

A Hamm's Beer/Cubs WGN-
TV Schedule for 1969.

First row of Cubs from left: Shortstop Don Kessinger; roving minor-league pitching coach Fred Martin; and second baseman Glenn Beckert. Second row of Cubs from left: 1969 rookie pitchers Jim Colborn and Joe Decker and starting pitcher Ken Holtzman (all photographed after the 1969 season). Third row of Cubs from left: Rookie catcher Ken Rudolph; utility infielder Paul Popovich; and bullpen coach Verlon (Rube) Walker.

Two shots of second baseman
Glenn Beckert, pre-1969.

Starting pitcher Bill Hands (pre-
1969 road uniform); first
baseman/outfielder Willie Smith;
and manager Leo Durocher.

Vendor Lloyd Rutzky in the 1970s, when
beer was priced as low at 20 cents. He
was still on the job in 2018 after 53 years.

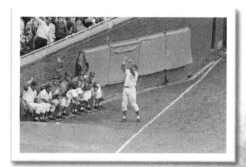 

Left: Starting pitcher Dick Selma leads cheers for the Left
Field Bleacher Bums from the bullpen in 1969. Right: The
voice of play-by-play man Vince Lloyd (center) helmed Cubs
radio broadcasts on WGN-Radio in 1969. Lloyd is flanked here
by third baseman Ron Santo (left) and first baseman Ernie
Banks (right)

From left: Ernie Banks (pre-1969); Don
Kessinger (1972 or later); and rookie
outfielder Oscar Gamble (1969).

From left: Hall-of-Famers Billy Williams, Ernie
Banks and Fergie Jenkins at a Wrigley Field
ceremony, decades after their playing days.

In Appreciation Of
"Dag" Ron Santo

By August 1969, Ron Santo had already contributed enough on his resume to eventually be a serious candidate for the Hall of Fame: 5 Gold Gloves for fielding excellence at third along with a string of 30-homer, 100-RBI caliber seasons as the best offensive third baseman of his era.

Santo, nicknamed by teammates as "Dag," short for "Dago," the epithet-like description of an individual of Italian descent in those politically incorrect days, led the National League in RBI going into the stretch after ranking one-two with Ernie Banks for much of the first four months. He was the cleanup hitter on the NL's winningest team. There was little more he could humanly do as a big-league player.

Emphasize "humanly." Santo was a human with all the accompanying faults, not an automaton. As things warmed up, both in climate and pennant-race pressure, many fans and some media expected Santo to be physically and emotionally more than he could be.

When he drove in 123 runs in '69, many around baseball looked at some failed RBI chances and figured he should have driven in 150. If they expected him to stay out of double plays, then they should have given Santo, one of our slowest baserunners, an elixir for speed that has yet to be invented. If they expected the heart-on-his-sleeve wearer to react with equanimity after Don Young failed to snare two ninth-inning fly balls in my July 8 loss, then they should have cast the first stones as if they would not have also popped off in the sorrow of a shocking loss.

Even the manager who he heartily endorsed through 1970 took shots at Santo. Leo Durocher wrote in his biography that stereotype: "Santo was not a clutch player." How could you not be clutch if you drive in 97 or more runs almost every season and play at least 160 games? Baseball is a cruel game in one way with its built-in failures, such as the very best hitters making outs 2 of every 3 times at bat. Another is how it hangs stereotypes that are tough to shake for the top stars.

"Right from the first, other baseball men whom I respected began to tell me that I was never going to win a pennant with him," Durocher penned about Santo. 'Sooner or later,' they would say, 'Santo is going to come up with the game on the bases and 9 times out of 10 he's going to kill you.' Five runs ahead and he'd knock in all the runs I could ask for. One run behind and he was going to kill me."

That attitude was picked up by opposition players and even several Cubs. But if Santo had so many flaws, why was he the franchise's starting third baseman for 13 ½ years, outlasting Durocher? On the index cards on which General Manager John Holland's assistant and team Traveling Secretary Blake Cullen kept, it said the

Santo makes a catch...in a clutch!

Cubs' brass evaluated us versus other comparable players in the league, and Santo still was rated the best third baseman. He only departed after a Phil Wrigley-mandated housecleaning after the 1973 season.

And the images of Santo were formed without all the available facts for the public. At that point, Santo had not revealed his Type 1 diabetes, then called "juvenile diabetes." He suspected, but couldn't quantify, the specific effect of fluctuating blood sugar on his baseball production. He could not specifically measure his condition during games as do modern-day athletes. But with what we know now about Type 1 diabetes, for Santo to amass his impressive numbers while afflicted with his disease getting less-than-required treatment and amid the tough playing conditions of the time was still 150 percent worthy of Hall-of-Fame induction that unfortunately came posthumously in 2011.

In his own words, the man who totally rehabbed his image and then some as Cubs radio color analyst from 1990 to 2010 described his daily challenges of injecting himself with insulin, but only using educated guesswork to determine if diabetic symptoms were coming on fast during games.

"If I was in a hot streak I would be on base all the time, and then I'd take less insulin the next day," he told Michael Glab of the Chicago Reader on September 22, 2000. "You don't know how tough it was. It took me four years to adjust to the two-hour time difference in California, one hour in the east. Day ball was perfect for me. I could regulate things--get up in the morning, have my insulin at eight o'clock, eat a big breakfast, come to the ballpark, work out, have a candy bar or a Coke before the game, and then after the game get a Coke in me."

I'll keep saying it as long as I can, but I can never forget the middle-innings sight of clubhouse boss Yosh Kawano bringing a candy bar and Coke from the clubhouse as Santo's insurance policy in case diabetic reactions came on quickly. We didn't quite understand it at first, but later, when Santo revealed his disease, we could put it in perspective.

"He was the greatest third baseman I saw play the game. He had 100 assists more than (Baltimore all-time great Gold Glover) Brooks (Robinson) three years in a row," said our lefty teammate, Rich Nye.

"How could he not get into the Hall of Fame (in reasonable time)?"

Who knew when a slow bat on a particular day might have been attributed to a blood-sugar drop or other symptoms? Or a drop-off in road numbers could have been affected by the time-zone changes to his body chemistry?

How about the famed game on September 25, 1968, when severe diabetic symptoms were oncoming faster than Santo could have anticipated in the bottom of the ninth with the Cubs trailing 1-0 and none out? Standing in the on-deck circle as Dodgers starter Bill Singer was intentionally walking Dick Nen to load the bases, Santo refused to beg out of his at-bat, despite blurred vision being one of the most serious symptoms. And so Santo stepped in and saw three baseballs from Singer on one pitch. Eager to get back to the dugout for his emergency treatment of a candy bar, he swung at the middle ball. Amazingly, his strength had not ebbed and he powered a walk-off, grand-slam homer. Santo was desperate to get back to the dugout, as Nen trotted slowly around the bases in celebration, with Santo unable to pass him legally on the bases, even to quickly get his sugar fix.

Santo was described in the Chicago Tribune game story by George Langford as a "brooding facsimile" of his status as a Cubs hero due to a subpar '68, in which the third baseman studied film of his hitting and scheduled a post-season eye exam. Afflicted physically and always mindful of slumps, Santo still had the ability to come up with dramatics. And if he could do this with severe symptoms coming on and be in danger of passing out, what could he have accomplished without diabetes?

When Santo finished his 1993 autobiography, *For Love of Ivy*, he talked about something he never dwelled on while he wore a baseball uniform. "I never thought about diabetes affecting my career," he analyzed. "I am so surprised that I put up the numbers I have. I wonder what kind of numbers I would have put up without diabetes. There were plenty of times I couldn't tell my sugar was low, so all of my faculties were not working 100 percent. You're a little slower thinking, you have a little slower reactions. I might have played longer, too."

And Santo shared this wonderment with his family.

"Lots of times," said oldest son Ron Santo, Jr. "My mom (Judy Santo) always said there would have been no telling what numbers he'd put up if not for diabetes. He got fatigued or tried to control its symptoms. He had good days and bad days. Coming from different time zones, it was a big deal to get his sugar back to where it was."

Diabetes likely cut the length of Santo's career. In his final four seasons with the Cubs, from age 30 onward, he dropped to a lower level of production from his 30-homer, 100-

RBI standards. Now he was more of a 20-homer, 80-RBI guy. In his final Cubs season in 1973, he batted .300 well into mid-summer. But Santo slumped to .267 and finished with just 77 RBI, despite batting fourth or fifth most of the time.

The sum total of Santo's career was surely amazing, even with diabetes tugging at his reactions far more mildly than it would affect him later in life, when he had both legs amputated and endured bouts with heart disease and cancer. I just knew him as one of baseball's best all-around players when I endured a rather rude introduction to Santo as a Phillies rookie on September 21, 1965, at Wrigley Field, before just 892 fans.

Summoned by manager Gene Mauch in a 5-5 game to pitch the bottom of the eighth, I walked Williams with 1 out, then served up a wind-blown homer to Santo for the game-winner. That was my first loss in the majors, and so the Cubs thus became, ironically, the only National League team I never beat during 10-plus seasons in the league.

As a player, Santo made up for any lack of homers with clutch plays, both at bat and in the field. The only thing he could not do was run. As evidenced by all those double plays he hit into, he was simply slow afoot.

If dealing with diabetes and critics wasn't tough enough, Santo attracted baseballs to parts of his well-muscled torso as our cleanup hitter. One ball thoroughly got away on June 25, 1966, a fastball that struck him on the cheek from the Mets' Jack Fisher. The right-hander immediately hollered to Santo, who was placed on a stretcher, that he was sorry for the errant pitch. Santo missed just a week, the only time between 1962 and 1969 that he failed to log 160 games played, diabetes or not.

The likes of Hall-of-Famer fireballers Bob Gibson and Don Drysdale allegedly threw deliberately at Santo, but he knew it was part of the game. And in 1969, he appeared to become a specific target of the Mets' aces. Tom Seaver hit him in the leg to light a fire under his upstart teammates earlier in the season at Wrigley Field. During the 'Black Cat' series in September at Shea Stadium, hard-throwing lefty Jerry Koosman took his turn, drilling Santo on the arm to demonstrate the Mets were for real and ready to win. And they had good reason to throw at Santo. In 204 career games against New York, he slugged 27 homers, drove in 119 runs and batted .282.

The Mets also seemed particularly ticked off by Santo's home-victory heel-clicking, although according to Santo, he never meant it as a disrespectful gesture toward beaten opponents. As the most publicly emotional of the Cubs who had a pair of 103-defeat seasons under his belt, he simply let loose with long-repressed joy.

No matter what though, Santo was a sight to behold, more times than not winding up with the filthiest Cubs' uniform on a daily basis. He not only was diving every which way at third, but he was also applying dirt on his hands, up into his arms, for a better grip on the bat. Combined with his excitable personality, Santo was an easy target for team humorists and how the excitable Santo became the straight man for WGN-Radio booth partner Pat Hughes' wry humor. Getting Santo to react to a challenge, such as to list all the animals he could think of with three-letter names was priceless during a blowout loss. Even funnier was getting his goat (not the famed Billy Goat) on the team bus or in the clubhouse.

Added Nye: "He was this hot-blooded Italian personality. He'd get hot over little things, like why doesn't this bus have air conditioning? As an announcer, he totally mellowed. He didn't mellow while a player."

The ultimate way to aggravate Santo was simply to lose. "My dad was never happy about losing – he was always that way," Ron Santo, Jr. said. He took losses harder than any other Cub. Second son Jeff Santo recalled how he'd want to catch another ride home, rather than ride with his dad after losses. "He'd be a bear to drive back with," said Ron, Jr. "It was quiet in that car."

And he never changed through the decades. On September 23, 1998, Brant Brown dropped a fly ball in the Milwaukee County Stadium sun field in left that would have been the final out in a Cubs win. The misplay shockingly allowed 3 runs to score in what would become an 8-7 loss to the Brewers amid the last week of the wildcard race. The error hit Santo hard in the radio booth. "He looked like he was shot," recalled Hughes. Santo had to be consoled almost even more than Brown after what Jack Brickhouse would have called a "disastrous turn of events," and Santo's famed "noooooooo" call in the background of Hughes' call became an instant Chicago radio classic.

Santo could never stray from his attachment to the 1969 Cubs, no matter how many around baseball thought that season was a sensitive subject for him.

"Everybody asks me, what did the '69 Cubs have that everybody remembers us?" Santo said, "I tell them, 'We related to the fans. We signed autographs. We talked to them.' In those days you needed fans. Players today with all their money, it's different."

He still easily bridged both eras though. And despite all the doubters and critics, his plaque is right where it should have been since the 1980s – near mine in Cooperstown.

Dirt from the fans...

1969 was my third season vendin in Wrigley Field. I worked all over the lower and upper grandstand and began keeping a diary so I had a record of what I did as a vendor in 1969. For the Billy Williams Day doubleheader on June 29, I made $87.90, which was pretty darn good. Remember, many breadwinners were happy to earn $200 a week for their office or factory jobs then. I worked 73 dates at Wrigley Field in '69. That included six doubleheaders. Attendance was so good that sometimes they had to open the gates as early as 9:00 A.M. due to the mobs around the ballpark. By 10:30, the unreserved grandstand was full while the reserved box seats were still empty. So you could start selling your Frosty Malts three hours before the game. You could sell out of product by early in the game. Sometimes they'd reorder and the Borden's truck would show up during the game. The vendors would load up their cases straight from the truck.

-Lloyd Rutzky, Bartlett, Illinois

Chapter 15

The Ups And Downs
Of A 21-Win Season

If you could totally dominate every top opposing hitter, you'd go undefeated. And that does not happen in baseball, the ultimate game of failure, where the batting champion fails two of every three at-bats and the winningest teams still lose around 60 games a season.

I finally pushed my victory total one better off the 20 mark in 1969, but could I have done more? Certainly. Was I yet a finished product at 26, ready to write in my first book that I was "like nobody else?" Not quite yet.

If I only knew in 1969 what I did two seasons later, when I won the Cy Young Award with control and endurance feats that I don't feel will be matched anytime soon. Or in 1974, when I won a career-high 25 games pitching for the Texas Rangers in an entirely new league.

Teammates and fans had huge expectations of me in 1969, and rightly so. "He can do exactly want he wants to do," said Ron Santo after my headline-making outing on June 25, although not for all the right reasons. "All he's got to do is want to do it because he's great. He's Fergie Jenkins."

I had been the first Cubs pitcher since Lon Warneke in 1934-35 to win 20 games in two consecutive seasons. I was coming off a 20-win season with a career-low 2.63 ERA that showed I could have done even better if not for five 1-0 losses. After striking out 260 (7.6 per nine innings) in 1968, I had grand dreams of taking the next step to fan 300, edging into Sandy Koufax or Sudden Sam McDowell territory.

I did not possess Koufax's or McDowell's near-100 mph fastball, but did not need to. Through 1969, I was still learning the art of pitching, with razor-sharp control when all my stuff was working. Koufax said his best pitch was "strike one," and I heartily agreed. Speed was hardly everything. By '69, I had honed a hard-breaking slider as a strikeout pitch. And when mind and body were coordinated, I was tough to beat.

On August 16, 1969, I pitched what turned out to be my single-season, career-high seventh shutout to lock down my 17th victory. And I learned to make quick work of opponents, better to keep my fielders on their toes and enable them to get a full night off in San Francisco. Despite issuing an uncommonly high 6 walks, I still recorded a 2-hour, 21-minute game, about 15 minutes more than I preferred.

A month later, I had endured one of the roughest patches of my career, at just the wrong time, but that's the nature of the game; you're never totally a finished product. If I had stopped learning, picking up a little thing or two any time before my final game on September 26, 1983, at Wrigley Field, I'd have been doing myself, my family and my teammates a disservice.

So I look at the package I offered the baseball public in 1969 as a work-in-progress, even as the Cubs' certified ace. Since we've mentioned Koufax, in his fourth full season in the majors in 1959, Koufax, as many called him, astounded the world with an 18-strikeout game and a brilliantly-pitched 1-0 loss to the White Sox in the World Series. But he was still viewed as wild and inconsistent and a year later threw his equipment in the trash in frustration at season's end.

Like Koufax would, I had overcome the first big barrier and it was in my rear-view mirror by '69, that being Manager Leo Durocher's confidence. He had a hunch in 1966 I'd be a successful starter and acted accordingly. I never missed a scheduled start under The Lip. If anything, under the gun, Durocher tried to get too much of a good thing.

If anything, under the gun, Durocher tried to get too much of a good thing.

Pitching in a rotation in the 1960s was radically different than today. Rotations usually were four deep with starters going on three days' rest. The Cardinals' Bob Gibson was the only prominent starter with four days' off between outings. Gibson made 34 starts, a 21st-century workload, in his 1.12 ERA season in 1968. Who was to argue with that kind of success? The additional rest obviously helped, as Gibson completed 28 of those starts in '68. A fifth starter usually was deployed for the second game of a doubleheader or when the schedule otherwise became jammed up with as many as three weeks without an off day on the schedule.

Lineups were somewhat thinner than today's offensive-oriented game. A starter could ease up on the gas for two or three hitters in a lineup besides the pitcher. Few catchers were huge offensive threats like the up-and-coming Johnny Bench. Middle infielders were usually slap hitters or the proverbial "good-field, no-hit" types. And some center fielders were not offensively robust.

Subsequently, no starter could afford to "5 and dive" with only 9- and 10-man pitching staffs. A starter who did not display late-inning endurance often found himself an ex-starter or traded. The macho creed of pitchers endured, including pitching through tiredness and soreness that, in my opinion, would toss a present-day starter onto the disabled list. We worked on one-year contracts and we were only a few years' removed from an era when farm systems had Class B, C and D teams. Job security always was in the back of one's mind.

Our arms were trained from the start to go on three days' rest. Our workouts were oriented as such. On our "throw" day between starts, we'd pitch live batting practice instead of simply working in the bullpen. Throwing to your own hitters was a good way to sharpen your control and work on the touch and feel of breaking pitches, as your hitters requested them.

Warming up for a start, I'd throw up to 100 pitches in the bullpen. I'd throw five minutes each of of fastballs, curves, sliders and changeups. The last 20 pitches would be at full bore, as if I was already working the first inning. Santo and Billy Williams often stepped into the would-be batter's box to provide a more accurate gauge of how my pitches were coming in. My windup had been fine-tuned in the second half of my rookie season in 1966 by then-pitching coach Robin Roberts, with Becker providing reminders constantly in subsequent years.

I used the fastball motion with the same arm release in throwing the slider, my "out" pitch. Geared for the fastball, the hitter had to commit and the ball would dart under or away from his bat if the slider worked properly. I was the guy everyone said had the control great enough to be able to throw to all parts of the strike zone – and a pitcher against whom a hitter could not afford to take pitches.

Radar guns were not perfected yet, so it's only an educated guess of the speed of my best fastball. I'd say the low 90s was my "heater – although not in Gibson, Tom Seaver or Nolan Ryan giddy-up fastball territory. Bill Singer of the Dodgers also threw hard, with teammate Don Drysdale adding the illusion of more speed to his fastball with that deceptive sidearm motion. But I did not blow guys away with three straight crackling fastballs. The style I developed was to work the strike zone up and down, in and out and not miss because I couldn't throw in the high 90s.

But a control pitcher like me could sway umpires simply by being around the plate. If you were consistently on the corners, you could almost subconsciously get the umps to slightly expand the strike zone to help you. Your reputation of possessing control would help you, and I found that out in my first 20-win season in 1967. I remember really good ball-and-strike umps like Augie Donatelli, Billy Williams, Doug Harvey, Lee Weyer and Chris Pelekoudas. When you had a duel of me versus Gibson, both masters of control and fast workers, the umpires certainly weren't going to get picky in calling strikes, in my opinion. They're human, after all.

By 1969 though, I had developed an interesting pattern where sometimes I was shaky in the first inning, giving up a couple of runs or even a bit more. Perhaps I needed to warm up even more, or it simply took more repetition for the slider to locate better. Whatever the reason, I was able to settle down, prevent further damage and allow our lineup to catch up. The ability to survive rough starts and then lock down to last 9 innings was a key to winning 20 games six years in a row.

Of course, a 1960s pitcher was hardly as fast or as crisp in the eighth or ninth innings as he was in the first. To complete games, one had to adjust the repertoire, so I'd throw more off-speed sliders with the fastball as a 'show-me' pitch.

And to finish 9 innings, your legs had to be in shape and Becker made sure of that attribute. He was hardly a technocrat as a pitching coach, but his top characteristic was making we pitchers run…and run…and run.

The workouts paid off though in performance and endurance, at least for much of the season. I spun two shutouts in April, 1-0 over the Cardinals and 10-0 against the Phillies, my original team, against whom I was particularly determined. Two more blankings were recorded in May against the Padres and Dodgers, respectively, the latter taking advantage of Dodger Stadium's 'pitcher friendly' dimensions at night. I nailed the Phillies again, 1-0, in the first game of a doubleheader before the All-Star break, then pitched back-to-back shutouts against the Padres and Giants on our mid-August final West Coast swing. In every duel against Gibson, you felt you needed shutout stuff, yet I gladly took the 1-run Gibson yielded in consecutive winning starts against the defending MVP on June 29 at Wrigley Field and July 4 in old Busch Stadium.

But my old bugaboo from 1968, the 1-0 defeat, visited me again on June 17, 1969, in Pittsburgh's Forbes Field at the hands of giant Pirates lefty Bob Veale and reliever Bruce Dal Canton. The first game of that twi-night doubleheader was an exercise in stranded baserunners for both teams.

And the Pirates fast became my National League nemesis. I'd finish in 1983 with a 14-23 lifetime record and 3.30 ERA with 43 starts against the Buccos, who justifiably earned the nickname "Lumber Company" in the years after 1969. They weren't just free swingers and bad-ball hitters who could golf a pitch off the ground into the outfield. The Pirates carefully took the measure of someone like me and adjusted accordingly. Outfielder-first baseman Al Oliver, one of the true gentlemen on that club, along with Willie Stargell, provided their scouting report on me.

"One thing about a guy like Fergie is those guys are around the plate," said Oliver, who eventually became a teammate on the Texas Rangers. "They throw strikes. If you can't hit a strike, you shouldn't be in the game.

"Fergie did like to throw the slider down and in on left-handed hitters. To his credit, he was able to get it in the right spot on most. The slider looked good to hit until you went after it. I felt he would rather make a mistake away. It didn't matter who pitched against us, any of the Hall-of-Famers at the time. We wanted our hits so bad.

"I know I beat him with a ninth-inning single when he had a 14-strikeout game (the second-to-last day Forbes Field was open in 1970). With a quick bat, I could wait until the last second and try to take it up the middle or to the opposite field. But if Fergie struck out 14 of us in one game, he was pitching."

So Oliver's productive lineup brothers provided ongoing lessons in crisis management on the mound for me. But in 1969, they were the backdrop in developing a more even-keel attitude when things did not go well for me. Sometimes you learn by making mistakes or by going through failure, and those experiences came in handy in future seasons, most notably my Cy Young Award Cubs season in 1971.

So what would cause an uproar by Durocher and some of my teammates in the middle of the first 2-hitter of my career against the Pirates at Wrigley Field on June 25, 1969?

Well, a temporary loss of concentration, a mental hiccup. I had another thread on my mind going into that Wednesday afternoon start because I had not thrown a baseball since the previous Saturday due to occasional pain on the inside of my elbow.

Three weeks later though against the Pirates, I led 3-1 in the top of the sixth, with only one pitch on which I felt any pain. I struck out the first two Buccos, but then Matty Alou, one of the game's top pests with his chopping swing, bounded a double over Santo's head into left field. Free-swinging Richie Hebner, who had accounted for the Pirates' only run earlier with a homer, then grounded to Ernie Banks at first. As I ran to cover the bag, I dropped Banks' throw for an error, and so what should've been the easiest of third outs surely ticked me off. I then did something very uncharacteristic for me: I walked Roberto Clemente on 4 pitches, a Hall-of-Fame opponent who often swung at bad balls. The final pitch popped out of Hundley's glove, rolling to the screen for a wild pitch as Alou scored.

The sequence attracted the attention of our entire 'Million Dollar Infield' and Durocher, all of whom converged on me at the mound. Durocher let loose with a few of his profane specialties, later explaining, "You couldn't print what I told him, except that I said he had gotten lazy." My usual in-game discourse with Durocher was the manager sidling up to me on the bench in the late innings while we batted. "You all right, big fella?" he'd ask, probing for any doubt that I could complete the game. I usually responded all was fine. But on this day, something was off.

Except Durocher was not the type to provide a shoulder to cry on. I wasn't the first pitcher to get a Durocher tongue-lashing on the mound and by far would not be the last. Durocher did the same thing to Bill Hands and Ken Holtzman. He'd pick a time to just let you know who's in charge. You couldn't afford to think that just because you were winning ballgames that you were in charge.

Durocher was not the type to provide a shoulder to cry on.

Other words were exchanged in mound scrums. though apparently some lit a fire. Stargell may have menaced many pitchers just by walking up to the plate, his twirling bat seemingly a toothpick in his arms. But I was always more confident against 'Pops' than against Clemente. I struck him out to end the rally and retired the last 9 in a row to finish out the 5-2 victory. But remember the time frame. Nothing in baseball is automatic, and you are always in the process of learning how to pitch out of tough situations, especially ones you helped create.

Santo claimed he told me on the bench after that inning: "You struck out 3 (in the sixth) because you wanted to." I told writers at the same time I accepted responsibility for dropping the ball at first, Banks' throw hitting me squarely in the glove's pocket.

"Maybe you have to get him mad sometimes to really get him going," theorized Durocher.

The Chicago Tribune's secondary headline on the game said it all: "Teammates Praise Fergie, But Scold Him For Letdown." Winning solves all problems. But the memory of the incident faded and eventually I would experience a "conversation" with the manager that would classify his June 25 communication as "Leo Lite."

Fast-forward to the afternoon of Saturday, September 6, at Wrigley Field. The Pirates had thrashed Holtzman in a 9-2 victory the previous day. The Mets were starting to really breathe down our necks. The Pirates had lost the previous 6 games at Wrigley Field that season while verbally roasting us while we lost at Forbes Field, so they did not lack for motivation to kick our butts. In the second inning, somehow Jim Hickman and Don Young got mixed up on a pop fly to center by Gene Alley. Had the ball been handled cleanly, that would have been the third out. Instead, the ball fell safely with 2 runs scoring amid a 3-run Pirates rally. The next day, the Chicago Tribune ran a photo of the misdirected outfielders with an arrow superimposed on the ball, showing where it landed.

I allowed doubles to Oliver and Manny Sanguillen and a single to Carl Taylor, good for two more runs thereafter, before Durocher pulled me. The Pirates went on to thump us again 13-4, giving the pursuing Mets even more inspiration.

I was obviously perturbed by the outfield goof-up and it carried over into the next inning. I did not stick around for the post-mortem with teammates and writers after the game – a very uncharacteristic action for me. If I was upset, figure Durocher's emotions were doubled. The measure of maturity is sticking around to face the music.

Durocher made sure I quickly understood his displeasure about my fast exit before the September 7 game. Described in one account as a "heart-to-heart talk," you can rest assured it was one-sided, with Durocher doing the talking (or yelling) and me doing all the listening. If anything came from the heart, it was from the manager's. And Durocher, never keeping a player's foibles within his office, aired it out in front of the entire team.

If you were in Durocher's core group in the lineup, in the rotation or at end of the bullpen, such assertive communication did not cost you on the field. The manager had you right back in there. In my case though, I believe Durocher wanted a bit too much of me in '69. For the second year in a row, I led the NL in starts with 42, two more than in 1968. I also added a 1-out save in a 9-8 victory in Cincinnati on June 14 – the day after I went 5 innings in a no-decision during a 10-inning 14-8 triumph.

On July 25 against the Dodgers, Willie Crawford hit a line drive to the mound that I tried to stop with my pitching hand. The liner bruised my thumb, but I was removed to make sure nothing was fractured. But in 1969, Durocher figured I had relatively few pitches under my belt and he pondered bringing me back for the July 27 start, also against the Dodgers.

But The Lip sneaked off unannounced to his stepson's Parents Day at Camp Ojibwa on July 26, leaving third-base coach Pete Reiser in charge of the team. Reiser dutifully followed his boss' recommendation and put me back on the mound for the final game of the 4-game Dodgers series. I could hardly argue, given Hands was sidelined with a throat infection.

But the short-rest routine did not work. I gave up 10 hits and 5 runs with 3 walks in 4 1/3 innings in a 6-2 loss, as Don Drysdale recorded his 209th and final big-league victory.

But the two losses in the same series must have been in the back of my mind a month later when I declined to take the ball on short rest as the season's dog days were at their peak.

I threw 72 pitches in a 3 2/3-inning stint in which I yielded 6 runs on 8 hits amid a game where the Cubs came back to win 10-9 against the Astros at Wrigley Field on August 24, 1969. I told Durocher and pitching coach Joe Becker I simply needed my usual three days' rest with some 250 innings already under my belt. Ignoring the pitch count, Durocher and Becker looked at the less-than-four-inning outing and figured I could go again on August 26 against the Reds at home.

I took my normal turn in the final game of the four-game Reds series on August 28 after the visitors had belted around our staff for 33 hits in the first 3 games, and the working-in-turn clicked. I restored order with a 5-hit, 8-strikeout, no-walk 3-1 victory. However, Becker did not necessarily agree the normal rest helped. "It's just a state of mind," he said afterward.

Two weeks later, I couldn't turn down Durocher, claiming I again needed normal rest. His stern lecture following the September 6 debacle against the Pirates was still ringing in my ears. Durocher also held his most explosive team meeting to date before the September 7 game, in which several players thought the manager called me a quitter.

Once matters cooled down though, I was able to gather my thoughts to writers:

"I definitely did not quit (September 6)," I said with what was described as "calm conviction" in published accounts. "I admit that I did lose some concentration. But I never quit on this club…(Durocher's) got a right to handle the situation his own way. I know what my job is, and I'm not going to say anything. I want my five more starts."

More important things were on the agenda anyway, instead of ruminating over Durocher's tongue-lashing. The big two-game series in Shea Stadium loomed and Hands was locked in to face Jerry Koosman for the Monday, September 8 opener. Holtzman was at first scheduled for ace Tom Seaver in the second game, on Tuesday, September 9. However, Durocher calculated that Holtzman would have to miss his Saturday, September 12 start in St. Louis due to Rosh Hashanah, the Jewish New Year. If he pitched Holtzman on Wednesday, September 10, in Philadelphia, he'd be able to also work the final of the 3-game series in St. Louis on Sunday, September 13. That left a hole in the rotation against Seaver and who was I to turn down that dramatic job?

Well, I took the ball. The black cat appeared and so did the Mets' bats. Observers thought I had decent stuff, but I gave up all 7 runs, 5 earned, in 7 innings in the 7-1 loss that dropped our first-place lead to a half-game. I also failed for the second straight start to notch my 20th victory.

Looking back from the hindsight of many decades, I likely fell victim to overwork. Those two extra starts compared to 1968 probably took their toll. My ERA inflated from 2.72 after my seventh shutout on August 16 to 3.24 going into my final start, the 2-0 loss to Dock Ellis in Pittsburgh on September 26. Five days earlier, I captured my 21st victory in a complete-game, 4-3 victory over the Cardinals at Wrigley Field. I had dominated St. Louis all season, but several prominent Cardinals stated I did not show them my best stuff in this game.

I could have requested one more start in the season's final series against the Mets at Wrigley Field, October 1-2, but enough was enough. I finished 21-15 with a 3.21 ERA and an NL-leading 273 strikeouts. My stated mid-August goal of 300 strikeouts fell short to a weaker flesh despite a willing spirit.

The lessons of '69 were learned. I was better able to control my emotions and simply push on from setbacks the next year. In 1970, I began 4-7. People wrote off my 20-win goal too quickly. But I then pitched up to my standard and won 9 of my final 12 decisions to finish 22-16, setting the Cubs season strikeout record of 274 in the process.

"I didn't pitch well at the finish (in 1969)," I said in reflection nearly a year later. "This time I'm not overthinking – but I remember what happened. I feel different this time."

Just like completing 9 innings, finishing out seasons required a change in pitch selection. I'd become more of a breaking-ball pitcher and used more sinkers, but my best average strikeout per game usually were not in September. You did what you needed to do to make all your starts, even if the arm begged for the off-season.

My strong finish in 1970, incorporating the approaches of maturity, kicked in further for 1971, when I put everything together for my 24-13, 2.77-ERA, Cy Young Award season, throwing 30 complete games in 39 starts. I won my final three decisions in '71.

Even in 1972, when shoulder soreness began barking at me in August, I was able to work around the malady enough to shut out the Mets for my 19th win on September 4, and then finally record my sixth consecutive 20-win season against the Phillies. I tried to gut my way through two more losing starts, but management then shut me down for the season, costing me a pair of additional starts.

The moral of the story is simple; no one is perfect, particularly an athlete who has to be finely tuned at the highest competitive level. Listen to your body and stand up for yourself, but also be ready to make sacrifices in tough situations. I needed the ups and downs of 1969 to get to more than 3,000 career strikeouts and fewer than 1,000 walks, 284 victories and the Hall of Fame.

Phil Wrigley, Bleacher Bum?

Some of us Cubs actually claimed to have met team owner Philip K. Wrigley by 1969. The chewing gum magnate who had run the Chicago National League Ballclub since 1932 wasn't just a disembodied quote in reporters' stories. A few of us met Wrigley at January rumor-driven, hot stove-league press luncheons. Several others were admitted to his Wrigley Building inner sanctum discussing business ideas.

Overall though, Wrigley was notorious for supposedly never visiting the ballpark he personally owned in totality. The Cubs' team was formally owned by stockholders, of which Wrigley was majority holder. Yet the 55-year-old ballpark in '69 was totally a family possession, passed down from William Wrigley Jr. and eventually sold in a separate transaction when the Cubs were acquired by Tribune Company in 1981.

Wrigley was described as a shy man with few personal friends. But he did not shy away from newspaper or magazine interviews. He was easily accessible by phone at his office or Lake Geneva, Wisconsin, estate. During one managerial change, he instructed an assistant to carefully record all callers so their messages could be returned in a timely manner. Wrigley's accessibility as a captain of industry, running the most prominent gum company, bought him easier treatment from the media than his long track record of Cubs failure might have warranted. When he told a group of reporters in 1934 that he knew little about baseball, the scribes asked him to stifle that sentiment again in public. They liked him and would thus protect his blissful ignorance.

At Wrigley Field, he simply did not want put upon his staff and players by publicly appearing as P.K. Wrigley. A mob scene would have quickly commenced around the big boss and that's the last thing he could have handled.

And yet there's strong evidence that despite Wrigley's repeated denials, he likely watched us in person, incognito, any number of times, including from the bleachers. At age 74 in 1969, Wrigley easily could have passed as one of the many senior citizens who attended our matinees. All he needed was sunglasses and a hat with the brim pulled down. The Cubs held a Senior Citizens Day on each home stand and a regular group of senior gamblers gathered in the right-center field bleachers, directly in the line of sight of the pitcher and catcher. As I wound up and threw to Randy Hundley, those bettors 350 feet behind me laid money on whether it would be a fastball, a curve or a slider, a strike or a ball, and who knows what other categories of baseball could attract the cash.

Our fast start and mid-season dominance in first place must have attracted Wrigley for his own personal viewpoint, as rumors circulated Wrigley had visited his ballpark. Noted newspaper jokester David Condon of the Chicago Tribune, who would soon spread the myth of the Billy Goat Curse, used his July 16, 1969, "In the Wake of the News" column to search Wrigley Field and its environs to ask a cross-section of people if one of them was Wrigley in disguise.

"Some claim his disguises were so effective that Andy Frain ushers have vacated him from a seat for which he was unable to produce a ticket," Condon wrote.

The corpulent columnist and his trusty cigar first stopped at the convent parking lot on Grace Street, now a main Wrigley Field lot with redevelopment pushing parking further away from the ballpark, but Sister Mary was not Wrigley. He also asked 43-year-ballpark hot dog vendor George Levin and beer vendor Ira Levin, who had just hustled 20 cases of beer to make $30, if either of them was Wrigley. Also quizzed whether they were Wrigley were Bob Weber, who vended novelties by the Waveland Avenue firehouse; the Rev. Steven Kose, from downstate Gilman, Illinois, and Davenport, Iowa's Delma Peterson, who said she and her posse recently traveled to St. Louis to cheer me on, pitching against Bob Gibson. Condon's list of suspects also included: Rosie Laverde, a waitress at The Cottage, which had drawn a lot of our post-game business; Clarendon Hills second-grade teacher Norma Ferguson; and Burns Security Sgt. Roscoe Smiley.

Even celebrities were earmarked for inspection. A sunglasses-wearing man entering the ballpark was famed Chicago Sun-Times gossip columnist Irv Kupcinet. Condon finally ended up in the visitors' clubhouse, where he proclaimed that the towel-garbed Yogi Berra, just out of the post-game shower, was not Wrigley.

Condon played a lot of things for laughs, including barnyard animals affecting our fates. But three decades later, the columnist just might have been on to something. Wrigley's protestations and other reports he avoided the ballpark may have been a clever misdirection play.

In fact, one of my 1972-73 Cubs teammates Pete LaCock, a true free spirit, told my co-author that while walking down Michigan Avenue one day, LaCock, on an impromptu basis, entered the Wrigley Building and, cold, asked to see the Big Boss. Informed one of his players was at the door, Wrigley said, sure, come on in. In the conversation between respective senior citizen and baseball hippie, LaCock says he was told by Wrigley that he watched games from the bleachers. In his clandestine rounds, perhaps Wrigley kept enough of a distance from the likes of Bleacher Bums Mike Haley and Mike Murphy, who surely would have sniffed out the disguised Lord of the Game.

In the same flurry of research, Castle was told by Salty Saltwell, the longtime director of Wrigley Field park operations (including in 1969), that Wrigley asked him questions about ballpark goings-on that could only be gleaned from the owner's personal observation. Saltwell also revealed that Gus Settergren, Wrigley's chauffeur and close friend, dropped off the owner two blocks from the ballpark – better so he could mix in with the incoming crowds.

More recently, Bill Hands claimed he once spotted Wrigley sitting in the grandstands. That synched with a report of a Wrigley relative who claimed P.K. took him to the ballpark to sit in the back of the grandstands, far from the family's box seats.

Mostly forgotten in 1969 was Wrigley's own admission 11 years prior in a *Sports Illustrated* profile: "Generally, I sit up in the grandstand where the real fans are. I don't like any special treatment."

P.K.-as-Wrigley Field-attendee thus makes perfect sense when his appropriation of more than $8,000 of Cubs funds to send 65 Bleacher Bums to Atlanta for a 3-game series on August 29-31, 1969, is considered, because he watched the Bums, perhaps up close-and-personal. But repeated incursions onto the field, culminated by riotous on-field demonstrations on September 2, 1969, and at the 1970 home opener, eventually soured management on a too-close relationship with fans.

But Wrigley's stewardship of the Cubs in 1969 was a double-edged sword. His ticket and broadcast policies enabled us to start the summertime attraction that continued through the decades and, with necessary enhancements, basically doubled in attendance to the present day.

Keeping 22,000 seats on sale for day-of-game only – and announced frequently by the WGN broadcasters – enabled any kid to wake up and decide on the spur of the moment to go to Wrigley Field instead of buying tickets months in advance. Ticket prices were low and when they increased, did so only incrementally – 25 cents at a time. Most fans could afford $1 for bleachers or $1.75 for seats in the shade in the grandstands. Splurging for $3.50 box seats was a special occasion.

Keeping an all-daytime schedule promoted attendance by teenagers not needing an older companion to escort them to games and all-female family delegations not having to worry about taking public transportation at night. Wrigley also continued his "Ladies Days," started in the 1920s by William Wrigley Jr., his father, which on Fridays filled the ballpark to overflowing in the summer. No wonder we always had a high percentage of multi-generational female rooters.

Meanwhile, fans across the Midwest whose interests were whetted by the new WGN-originated TV network, could make a day trip on the interstate highways to Wrigley Field without worrying about coming back home well into the wee hours. Wrigley had allowed all home games to be televised since the dawn of the medium in 1947. When the White Sox split off from their shared agreement on WGN-TV in 1968 to go to a UHF station, Wrigley responded by giving the go-ahead to dramatically increase the universe of televised Cubs contests by adding the majority of road games to the TV schedule. And the timing was perfect, what with our emergence as a contender.

As an experienced gum peddler, Wrigley had long aced his Marketing 101 course. People of a certain age not only recall our 1969 dramas, but also the assorted Wrigley commercial jingles for Juicy Fruit™ and Doublemint™.

Yet a baseball-savvy owner realizes that to win, you had to be better in scouting and player development -- except he tried his unconventional College of Coaches and an athletic director. But the sour on-field results showed Wrigley had not gotten out of Baseball 101. And, for a captain of industry, he was surprisingly willing to leave tremendous revenue on the table by not installing lights to boost the crowd count and TV ratings when a full house was not possible for weekday games. In turn, the lack of home night games likely had a negative effect on Cubs teams' effectiveness in the second half of seasons over decades to come after 1969, with the daytime only schedule being blamed by media and fans for what they termed the team's inconsistency and lethargy.

"I'm living for the day when the Cubs have enough money to put in lights (to finish late-afternoon games and for November-December Bears games)," he said in 1968. "I hope we make the money for many improvements."

I'm living for the day when the Cubs have enough money to put in lights.

But the modest man's first choice was to be a more detached owner. Phil Wrigley's preference was tinkering with devices – he said he'd have wanted to be a garage mechanic. Great with his hands, he was put in charge of the Wrigley Gum Co. and ranged worldwide to look over the chicle assembly lines.

But when his father died suddenly in 1932 and talented, innovative Cubs president William L. Veeck Sr. died at age 56 nearly two years later, a reluctant Wrigley had to install himself as a hands-on Cubs president. He was upset at his inability to find "another Bill Veeck." Indeed, the elder Veeck's passing due to fast-spreading leukemia could be classified the most catastrophic event in the Cubs' 20th-century timeline. He was thus unable to train his future-maverick son, Bill Jr., to take over as president, a move Wrigley likely would have signed off on.

Phil Wrigley maintained his father's beloved ballpark, which had been expanded to its present capacity via the addition of an upper deck in the late 1920s. He added the famed ivy-encrusted bleachers and landmark manual scoreboard in 1937. He rebuilt the upper deck in 1967-68 and ordered lower grandstand seating down the lines to be turned toward home plate. Overall, the Cubs spent enough each off-season to keep patching Wrigley, so it did not suffer the fate of crumbling old Comiskey Park on the South Side in the 1980s. The ballpark held up enough to endure its major reconstruction under the Ricketts family ownership in the mid-2010s.

Wrigley also continued his father's wide-open broadcast coverage, which featured under-market rights fees. The Cubs subsequently collected hundreds of thousands of dollars less in annual broadcast rights than the crosstown White Sox.

One tactic in an attempt to duplicate his forebear's success failed though, as the elder Wrigley hired the elder Veeck, a baseball writer for the Chicago American, to run his ballclub. By 1929, the Cubs possessed a Murderer's Row lineup, drawing all-time major-league record attendance. More than a decade later, Phil Wrigley tapped another writer, Chicago American scribe James T. Gallagher, to serve as general manager. But there would be no Second Act. Gallagher presided over a wartime pennant in 1945, aided by Stan Musial's single-season absence from the Cardinals for Navy service, along with a steady decline over impact players coming up from what passed as the Cubs' farm system. For every star like Andy Pafko coming up, there were far more pedestrian Wayne Terwilligers and Roy Smalley Sr.'s having to fill roster spots.

Gallagher eventually yielded to Wid Matthews and then John Holland running baseball operations. Promoted from running the Triple-A Los Angeles Angels late in 1956, Holland and Wrigley became joined at the hip. Holland had to call the owner after every game and somehow Wrigley did not fire him despite just one winning season between 1957 and 1967 and a pair of 103-loss campaigns. "I have a fine man in John Holland," Wrigley said, adding his vice president was respected throughout the game.

A downward spiral began, causing the Cubs to be stuck in the mud of the National League's "second division" until our core assembled in 1966-68. Wrigley insisted the Cubs had to pay their own way, and he would not subsidize them out of his own pocket. And the more seasons they lost, the more money the franchise lost and the more clampdowns on spending had to be instituted. When the process of scouting was 'every team for itself' in the pre-amateur draft era, Cubs signing bonuses were typically smaller than that of the Dodgers, who typically led the majors in attendance in Los Angeles. The process so frustrated 1963-65 manager and 1977-81 General Manager Bob Kennedy that he said in the late 1990s he wished the Cubs had been owned by the gum company, not the individual Wrigley. The company had a robust $100 million in revenue in 1962, for example.

One financial snapshot showed how the Cubs lost and spent money in the first College of Coaches season in 1961. The Cubs lost $396,000 on team operations in 1961. But the sale of five players – including future manager Don Zimmer -- worth $225,000 in the expansion draft to stock the New York Mets and Houston Colt .45s (now Astros) turned into a paper profit of just more than $29,000. The Cubs lost a shade under $1 million in "direct baseball operations," but the team garnered $603,000 from local and national radio-TV rights plus the annual rental of Wrigley Field to the Bears.

The Cubs also blamed uncommonly large player bonuses for the '61 deficit. They had paid out $125,000 to 17-year-old Danny Murphy (.171 with 3 homers in 49 games from 1960-62) and $60,000 to first baseman Mack Kuykendall (who rose only as high as 17 games in Triple-A in 1963).

But winning had the opposite effect. All the ruckus we stirred up in 1969 generated a profit of nearly $1 million for Wrigley.

Still, the owner clung to unusual ideas amid the upswing. And no dynamic, independent baseball man was on board to persuade the owner to plow the profits into building up the organization to Dodgers' and now Mets' levels. Holland was a prime example of loyalty being rewarded with longevity. Others below Holland rarely were fired and were simply recycled up and down the Cubs system. I was always curious to see what Wrigley would have done had we gone to the World Series in 1969 and really increased the cash flow, with a projected 2 million attendance the next barrier overcome.

Wrigley was constantly bothered from all sides about installing lights. He definitely planned night baseball for the 1942 season after a two-year performance and attendance decline. But Pearl Harbor persuaded him to donate the steel for the light towers to the war effort. Interestingly, Wrigley applied for lights, supported by wood poles, to the War Department, over the next two years, but he was turned down. Then, starting with the pennant season in 1945, the Cubs drew at least 1 million for every season but one through 1952. The urgency to install lights was gone, even as every other big-league franchise installed lights. Wrigley became ingrained in the daytime schedule and the Cubs came close to 1 million only once the rest of the 1950s, but Wrigley still held fast to 1:30 or 2 p.m. games.

With summertime weekday crowds growing during our mid-season surge in 1968, Wrigley backed the team's outlier lightless status in a sit-down interview in the Wrigley Building Restaurant with Condon, who called the owner "baseball's distinguished free thinker" in his August 15 column. He asked Wrigley what his biggest was satisfaction in the ongoing revival.

"The crowds at Wrigley Field have justified my belief that a contending team doesn't need night baseball," he replied. "The Cubs have done so much research to prove a city the size of Chicago has many thousands of people who have time off during the daylight hours. Aside from the race track, there is no place for the sport fan in this group to enjoy himself. Except baseball."

Then Wrigley offered up an odd narrative about the appeal of being a runner-up.

"Actually, I suspect second place is the ideal spot if you're an owner. Once you win a couple of championships, once you dominate the league, fans will turn against you. I always felt the great support given to the New York Mets was largely due to a backlash at the New York Yankees."

Years before, Cubs broadcaster Vince Lloyd was startled by a casual conversation with the owner, having asked him why the Cubs continually did not win. "We're not interested in winning, we're interested in entertaining," Wrigley told Lloyd.

Subsequent events may have proven Wrigley wrong. Although the all-day schedule did develop new fans when we won, the majority of the total populace still worked the traditional 9-to-5 hours, or some variation thereof and schools were in session during the day three out of the six months of the season, with many of the students having been shuttled off to camp during day games in the summer.

If Wrigley referred to "shift" workers with his study, he declined to mention that second shifts typically began at 3 or 4 P.M. Those workers did not have time to attend day games. They would have to leave mid-game and race to their factories or offices. Several Chicago Tribune sports staffers hung around in the right-field bleachers for day games in the 1970s, but those workers started at 6 P.M. in order to edit the final newsstand edition going to press around 1:30 A.M. They could not have come out to the ballpark for a full game if they began work two hours earlier.

It's likely that, by not having some weeknight games during the season, Wrigley cut off revenue from much of his fan base. In an ideal situation, the Cubs could not contend every year. Those 6,000 attendees for a Thursday game in August might have been 15,000 to 20,000 for a night game, given the Cubs fan base was never further away than their television sets.

Much was made years later about the heat of day games draining players, and to be sure, that was a factor. But the constant switching back from a 9-to-5 schedule at home to 4-to-midnight, "entertainer's hours" on the road – physicians call it "shift work disorder" – likely was a bigger influence on Cubs teams fading late in the season. I could sleep easily on any schedule, but other players needed a more consistent, less stressful-on-the-body routine. My best buddy Billy Williams tried to work with the day-ball schedule by going to bed at 10 p.m. nightly before home games. However, his "body clock" still told Williams it was time to hit the sack later in the day for the first night game (then usually an 8 p.m. start) on a road trip. The schedule would be more out of whack if we went to the West Coast straight from Chicago, with games starting at 10 p.m. Central Time.

The Cubs did get some relief when lights were installed in 1988. But still half of the home schedule was played in the day by the time the franchise won it all in 2016.

But Wrigley's second point about the advantages of second place came out of left field. He apparently did not talk to enough players. Rotation-mate Ken Holtzman said it best: you either capture the World Series or you're a runner-up no matter how many games you win or your final place in the standings. Every players' goal should be to win it all.

And winning never gets old. Ask any Cubs fan who would have never gotten bored with consecutive titles after 108 years in the wilderness. The dynastic Yankees surely were an exception, with attendance that did not fit the massive size of the New York market.

In our 45-minute rides in from the South Side to Wrigley Field, Williams and I often speculated the long-term boost to the Cubs had we won it all in 1969. Winning often is contagious and we thought we could have won several pennants. If we made almost $1 million in profits for finishing second in '69, imagine Wrigley's ledger book bulging with black ink from 2 million-plus regular-season attendance, increased broadcast rights and postseason revenue. He could not have insisted the Cubs were financially unable to improve the ballpark or the organization under those circumstances.

But every owner had his attributes and faults and Wrigley's stance seemed oriented to his ballpark and the scenario of a summertime picnic with baseball as its backdrop. He sweated small details. Chuck Shriver, our public relations director in 1969, recalled a session with the owner in his Wrigley Building office. Major League Baseball teams tried to standardize the size of their media guides around that time with a longer, rectangular shape. The Cubs' guide was smaller and square-shaped. The issue required Wrigley deliberating the change in all seriousness in the meeting, then reluctantly agreeing.

Better that Wrigley had a longer session to study the player development results of the game's best franchises of the era and the size of the scouting and instructing staffs, almost always bigger than that of the Cubs.

The presence of Wrigley as the owner presented tradeoffs. The Cubs became the flagship franchise we know today because of the accessibility of ballpark and bully-pulpit broadcast exposure just when we began winning. At the same time, an owner with potentially more personal resources than any other mogul in the game did not employ them enough on the field, in my opinion.

We couldn't be all we could be.

The Daily Life Of A
1969 Chicago Cub

If you had the impression the life of a ballplayer a half-century ago was akin to an imperial pasha, I'll disabuse you of the idea right now.

Sure, we had perks and privileges. We flew on chartered airplanes with a bus meeting us on the tarmac when we'd arrive in another city. Our luggage was delivered directly to our hotel rooms. We might get a break on a major purchase. Since I was Ernie Banks' road roommate and he co-owned a South Side Ford dealership, I got a discount on a brand-new, purple-and-white Thunderbird with a Landau roof. I saw the car in the showroom and boom! I had to have it. Sixties' home-run hitters drove Cadillacs, so Ron Santo – the highest paid Cub – tooled around in a Caddy. Billy Williams drove a Buick Wildcat, and picked up "Wildcat" as a nickname to go along with "Whistler," his Alabama home town, and "The Sweet Swinger." But none of us had exotic sports cars as expensive as a small home. Once in a while we'd be treated to a free drink. But you could not get away without tipping, and that gratuity had better be generous because the reputation of a skinflint ballplayer got around quickly.

We did not have a police flying wedge allowing us high-speed driving to and from Wrigley Field. We did not earn the salaries to live in downtown luxury apartments or sprawling city or suburban homes. My then-wife Kathy and I lived in a middle-class, two-bedroom apartment at 7800 S. South Shore Drive. I recalled rent being $400 a month, but I was able to afford living quarters in both Chicago and my hometown of Chatham, Ontario, thanks to my off-season Harlem Globetrotters work. My Cubs salary, finally in a decent range in 1969, was supplemented by $16,000 from the 'Trotters. I played 185 'Trotters games in three seasons, going to Hawaii and all over the United States and Canada. That money covered a lot of things.

I usually car-pooled to Wrigley Field with Williams, who had bought his home on South Constance Avenue a few blocks away in 1966, just in time for the famed Blizzard of January 26-27, 1967, and Williams shoveled his own snow. But at home, we were like 9-

to-5 workers, hitting the rush hour coming and going. Playing all day games at home had some advantages for home life, but it exposed us to the world of our fans – traffic jams.

Players going home to the north and northwest suburbs had a designated, unpublicized route to dodge expressway-bound jams on Irving Park Road. Berteau Avenue, an east-west street two blocks north of Irving, carried the likes of Ron Santo, Glenn Beckert, Randy Hundley, Ken Holtzman and Jim Hickman to the Kennedy Expressway. The Cubs commuters detoured south to get over the Chicago River on Irving Park's bridge, then returned to Berteau for the mile-plus journey to the expressway on-ramp. The route was an open secret, though. Neighborhood kids knew the Cubs were coming, and gathered at several intersections to snare autographs. Decades later, Berteau was again the likely routing for Santo the radio analyst when he proclaimed on the air he had a "secret" way of getting home.

I had an extra annual chore to work at Wrigley Field. Then and now, I proudly maintained my Canadian citizenship, but I had to obtain a work visa for 8 ½ to 9 months. In that era, that task was pretty easy, talking to 'someone' in downtown Chicago to obtain the document.

At Wrigley though, our parking lot was next to the Waveland Avenue firehouse and after our 1968 success, fans always waited for you there when you arrived, maybe some 50 to 60. Many would walk in with you – and what the heck, you'd take them in with you for free. And the ever-present Bleacher Bums were always there early.

The home clubhouse down the left-field line was infamous for its tiny dimensions. You might call it the Cubbyhole. High-school locker rooms were roomier, although some road clubhouses, like at Cincinnati's Crosley Field, might have been worse. But we did not get any breaks playing at Wrigley Field. A trainer later accurately described the players as sitting "butt to butt" by metal cubicles. If it was tight for 25 baseball players and four coaches, I cannot imagine 45 or more Bears players squeezing in for practice and games, as the Monsters of the Midway still called Wrigley Field home in 1969. Chicago Tribune writer George Langford recalled simply turning around in that locker room, rubbing shoulders with a Bear and getting his interview.

The locker room was accessible only from an entrance leading to what was known as the catwalk where fans sat to the left-field bleachers, or from a door in the left-field corner. Once we were on the field or in the dugout, it was a nice walk back to the locker room. There was no in-game clubhouse time, as is common today. Our locker room had been opened in 1960, taking over from the longtime second-floor clubhouse behind third base, similar in layout and size to the visitors' clubhouse behind first base. That little area was turned into security and concessions offices.

Amazingly, General Manager Dallas Green built a bigger locker room in 1984, under the stands, behind the home dugout, to supplant these cramped quarters. Groundskeepers then took over our old dressing quarters. By the 2000s, Green's replacement clubhouse was considered too small and eventually gave way to the palatial, present-day, underground Cubs quarters in 2016. Present-day players just don't know how good they have it.

Back in the day, though, each "locker" was simply a space containing a bar running through the chain-link dividers. Your mom taught you to hang up your clothes neatly, so we practiced what she preached on hangers affixed to that bar. We had one shelf across the top for incidentals and personal items. As we got ready for games, front-office people arrived with our fan mail, to which further cluttered up the small spaces. All we had to sit on were stools. Comfy chairs or a player's lounge were stuff out of science fiction. All the guys could do was sit around to read a newspaper or wait for another team meeting convened by Leo Durocher.

Scattered around were sandboxes into which players could spit or deposit their cigarette butts. No littering was allowed by clubhouse manager Yosh Kawano, who constantly swept the floor. It's in this locker room where I got the nickname "Fly" from 1967 reliever Dick "The Monster" Radatz, because I simply buzzed around my close-in teammates with nowhere else to go. Willie Smith and Rich Nye were my immediate cubicle neighbors. Williams, Santo, Ernie Banks and Glenn Beckert were always on one side of the rows of cages.

Santo and Banks – 1969.

The only other space to which we could go was Al "Doc" Scheuneman's trainer's room, which was off limits to the media. Also cramped, Scheuneman's space had one table and a whirlpool tub with white cabinets for his supplies. At most, two or three players could squeeze in and media-shy guys would try to wedge their way into the off-limits area. But Scheuneman had a policy – no rookies in the trainer's room, so I guess, by trainer's policy, youth made you exempt from injuries or rubdowns. One day in 1969, though, there was a huge jam by the trainer's room because – ahem - backup catcher Bill Heath had a huge boil on his rear end. Bug-eyed witnesses squeezing into the doorway gazed in amazement as Scheuneman lanced the angry growth, producing a mini-volcano of a pus eruption.

The bathroom and shower areas were equally inadequate. Space was at such a premium that some relief pitchers began filtering in during the eighth inning to shave before the mob scene commenced. Two sinks, one large mirror, two toilets and one tall porcelain urinal were all the facility offered. Only two of the six showerheads really worked. The guys had to shower in shifts, so you had to get in there quickly after the final out and the steam from the working showers drifted into the clubhouse. The room would subsequently get so warm that the door to the field was left open a lot.

But the man simply known to everyone as Yosh also had an equipment room in which he'd locate September call-ups, or else they'd double up in a locker. Bats, gloves, boxes of spikes and hats were stored in the room. If you had a heavily-stained hat, you had to exchange it with Yosh.

Another quirk was that all pitchers needed a windbreaker for the entire season to keep their arms warm between innings while pitching. Certainly, position players required a jacket for the cool months of April, May and September, but they were not provided gratis by the Cubs; they cost $20 from Yosh. Breaking in as a lightly-paid rookie, catcher Ken Rudolph gladly paid the charge. He hung his windbreaker at his cubicle for three months, almost afraid to wear the new shiny piece of Cubbie blue apparel.

"But one day, I came back from hitting, and the brand-new windbreaker is hanging up dripping wet," Rudolph recalled. "Glenn Beckert took it from my locker to work out. Yeah, Beck was known for being very frugal, tight. He borrowed a lot of stuff from guys. Well, he 'borrowed' mine."

Beckert, the best man for my 1993 wedding to Lydia Farrington, had humor, dry and otherwise, draped all over him. One time, as our team plane began descending for a landing, he commandeered the PA mic from the flight attendant. According to Chicago Tribune beat writer George Langford, 'Beck' advised, "Look horny, guys." No wonder they don't allow writers on the plane anymore.

Fergie in his Cubs' Blue Windbreaker.

The joke was on Beckert though and all of us trying to maintain our blood sugar as game time approached. Locker-room food choices were limited and spread out. "We didn't have a good lunch program. When you left home, that was it," recalled catcher Randy Hundley and Yosh was famous for providing his signature watery soup. Basically, if you wanted any protein, however greasy, beyond your breakfast at home, you had to send a clubhouse kid outside to a place like Yum Yum Donuts. Always before a doubleheader though, Yosh was nice enough to have some food handy – a piece of chicken or cold cuts. The age of proper nutrition or making sure you had energy and proper blood sugar in the heat of the afternoon was still years away.

Meanwhile, Santo had his Pros Pizza business that was included on the Wrigley Field concessionaire's menu. One promotional deal had players' faces rotating each month on pizza boxes. Sorry, Santo, the pizza kind of wilted and tasted cardboard-like when we had it after doubleheaders. You could not take that pizza out of Wrigley Field after games and eat it in the car or at home.

We also had a clubhouse Coke cooler where you slid bottles down to get them out. Yosh had a big sheet on the wall where you had to write that you took some pop. Post-game, beer and Seven-Up were available, especially when sponsors brought in samples. Players would take the cans of beer in sanitary socks to their cars post-game. Meanwhile, cigarettes were a part of clubhouse life and I'd smoke only after a stressful game.

Yosh strictly accounted for what we consumed in the Cubbyhole. "We got a monthly bill," recalled lefty pitcher Rich Nye. Yosh had it on the back of an envelope -- you had a Coke (on this day). For what you used, it was really $10, but for what you gave him each month, probably $25.

"He could run the U.S. government on the back of an envelope," said 1967-75 Cubs public relations chief Chuck Shriver.

Subsequently, players spaced out the favors they asked of Yosh.

"There were times when nobody had extra tickets," recalled Nye. "Then I'd go to Yosh. He always came through. When you expected him to do something, it was no. But when asked him on occasion, he helped. Knowing that, when he asked you sit and sign balls, you'd do it. He'd put out a minimum two dozen, and had them sitting on a chair."

But given the small square footage of our clubhouse, no wonder guys could not wait to get out on the field. We typically were dressed and out in the Friendly Confines by 9:15 or 9:30 a.m. for a typical 1:15 or 1:30 p.m. game. Yosh and Scheuneman typically arrived together, around 8 a.m. If I was pitching, I'd arrive a little later, around 10 a.m. Between starts, I'd throw batting practice in place of that day's between-starts "bullpen" session. Remember, we were on the field earlier because we also had infield practice in addition to three rounds of batting practice. Coaches Joey Amalfitano or Pete Reiser threw BP to the regulars. It was a long day overall.

Pitchers, however, typically did not get rubbed down by Scheuneman until at least the regulars' BP or soon afterward. At least we did not have the eccentric situation I witnessed when I first came to the Cubs three years earlier. Right-hander Bill Faul, by then noted for "hypnotizing" himself before starts, lay on the trainer's table listening to a record that fed into his self-proclaimed mental state. You could be sure Faul did not last long under Durocher.

And I'd always throw up to 100 pitches warming up in the bullpen, which was a relatively new thing. At Wrigley Field, starters used to warm up on mounds in front of the dugout. But after Santo tripped over it and made a fuss, they were eliminated.

Those dugouts were just as cramped as the clubhouse. They were not further expanded, via excavation, to reasonable big-league standards until 1978. Maybe you could get 12 to 15 guys, including Durocher and the coaches, in there at the same time. Some players spread towels to sit on the cement steps to the dugouts to avoid the crunch. Meanwhile, maybe six or seven pitchers could sit in the bullpen, brushing with the fans in the box seats. At most, they could barter for peanuts. No one could be sneaking hot dogs from fans, given how director Arne Harris could have his WGN cameras on a bullpen shot at any second.

Like clockwork, about the fifth inning of every game, Yosh came down from the locker room with a can of Coke and a candy bar for Santo. We did not have a firm awareness that Santo was trying to manage his Type 1 (juvenile) diabetes without the aid of present-day glucometers. He'd have to guess at his blood-sugar levels at mid-game and the Yosh-borne sugar fix delivery was his insurance policy. Santo would go into the runway behind the dugout to swig part of the Coke.

And after games, there was a technique to running the gauntlet to our cars by the firehouse. In an August 28, 1969, Chicago Daily News feature, sportswriter Bob Billings described how Kessinger, a gentleman, regretfully let down waiting fans on Waveland Avenue with this explanation, "I'm sorry. If I sign one I'll have to sign them all. I hope you understand." Billings described how a "couple of thousand" fans typically waited for us after a loss. If we had won, he estimated at least 5,000 frenzied Cubs worshippers and autograph seekers would be milling about, playing the "tougher, no-holds-barred rules" that had Beckert and others literally lose their shirts in the "300 feet of asphalt" between the left-field entrance and a car baking in the sun for six hours. On this day though, Beckert needed a police escort to get to his car.

In the Billings piece, I was described as one of the first out of the clubhouse. I must have had an appearance that day, as I normally hung around awhile after a win. I was depicted wearing a "bright blue shirt, red and blue striped tie, blue bell bottoms and navy blazer slung jauntily over his shoulder." No wonder Banks described me as a "mod" dresser he could not keep up with in one of his 1969 Chicago Tribune columns. Billings said I walked fast and did not stop, which I can confirm because a Cub player had to make a beeline for his car after a game, although, sometimes Kathy would have been waiting at the T-Bird.

Another tactic was described as keeping one's hands full, preferably with a liquid. Reliever Hank Aguirre left with a paper cup of something. "If they get too rough, some of them get splashed," wrote Billings. "Besides, how can you write when your hands are full."

However, the cup tactic apparently did not work as well for Willie Smith. A photo with Billings' article showed Wonderful Willie with a cup of coffee in one hand, a cigarette in another, but still engulfed by kids.

Billings' story stated Banks did not have to walk the gauntlet to the parking lot because his car was pulled up to the curb on Waveland Three police officers and their ballpark-area commanding lieutenant provided what Jack Brickhouse used to call on Bears radio broadcasts "blast blocking" to get Mr. Cub into the car, which was "whisked away fast," said Billings.

Durocher, meanwhile, made a grand exit an hour after the game. The left-field exit door would open as, "A sleek, black car backs out into the street," Billings penned. "Police swing into action clearing the street. The lord of the Cubs smiles through the dark glass brightly. He raises his left hand in an imperial wave and roars down the street."

Durocher zoomed off to his Gold Coast apartment and whatever after-hours rounds he had booked. If I did not immediately return all the way to the South Side, I could stop at The Cottage restaurant, one-half mile south of Wrigley Field on Clark Street. That was a popular ballplayer's hangout with good food. Visiting players and Chicago Bears often went there too. Legendary Wrigley Field public-address announcer Pat Pieper had been a waiter at The Ivanhoe, a restaurant-bar one block further south on Clark. And if I stopped downtown instead, I'd dine at Gene and Georgetti's or The Chop House. Then and now, Chicago had a lot of good steakhouses. The odd bar downtown might comp you the first round – "Fergie, you pitched a good game," but after that, you had to open your wallet.

Meanwhile, daily spring-training life in Scottsdale, Arizona, started even earlier – and ended earlier – than the 9-to-5 Wrigley Field routine. In 1969, before we had children, Kathy and I rented a one-bedroom apartment for six weeks just off Miller Road. For wheels, I rented another Ford.

You had to be at old Scottsdale Stadium at 7:45 a.m., and be dressed and ready to go by 8:30. The 3,000-seat ballpark was ancient. Both the floors and doors were wooden. The showers had wooden pallets, so you always had to wear shower shoes to avoid splinters and nails. The best ballpark in the Cactus League then was the Giants' stadium, also used for their Triple-A team, in Phoenix.

We only had one field with four mounds. But we did not have masses of players like today – just the 40-man roster and maybe six to seven guys who had extremely good minor-league seasons. We topped out at 19 or 20 pitchers. Even without the extra facilities of the lavish spring training complexes of today, I felt we got our work done.

For the first few days, before the regulars arrived, pitchers and catchers threw BP to each other. We were just running and throwing. I threw batting practice every other day, basically to Banks, Williams, Santo, Kessinger and Beckert. The other rotation starters also threw these BP sessions. I threw just to get my arm in shape. Early on, I threw mostly fastballs to the top hitters, as they wanted the ball pretty straight. I limited throwing curves to the bullpen. After about the third week, I'd start throwing sliders to the top hitters and they'd work on contact to the opposite field.

And there was always a therapeutic session was available at the Buckhorn hot tubs in Mesa. We'd wrap up in warm blankets post-game. Meanwhile, a main pastime of Cactus League players in the Phoenix area was somehow avoiding the two-hour trip each way to games in Tucson, at the Cleveland Indians camp. Later, the White Sox, Colorado Rockies and Arizona Diamondbacks set up shop in the state's second city. The expansion Padres set up even further away in Yuma, where the ballpark was on a military base. Durocher was pretty sharp to make sure the regulars could not skip those journeys. The players had to travel to and from Scottsdale in their flannel uniforms – not a great experience. If you were one of the early innings pitchers in a game at Tucson, you got a bit of a break. You could dash into the home clubhouse, take a quick shower and change.

The one road trip most players enjoyed was Palm Springs, where the Angels trained. That was a nice place and you got to fraternize with a lot of people. Durocher, of course, knew the celebrity set, led by Frank Sinatra, in the California desert resort city.

But with the early hours, there was little going out on the town and waiting 'til last call. Billy Williams and I usually had dinner at the legendary Pink Pony steakhouse in Old Town Scottsdale about once a week. Don't worry, we did not deke each other when the check came. We split the bill for our steak and beers. The Pink Pony, later supplanted by Don and Charlie's as the go-to baseball-themed restaurant in Scottsdale, stayed open until 2016.

Our hours and routines were a bit later on the road in the regular season. We turned from regular daytime workers into largely night-shift entertainers. Long distance, we were fortunate to ride mostly charter jets. Sometimes though, teams saving some pennies opted for commercial travel.

Many times we'd fly from Chicago to our first road stop the day of the game. Remember, most night home games began at 8 p.m. local time in 1969. And since visiting teams took batting practice last, we'd have most of the day to travel, get into the hotel and take a quick nap if needed. That was not strenuous travel, as Chicago was within a two-hour flight of all other NL teams except the West Coast clubs and Houston. Now though, Major League Baseball does not want to take the risk of a flight – and thus the game –

being delayed on same-day travel. I don't know how that's an advantage if the visiting team arrives in the middle of the night or even at dawn.

We'd leave through a special gateway at O'Hare Airport, with fans waiting to snare autographs. On board, I'd sit close to Williams and Banks toward the back of the plane and play cards. In that era, beat writers flew with us and the team broadcasters. I'd chat with the scribes on the plane and never felt I'd be misquoted. In 1984, Green allowed Chicago media to ride on the Cubs charter to and from the National League Championship Series in San Diego. That kind of relationship, dating back to when the writers rode trains with the teams, ended by the 1990s. The newspapers would be charged for first-class airfare if their writers wanted to hitch a ride. And the teams themselves did not want the writers to get that close and personal with players and managers. I felt the game had lost something with the team-media separation.

Anyway, many players would take cabs to and from ballparks, but I stayed on the team bus to save money. Durocher would stand by the doorway, and say, "Let's go, guys!" In Montreal and New York, though, I took the subway. Sometimes you'd be recognized, especially on the platform by Mets fans coming to Shea Stadium. No way would I ride with the Shea crowd back to Manhattan, where we stayed at the Waldorf. I took the team bus after the New York games.

Dining options were limited as per diem meal money of $12 a day did not permit you the prime steak or market-price seafood. Nye recalled splurging for an $18 room-service breakfast in New York. He had blown basically several days of meal money. Traveling secretary Blake Cullen typically dispensed the meal money from a valise. A typical request to Blake was, "I ran out of meal money – can you advance me some?" I don't think Santo, though, was cash-poor on any trip. He was the first guy I ever saw peel out a roll of $100 bills.

New York had the expected good eating despite the expense and everyone ate at Fisherman's Wharf in San Francisco. Houston surprisingly had some good places, which I discovered through my friendship with Williams, who had a lot of good friends in the city. Atlanta also had good eats. Ted Savage, a 1967-68 teammate and St. Louis-area native, was able to tip me off to good places in our archrival's area, so I used to go to clubs in East St. Louis, Illinois. For entertainment, St. Louis also had some good bands.

St. Louis and Cincinnati, of course, hosted the most road-tripping Cubs fans, although the hotel lobby in St. Louis always was jumping. But our fans also followed us to the Netherland Hilton in Cincy.

We did not face a Durocher curfew in smaller cities like St. Louis, Cincy or Pittsburgh, nor in Philly. They were not perceived as swinging towns. But Durocher tried to rein you in with a 12:30 a.m. cutoff in New York and Los Angeles, where the distractions were obvious and we had trouble with their teams. We also had a curfew in Montreal, and for good reason. Near our Queen Elizabeth Hotel was the 24-hour Chez Paree club, which had French-Canadian table dancers. The players raced to the club after games for entertainment before the curfew kicked in. Or maybe they stretched their wee-hours' time in Montreal. Durocher certainly did.

Beckert, one of Wrigley Field's merry men of '69, summed up our travels on the road the best: "Things happened on the road that I can't tell." But Beckert also insisted that life was not all late-night last calls and Baseball Annies offering temptation. "You always hear wild stories about the players," he said in 2003. "But you never hear about going to bed early and ordering room service, like we did all the time in New York. Yeah, even in New York."

If you could not slip out on the town, a lot of the top hotels had good bars or clubs. There, you'd often run into those Cubs fans who traveled well. A lot of their stories originated from those bars.

Where applied on the road, curfew was enforced. [Coaches] Reiser and Becker would knock on our doors to make sure we were in our rooms. I had to open the door to prove I was buttoned down for the night. In Los Angeles, though, road roomie Banks was absent. He'd often stay with relatives.

People would phone the room and ask if Banks was there. "Who is this?" I'd respond. They'd hang up. More often, Banks and I would tell the desk when we'd arrive: no calls. At that time, players did not register under aliases, as was common as the 20th century ended.

When my head finally hit the pillow, I got my rest. The concept of "shift-work disorder" has been floated as a reason why the Cubs did not win forever, playing that commuters' daytime schedule at home, then switching to the night shift on the road, constantly back-and-forth for six months, wearing out finely-tuned athletes, in my opinion. Williams, for instance, typically went to bed around 10 p.m. at home. But his body clock was still saying 10 p.m. on his first night of, say, a West Coast road trip, when he'd bat in the first inning against Juan Marichal, Gaylord Perry or Don Drysdale. By the time the Cubs players' bodies adjusted to local time, the road trip was half over and they might have registered some sluggish oh-fers. I can't say definitively if the schedule upheavals were a detriment. But I personally had no problems going to sleep, no matter where I was.

Overall, the daily life of a 1969 Cub wasn't too bad at all.

Dirt from the fans...

I worked at a hot dog stand behind the Cubs' dugout. There was a storage area behind with a ramp inclined towards a player walk area. There were also a few storage carts which were wooden on wheels for moving products throughout the park. One day, I went into the area and a cart got loose and could have continued down the ramp smack into the area. Adolfo Phillips was back there taking warmup swings with his back to me. I yelled out to him, "Heads up!" so he wouldn't get hit with the cart, proof positive that baseball is a game of inches more than you think.

-Larry Rosen, Managua, Nicaragua

"Hickman Did It Again!"

A long, long drive had a double meaning for the family of Gentleman Jim Hickman beyond his titanic homers onto Waveland Avenue and points beyond.

This extended drive was 500 miles, first in a Chevy station wagon with open windows for ventilation, and later in a Pontiac Grand Safari wagon with trimmings such as air conditioning. Starting and end points were Henning, Tennessee, not far from Memphis, and Chicago. One such jaunt may have promoted other long-haul destinations for baseballs off strongman Hickman's bat.

Occupying the wagon, plowing ahead on Interstate 57 at a steady 70 mph, was driver Nita (short for Juanita) Hickman and her four boys: Jim Jr.; Bill; Joey; and Mike. The oldest was Jim Jr., at 11 in 1969, charged with keeping order among his younger siblings, but who was really a "hellion" in his own words. The family made the trip around June 1 every season after school let out in Henning to join Dad, playing for the Cubs. "We fought and argued a lot, what normal kids did," said Jim Jr. "It wasn't constant. Mother held a pretty iron fist over us. I was expected to help keep order, but I instigated it. It was just mischievous stuff."

Nita Hickman made the trip deadheading 10 hours in one day, as there was no extra money for an overnight stop at a motel.

"Mother kept tabs on when we did stop to make sure we hit the bathroom," said Jim Jr. "Then she'd make an emergency stop if one of us really had to go."

And as a last resort, there was an emergency piece of equipment.

"We had one piece of necessary luggage," recalled Joey Hickman. "It was a Maxwell House coffee can if someone really had to go.

"And we made another stop if we filled up that can."

Those rolling hills in Tennessee and southern Illinois provided some scenic diversion. But once you hit those flatlands, 60 or 70 miles into Illinois, a numbing effect took place, experienced by every long-distance driver through the one of world's breadbasket.

"I turned 7 in 69," Joey said. "I remember driving through the cornfields of Illinois thinking, 'Man, are we every going to get there?' Mother would drive every bit of that at the 70 mph speed limit. In that Chevy, she did not let us roll down the windows so as not to mess up her hair. It got a little warm in the car."

But mass satisfaction erupted when Nita finally slowed down at the family's in-season home at the Old Ivy Apartments on Algonquin Road in northwest suburban Mt. Prospect. She was re-united with her guy, almost the ultimate strong, soft-spoken but not silent type. The boys had their father and Jim Hickman was whole in a way baseball could not do for him.

Yet something different was at hand when the Hickmans were all reunited in June 1969 after giving the Chevy wagon its rest. The strapping 6-foot-4, 200-pound outfielder's career had almost been trashed the year before, as the Dodgers had talked of outrighting him to Triple-A. Hickman talked of giving up his decade-long career in baseball that produced only a modicum of success.

But suddenly, after Dodgers broadcaster Vin Scully's recommendation to Cubs General Manager John Holland, Hickman found himself back in the majors as a Cub, coming over as the second wheel in a trade for closer Phil Regan. He was not a starter, just a spare outfielder, sometimes playing here and there in a platoon arrangement in right field. But when he comfortably made the Cubs again out of spring training in 1969, Hickman had a smidgeon of stability, so the arrival of Nita and the boys was the cherry on the sundae.

Things began to happen though as soon as the family settled into the apartment, with the boys dividing their time between Little League and hanging around the cubbyhole home locker room down the left-field line. He slugged his first homer of the season, a 2-run, pinch-hit job against the Braves at Wrigley Field on June 1. The ultimate family man, he surely was more inspired with a little extra step in his long gait when he'd arrive every day at Wrigley Field, hoping his name might be in the lineup if a lefty was on the mound.

But on a gloomy, rainy Sunday, June 22, at Wrigley Field, Hickman had come in mid-game as a pinch hitter and stayed in to play right field in the first game of a doubleheader, and he used his time well, slugging a 2-out, 2-run, walk-off homer in the bottom of the ninth off Montreal Expos lefty Don Shaw. It left all of us wondering why Expos Manager Gene Mauch didn't go to a righty to face Hickman, and preceding batter Ernie Banks, to try to cap the Cubs' 4-run rally, which touched off a wild celebration of our 7-6 victory. As fans jumped onto the field in typical 1969 celebration, Ron Santo was so jacked up he pounded the victorious slugger on his helmet, giving him a brief headache. And then Santo set off down the left-field line to perform his first heel-clicking, post-game demonstration of the season.

However, the weather was much different on Thursday, June 26. The hot breath of summer had arrived and the Cubs and Pirates sweated into the 10th inning, tied 5-5 in their flannel uniforms in 94-degree heat. Catcher Ken Rudolph, spelling starter Randy Hundley, walked with 2 out in the bottom of the 10th. Then Hickman lauched a Bruce Dal Canton service even further than his Expos bomb, far out onto Waveland, as Wrigley Field erupted again. In the broadcast booth, Jack Brickhouse tried to one-up himself on his previous walk-off call, exclaiming, "Hickman did it again!"

Twenty-five years later, in true laconic Hickman manner, he explained why he muscled up, especially in the sultry late afternoon against the Pirates.

"I can remember a couple of days that were pretty warm. I wanted to get out of there (by ending it with a homer)," he said later with a hint of a chuckle.

And, yes, Gentleman Jim did not want to disappoint in the clutch – especially himself.

"The fear of failure motivates you as much as anything," he recalled. "A player of my caliber, I was just glad to be there."

After Hickman gave the Waveland Avenue ball hawks more souvenirs, all was right in the Cubs Universe, again, in 1969.

The two walk-offs were just the appetizer for one of the most inspiring stories in Cubs history that began with Gentleman Jim practically carrying us on his back the entire month of August, then continuing into another season as he proved to be one of the best clutch hitters in team annals. Another month would have to pass after the blast off Dal Canton before Leo Durocher switched out Willie Smith for Hickman for a starting corner outfield job. But once Gentleman Jim got a few starts in a row, there was little holding him back. Like a release of all frustrations up to that point in his career, he let it all out with 10 homers, 25 RBI and a .315 average in August alone.

Such an offensive outburst cemented a special affection Cubs' fans developed for Hickman, only slightly less intense at the time than for his better-known teammates. We loved the man from the first day he set foot in our clubhouse early in 1968. He did not always come through in the clutch in his six Cubs seasons. But when he did, you never forgot his feats. If you talk about dignity and quiet strength, you looked no further than the Man from Henning with that trusty station wagon in the players' parking lot, hauling those active boys to their summer playground.

We got to know him as Gentleman Jim for his demeanor. That nickname spread to the general public, although within the family, he was "Big Jim."

"That started when I was young in our yard, and Mother started that," recalled Jim Hickman Jr. "My name was Jim, also. So they called me Little Jim and he was Big Jim. The grandkids also called him Big Jim."

Coming to the Cubs, Gentleman Jim made the same impression on us, the fans, the media and especially Durocher that was already ingrained in Henning, a tiny town of under 1,000 whose later claim to fame – after Hickman's career ended – was briefly hometown to Roots author Alex Haley.

"Jim Hickman was the most selfless man I have ever met," said Jim Peyton, a lifelong friend – directly to Jim Hickman Jr. and then the entire family. Later becoming a minister, Peyton officiated at his 2016 funeral.

"He was the most humble man I have ever met. Those are two of his greatest qualities, along with his gentlemanly-ness."

Gentleman Jim left us at age 79. Nearly two years earlier, in August 2014, co-author George Castle conducted the last in-depth interview with the reflective senior citizen by phone from his Henning home. When the chat was published at www.chicagobaseballmuseum.org, the website of the Chicago Baseball Museum, a record number of page views for the web site were recorded. Cubs fans of a certain age and others who simply loved great players in franchise history never forgot Hickman. They flocked to his recollections and "where are they now?" status. We will re-publish many of Gentleman Jim's comments here, along with remembrances from those who knew him best.

To his last day, Hickman treasured his time with the Cubs. He previously had been tagged as an Original Met, playing as a rookie on the comic 120-loss stumblebum expansion team in 1962. Playing in the old Polo Grounds, then the newly built Shea Stadium, in his first four seasons, Hickman slugged 56 homers with mediocre RBI totals and batting averages as a semi-regular outfielder, while also playing a bit of third and first base. Manager Casey Stengel liked the quiet striver and the feeling was mutual. But no one in the lineup really thrived through these dark-age campaigns that still endeared the Mets to very loyal New York fans who missed the Dodgers and Giants. The Mets blue-and-orange colors paid homage to the teams that had fled to the West Coast in 1958.

Gentleman Jim's modest production declined to near-rock bottom in 1966 and 1967 with the Mets and Dodgers. So the trade to the Cubs was a fresh start. Decades later, Gentleman Jim said they were the highlights of his career.

"It was a great honor to be able to play on that club with all those players," he said. "That was part of it. I was just happy there. I knew if I didn't do it, one of those other guys was going to do it. I just want to say this – those were the happiest years of my life. I couldn't have played on a club with 24 better guys. Everybody loved each other."

It was a great honor to be able to play on that club with all those players.

"Dad was a real patient man, always relaxed," said Jim Hickman Jr. "He looked at it as 'I get to play baseball today.' That sounds like a store-bought answer, but it wasn't. He felt blessed to play every day. He never let things get to him."

And when Hickman amply supplemented the longtime 3-4-5 trio of Williams, Santo and Banks with his run production spree in 1969's dog days, the established Cubs felt the cavalry had come over the hill – even if the new big bopper seemed to dawdle getting onto the field for batting practice.

"Before Hickman came over, it was just us Big Three," said Williams. "When Jim came over, he solidified a good team. He pushed the three of us. He had a tremendous year."

Coming in late on August 2 at Wrigley Field in his role as a frequent defensive replacement for Willie Smith during the latter's 1 ½-month stint in the lineup, Hickman got a 2-run pinch single off Padres reliever and 1968 Cub Frank Reberger in a Cubs' win. The next day, Gentleman Jim was finally promoted from his part-time status, on Sunday, August 3, 1969, as it turned out, against former teammate Joe Niekro, at Wrigley Field. He started for the second straight game against a right-hander the next night in Houston against the Astros' Tom Griffin. The lineup newcomer got 2 hits and proved Durocher's hunch right.

"It would be his hottest month," said Jim Hickman Jr. "But it wasn't a big thing for our family. Dad took the attitude he was doing what he was supposed to do. He had us feel like that. It was just another day in the park."

The family close at hand combined with the Cubs' first-place status was first time he had ever experienced a season where every day counted. For decades afterward, all comers came to Hickman to ask how he flipped his "on" switch.

The big man's new status as a regular permitted Nita and the four Hickman boys to establish a set routine that lasted four-plus seasons. Jim Jr. in particular hung out in the cubbyhole clubhouse, and the boys got to shag a few flies in Wrigley Field. Younger and more impressionable, Joey Hickman had his own special impression of the raucous Bleacher Bums of the day.

"I was afraid of the Bleacher Bums," he said. "Every time (Ken) Holtzman threw a game, they would stand on the wall. I was terrified because I thought they'd fall on me."

Not all the boys rode with Dad to Wrigley Field. He car-pooled from Mt. Prospect with the likes of Bill Hands, Paul Popovich and Hank Aguirre, and in 1970, with newly acquired Johnny Callison. He was a true working man, doing the 9-to-5 shift on the job, then coming home in his important role as a father. Modest by nature, Gentleman Jim generally shied away from after-hours appearances in favor of family life. He'd sign autographs on the way to his car by the firehouse – "I don't ever remember him not signing for anyone who asked," said Jim Jr.

Once Gentleman Jim got out of that car at home, he turned off baseball. He was the antithesis of a fellow son of the South, Hundley, that is, who, as catcher and team leader had baseball on the brain, 24-7.

"When the game was over, he left work at work," Jim Jr. said. "Home time was home time. He'd spend time with us. He didn't get out, otherwise he'd get mobbed. He was a very humble guy."

To any impressionable young Hickman, the old man had the same job as any other father.

"I thought every dad played baseball," Jim Jr. said. "When we started playing Little League baseball up there, my coach's son was my best friend. I asked what his dad does, who does he play for? He said he's a plumber. What the hell's a plumber?"

As a result of their father's spreading fame, the Hickman boys had a special educational arrangement so that they did not have to rush back to Henning to start the new school year and be separated from Dad. They began their school years near their suburban home, then transferred to their regular Henning school immediately after the season concluded.

"My dad became such an icon in Henning no one (at the local school) minded," Jim Jr. said.

And yet, despite his Redbird roots and identification with the Amazin' Mets and their expansion, bumbling legacy, Hickman, the rest of his life, felt he was a true-blue Cub.

"No question, I think of myself as a Cub," he said years later. "Everybody knows I feel that way. That was a great place to play and a great city.

"Anyone who's ever been there wants to come back."

To us, Gentleman Jim has never left.

27 Batted Balls For Outs –
A Holtzman No-No

You can't make this stuff up:
    •   Ken Holtzman, a strikeout pitcher, tossed a no-hitter without a single strikeout on August 19, 1969, against the Atlanta Braves at cozy Wrigley Field. Consider the long, long odds against a no-hitter itself, then multiply them into astronomical territory when Holtzman got all 27 batters to to put the ball in play for outs.

    • The most dangerous of the hitters, Hammerin' Hank Aaron, by all logic should have broken up the hitless gem with a seventh-inning homer, which would have in the end upped his all-time total to 756. Aaron rated his connection the hardest-hit ball of his 23-season career. But the ball literally took a left-turn – taking a page straight from "Angels in the Outfield" -- after it passed over the left-field bleacher wall where it curves outward. Tracking the ball every foot of the way, Billy Williams caught it, staggering backward. Aaron was tied for second all-time with Mike Schmidt among visiting players with 50 homers in Wrigley Field.

    • Aaron also raked Holtzman lifetime. But, sure enough, he came up to bat again in the ninth inning, standing as the last man between Holtzman and his first no-hitter. Holtzman fell behind 3-and-1. Three pitches later, Aaron made contact again...

    • The no-no required two catchers to handle Holtzman. Starter Bill Heath suffered a broken hand on a foul tip in the eighth. Little-used Gene Oliver finished up.

We'll take you through the play-by-play, the outcome of which convinced so many fans and media at the time that the hand of Providence was resolutely on the Cubs' side in 1969. They reasoned, not crazily, that only heavenly interference could have rigged the result the way it took place, figuring the all-contact no-hitter and hardest of contact for Aaron. And such experienced Cubs observers as WGN-TV sports editor Jack Rosenberg felt we were fated to make the playoffs, reaching a season-high 32 games over .500 at 77-45, after watching Holtzman pull off the near-impossible.

Setting the stage is easy for re-creating that sun-splashed Tuesday afternoon before the largest weekday crowd we had drawn to date – 41,033. The SRO throng had turned out in celebration of a season shifted into higher gear.

We had just gone 7-4 on a very tough road trip, coming home with an 8-game, first-place lead. We had just swept 3 games in the Houston Astrodome, which had been a chamber of horrors for us since it opened in 1965. Then we held our own on a three-city West Coast swing, always a trail of tears with the time-zone change and lots of good pitching arrayed against us.

Although the Mets had established themselves as a contender, they had slipped back to third place, 10 games out, behind the Cardinals on August 13. We always thought the two-time NL-defending champion Cardinals would make a run at some point, and that was our mindset. So was colorful Cardinals announcer Harry Caray. Aiming his post-game taunts northward through the summer heat at night, knowing his 50,000-watt KMOX-Radio signal would be picked up in Chicago, Caray clucked as the Cards cut their deficit against us to single digits: "Are you listening, Cubbies? Are you listening, Cubbies? The Cardinals are coming, tra la, tra la…"

Diehard Chicago fans' blood boiled hearing Caray, not realizing he'd be their pied piper and most popular Cubs figure just a mere 13 years later. But concerns about our first-place standing weren't as aggravating as listening to Caray. Starting August 19, we had an 11-game home stand against the Braves, Astros and Reds, while the runner-up Mets soon would challenge their body clocks and outpitch their hosts with their own trip to Los Angeles, San Francisco and San Diego.

We had a partial off-day on Monday, August 18, having arrived in the wee hours from San Francisco after a Sunday doubleheader. But we also had been mandated to show up at night to play the White Sox at Comiskey Park for the Boys Benefit Exhibition Game, which had generated controversy when Manager Leo Durocher first declined to play a core of six regulars, to give them a rest. Durocher then relented though, letting the regulars play 4 innings and we won 2-0, in a game that raised funds for boys' baseball teams in the Chicago area.

As usual, although this time for what would turn out be Holtzman's special day, thousands waited for the gates to open at 10 a.m. to claim one of 22,000 unreserved grandstand and bleacher seats. One of the early arrivals was 14-year-old David Fletcher of west suburban Glen Ellyn, who, like many loyal fans, endured a long commute to Wrigley Field. He was rewarded with a good seat.

"I sat in the first row of what is now Section 226 on the first-base side with a direct sight line to the left- field bleachers and the rooftops overlooking Waveland Avenue. I had an unobstructed view because I was right above the main concourse aisle. I had seen at least 30 games that year, traveling to Wrigley Field after taking a yellow-colored Northwestern commuter train from Glen Ellyn to Oak Park, transferring to the Lake Street

L to travel to the State-Lake station, and then make another switch to the Howard L subway for the final leg five miles north to the Addison stop.

That fateful day I had gotten to the park early to grab a prime unreserved seat for the first-game of a 3-game series against the Braves, who were battling for (and would eventually win) the newly created NL West division title. The buzz at the ballpark was incredible and portended what the post-season would be like at Wrigley Field that had been shut out from the promised land since 1945."

But Holtzman was due for a superb game, in my opinion. He had begun the season 10-1 with five shutouts, but had slipped to 13-7 coming in. Opposing him was Braves knuckleballer Phil Niekro, headed for his best season with 23 victories. One interesting factor working against Niekro though as the game began was the notorious 16 mph wind blowing in off the lake, with a temperate 76-degree, game-time temperature. Knuckleball pitchers usually want the wind to be blowing against them to create more resistance and make their fluttering pitches dance even more.

Holtzman was due for a superb game.

But the first inning turned out to be an even worse confluence for Niekro, who threw a low knuckleball to Ron Santo with two men on, and with a "short swing," blasted the pitch through the wind onto Waveland Avenue for a 3-0 lead. The clout was Santo's first-ever homer off of Hall-of-Famer Niekro.

"I never hit that guy," Santo would say two hours later. "He got two strikes on me with knuckleballs and I knew I'd been in that spot before…I knew it was gone as soon as I hit it. I'm elated."

Soon afterward, Holtzman discovered his curve and changeup were not really working. Taking a page from Sandy Koufax in Game 7 of the 1965 World Series and opted to throw what he termed later "maybe 96 to 100 percent fastballs."

And something special seemed to be in the air from the very first hitter. Second baseman Glenn Beckert moved nicely to his left to throw out Felipe Alou. Two innings later, Beckert went to the end of his range to snare an Alou grounder headed for right and from practically behind first base, again nipped him at first.

"The high grass slowed it up a bit, but, still, it was right in the hole and I didn't know if I could get it," Beckert would tell the media afterward. "But you don't give up…When you're going for a pennant, they're all big plays."

Several Braves afterward claimed Wrigley Field groundskeeper Pete Marcantonio had purposely let the grass grow long while we were on the road trip. But the ballpark always had been known for thick grass, so who could have known the difference?

Shortstop Don Kessinger had to use a bit of his boarding-house reach to his right to throw out Niekro at one point. Third baseman Santo waited for a high chopper from Felix Millan, then used all the gun in his arm to retire the No. 2 Braves hitter at another juncture.

On that afternoon and again 50 years later, Holtzman knew how much his defense had bailed him out.

"Both of my no-hit games (the second was June 3, 1971, in Cincinnati) were like all no-hitters: decently pitched games with an extraordinary amount of luck. Also, the defense has to be air-tight and Beckert surely made some great plays during that game."

Leading off the ninth, Alou was involved in another near-miss, as he sent a popup into short center field. Both Kessinger and center fielder Don Young pursued the ball and the proverbial Jack Brickhouse call of 'Alphonse-and-Gaston act,' 'I've got it – you take it,' was about to take center stage when Kessinger snatched the ball away from Young, who fell to the ground and barely avoided the collision.

"The crowd was making so much noise we couldn't hear anything out there," Kessinger explained later. "Don says he called for the ball, but I didn't hear him. And that wasn't a spot where I wanted to back off and let the ball drop. If it was going to drop, I'd rather Don had run right over me. Then one of us would get an error."

The only Braves to reach base were on walks to Gil Garrido in the third, Bob Didier in the fifth and Rico Carty in the seventh.

Holtzman also had to throw to the backup of the backup. Didier fouled a pitch off Heath's hand in the eighth and the catcher had to leave, his injury soon diagnosed as a fracture. Oliver, a favorite of Durocher, admitted he was nervous because he had caught only 10 innings all year.

But all these sidebars, even the spectacular Beckert play, paled in comparison to the astounding turn of events leading off the seventh with a certified Cubs Killer in Aaron coming to bat. Getting through Aaron to pitch a no-hitter at Wrigley Field was tough enough, yet when the man with the quickest wrists this side of vintage Ernie Banks connects as only he can, you logically have no chance.

"Tremendous hand elasticity," '69 Cub Nate Oliver said of Aaron's origin of lightning-fast bat speed. Nate Oliver's former Dodgers teammate, Sandy Koufax, had admiringly called him, "Bad Henry."

And Aaron had good looks at Holtzman. Lifetime, including two seasons against Holtzman in the American League in 1975-76, 'The Hammer' hit .304 (17 for 56,) with 4 homers and 13 RBI.

But Holtzman's definition of "extraordinary" luck though doesn't begin to describe what happened. Aaron got his very best swing on Holtzman's fastball, the very, very best of his career, according to Aaron's own comments at the Civil Rights Game festivities at Guaranteed Rate Field in Chicago in 2013.

"The thing I remember the most about playing at Wrigley Field is hitting probably the hardest ball I've ever hit in my life off Kenny Holtzman when he pitched a no-hitter," Aaron said. "I thought for sure I hit a home run. Sure enough, the wind blew it back to Billy Williams."

Responded Holtzman to his Aaron's recollection: "I have no reason to disbelieve him, but the same wind didn't seem to stop Ron Santo's blast in the first inning, so he must have absolutely crushed Phil Niekro's knuckler."

Holtzman left out one detail – Santo's clout was a line drive. Aaron normally hit the proverbial frozen ropes for homers, not high-arching ones like Jim Hickman, or renowned-slugger Dave Kingman-style ICBMs. He usually did not hit them 400 feet. But on this day, he scalded Holtzman's fastball and got it up, up and up into the wind, headed toward the last bleacher section before the concave curve of the wall, 75 feet from the foul line.

And Brickhouse's voice had the ultimate tenor of foreboding in the two seconds of his play-by-play:

"That's well hit…and there, I believe, goes the no-hitter…Caught! Caught by Williams! Whooo, boy!! Oh man. That ball looked like it was really gone when it left here. When it got out there, it hit the invisible shield. The wind, which is blowing in at 15 mph, caught it…"

Observing in a direct sight-line to the ball from his first-base grandstand seat, young Fletcher at first believed he was thwarted in his desire to see a no-hitter.

"Aaron's high drive immediately took the air of out of the crowd, certain that Holtzman's no-hitter was over," he recalled. "I had a direct sight-line to the ball from my vantage point and Williams did not give up on this blast. He ran back to the well in the left-field bleachers where the bleacher wall curves in front of the catwalk and waited against the ivy. Though the high-arching ball appeared to be headed for Waveland Avenue or beyond, the 16 mile per hour wind roaring in from center field knocked the ball down and literally blew it back in the ballpark into Williams' glove."

After the game, Holtzman recalled a tense wait for the outcome of the blast: "The ball was suddenly suspended up there – it seemed like 40 seconds between the time it left the bat and the time it started coming down – and finally it just dropped into Billy's glove."

But was the explanation that simple? How could a ball hammered so hard by the man many still consider baseball's home-run king simply die like that and find Williams as if the ball sought out his glove?

Anyone preserving the color videotape on a DVR or laptop can perform a stop-action view of the play to figure what happened. The WGN high home-plate camera showed Aaron really crushing the ball as it headed on a high arc toward the bleachers. Fans in the last section, ground zero of my friends in the Bleacher Bums, looked straight up expecting to get an unwelcome souvenir. Williams raced back to the curve of the wall and momentarily braced himself against it.

Suddenly, everything went nuts, as the ball was hung up after passing over two rows of bleachers, in the estimation of closer Phil Regan, watching from the bullpen. The Vulture also made the claim it took a left turn at this point.

Williams knew never to give up on a ball that was not clearly out of the park with a strong wind blowing in. He noticed the abrupt change in direction and he suddenly backpedaled at least six steps on the warning track. Brushing the vines, he reached up and caught the ball leaning backward. It virtually appeared as if some kind of giant hand simply swatted it straight down into Williams' glove.

"It was out of the ballpark," Aaron said. "I don't know how it stayed in the ballpark. Somehow it came back and ran in that little trough where Billy ended up catching the ball."

Williams grinned from ear to ear and gestured across his chest in triumph. Making it to second, Aaron crossed back the infield near the mound. His and Holtzman's eyes met. No words were said and none needed to be as Hank's quizzical, puzzled look said it all. Something seemed up beyond the control of mortal men.

In the dugout though, we knew what was up. Holtzman put on his final baserunner immediately after the aborted Aaron blast. But after the inning, the dugout was so small there was no room to give Holtzman space, to keep a baseball-traditional distance from a pitcher flirting with a no-hitter. So he sat by his catcher, as per Durocher's instruction.

Holtzman pitched an uneventful eighth and then, going out for the ninth, our hearts dropped for a half-second when Kessinger and Young dodged a collision, with the former firmly hanging onto the ball. A grounder to Santo was a sure second out. Now came the duel of the season in baseball – Aaron vs. Holtzman for the no-hitter.

None could describe it better than Brickhouse, who is riveting even in print form with no audio or video here:

"We have one of the great confrontations of the season. One of the most dangerous hitters in modern baseball history…There's a strike, strike one…The crowd is going wild on every pitch…WGN Television, Channel 9…baseball, excitingly, importantly, dramatically yours on Channel 9…"

Holtzman ran the count to 3-and-1. That only heightened the heart-palpitating drama.

Oliver went to the mound and asked the lefty if he'd rather not tempt fate, and simply walk Aaron. His response: "If he gets a hit, he gets a hit."

Up in the booth, Brickhouse uttered what was on countless rooter's minds: "There are a lot of people here right now who'd rather see ball four than see him groove one."

Holtzman threw a strike. Aaron fouled it off. Brickhouse called Holtzman's strategy a demonstration of real pitching class to challenge Aaron on that pitch.

The announcer had called four previous no-hitters, three in Wrigley Field., but Aaron, who had 31 homers at the time, was all-time baseball royalty, so Brickhouse rode the wave with the full count as TV sets flicked on within the 75-mile signal range of WGN's tower in the pre-cable days:

"…41.033 just delirious, hysterical with their excitement…Here we go! Foul ball. Whoo, man!"

Holtzman wound up again on 3-and-2 with his 112th pitch and Aaron swung. The ball did not go in the air this time, but Brickhouse milked every microsecond.

"Ground ball. Beckert up with it…the throw to Banks…It's a no-hitter! It's a no-hitter for Kenny Holtzman! Look at this. Oh, brother! It's a no-hitter hitter for Kenny Holtzman…Whooo, boy!!! And the fans are streaming onto the field…The Andy Frain ushers and the police are having a terrible time trying to contain them!"

Hundley leaps for joy after Holtzman's no-hitter.

The last 3 strikes earned Aaron an everlasting admiration for Holtzman for pitching bravery.

"The most ironic thing about that day is I made the final out," Aaron said. "So Kenny was not afraid to pitch to me. He came right back and got me out for the last out."

In the first-base grandstand, completing his neat scorecard of the game, Fletcher was too far away to be tempted to dash onto the field. Like tens of thousands of others, he simply stood there, transfixed by the wild celebration just beginning.

"From my vantage point, it was clear that Santo would be the first Cubs player to mob Holtzman. Fans streaked out onto the field past the Andy Frains (ushers) and I saw Holtzman get grabbed by one fan who seemed like he was choking him," he said. The jubilant crowd stuck around for at least a half-hour as Fletcher secured his scorecard and headed for the exits to begin his long journey home to Glen Ellyn.

Santo gets the first Holtzman hug after the no-hitter.

Meanwhile, quick on his feet, Santo was first to reach an ecstatic Holtzman and tried to leap into his arms. Next was Kessinger, then Banks, and Beckert -- recovered from his somewhat-nervous scoop-and-throw on Aaron – who tried to go around to get into the mass bear-hug. Two young fans, one in a sleeveless undershirt, also arrived at the same time to join the celebration but did not quite get to Holtzman. Hundreds of feet away, scores of young men lowered themselves from the top of the bleacher wall and dashed toward the infield ahead of the ushers and Burns security police pouring out of the entrance to the cubbyhole clubhouse in the left-field corner. Hundreds of fans soon mobbed the infield. We did our best broken-field running to get to the cubbyhole clubhouse before the full cascade of fans swept toward Holtzman.

Brickhouse had touted that WGN announcers Lou Boudreau and Len Johnson, the latter subbing for Lloyd Pettit on TV, were going down on the field to interview Holtzman in the manner Vince Lloyd had done for Cardwell in 1960 and Boudreau and Pettit for the Reds' Jim Maloney exactly four years earlier, on August 19, 1965. Lloyd managed to snare Cardwell with Arne Harris, then an assistant director, with several Andy Frain ushers somehow holding back the celebrating mob. But once Cardwell made his escape, the pressing masses snapped Lloyd's mic cord.

But WGN would not get Holtzman this time. Too many celebrants covered the infield and Holtzman was trying to seek refuge.

"The reason I didn't do live TV or radio immediately after that game," Holtzman recalled, "was the police had me surrounded in the dugout runway to escape all the fans who had crashed the field. I later did all the interviews in the dressing room so there was only a slight delay,

Holtzman now had a distinction in post-1900 baseball history. He joined Earl Hamilton (1912 Browns) and Sad Sam Jones (1923 Yankees) as the only pitchers to toss a no-hitter with no strikeouts.

The lucky lefty now had time to breathe in the cubbyhole clubhouse. His post-game smile and tousled hair, recorded by newspaper photographers then admitted into the locker room, told the whole story. Without TV cameras present to pin him by his locker, he was surrounded by a relatively small group of writers. The emotional Santo put his arm around him to celebrate. I rubbed his arm with mine for good luck for the next day's start, as I often did with my rotation mates. But like the billy goat continually being brought onto the field from 1982 onward, the attempt at good fortune did not stick. I gave up five 5 runs on August 20 against the Braves in a 6-2 loss.

About the seventh inning of the no-hitter though, player agent Jack Childers, who had been in the clubhouse before the game, raced back from his north-suburban Skokie office when he heard Holtzman had a budding no-no. He arrived after the last out. Seeing dollars signs ringing up, he called the local Pontiac dealers association from the only phone in the cubbyhole. Equally keyed up by Holtzman's feat, the man on the other end of the line agreed to a deal: Holtzman would get a free Pontiac in exchange for an endorsement. Childers shouted the deal to players' rep Regan, who was astonished at the news of the free car. The Cubs subsequently contributed $1,000 to the players' endorsement pool in honor of the no-hitter.

Later, Childers projected the pool would benefit $30,000 as a result of the hitless gem. I don't know if that actually happened, and Holtzman does not specifically remember the Pontiac. Still only 23, he grew up just a bit keeping his pitching composure, retiring Aaron under withering pressure and performing in a World Series-level supercharged atmosphere that afternoon.

"Pitching in front of large crowds during that entire year helped me later on, ironically, when I had the opportunity to pitch in many World Series games (with the Oakland Athletics), Holtzman said. "I think I learned how to concentrate much better on the task at hand and tune out the crowd noise. This helped in those postseason games which are more intense and pressure-packed than any regular-season game."

As on July 2, 1967, when we momentarily tied for first place with the Cardinals, most of the overflow house simply stayed put to soak up the supercharged atmosphere.

"The jubilant crowd stuck around for at least a half-hour," said Fletcher. No one would be especially late for dinner except those who stopped in at watering holes like Ray's Bleachers to stretch out the euphoria. Holtzman had done his deed in an even two hours starting from the 1:30 p.m. first pitch.

Fletcher had a lot to talk about hours later with parents Archie and Dottie, and siblings Sally and Tom. He no doubt chatted up the no-hitter with home-bound commuters pressing for details on his three trains.

"I secured my scorecard and headed for the exits to begin my long journey home to Glen Ellyn," he recalled of his happy self. The scorecard remains in mint condition after a half century.

"As a young sports editor for the Glenbard West High School paper, I got to interview Williams in 1971 in Glen Ellyn about 'The Catch,'" Fletcher said. "As he has retold countless times since my interview, Williams said he stayed with the ball, despite the fact it was seemingly a sure homer. 'The ball was already at least four or five rows in the bleachers as I continued to wait. Thank God the baskets had not been installed yet or that ball would have gone into the basket.'"

Anyone around the Cubs looked at the no-hitter as a positive omen, a positive portent. Higher powers were credited for taking our side. But sometimes a "go" sign is a big tease.

After they wrapped up their WGN broadcast amid the bedlam, Brickhouse and sports editor Rosenberg no doubt mentioned where they might be the first weekend of October – Wrigley Field along with Atlanta or one of several other NL West contenders in the race at the time.

"All I know is that on August 19, 1969, Holtzman, who was a strikeout pitcher, didn't strike out anybody in a no-hitter," said Rosey. "At the time, I thought this team was in. You can build anything you want in it. Baseball is known for teams that have streaks, and then fade, and how do you explain it?

"That's why you never take anything for granted in baseball – or in life."

Dirt from the fans...

"The highlights I'll always recall from 1969: hearing the public-address announcer, Pat Pieper, say, "Tention, 'tention please, have your pencil and scorecard ready and I will give you the correct lineup for today's ballgame;" Fergie Jenkins pitching inside, just as meaningful as Nolan Ryan, Don Drysdale, or Bob Gibson; Ernie Banks being a joy to se;e and Billy Williams being spectacular as the glue that kept them together; and finally, Ronnie Santo being so upbeat he made the clouds go away on an overcast day.

-Lennie Rubenstein, Indianapolis

Allies Among The
Ink-Stained Wretches

Who in the 21st Century would consider baseball beat writers an extension of the team they cover? I'd suspect you'd get a blanket "no" as a response.

The world has turned since 1969. Then, most Cubs' players believed the scribes, who had been nicknamed "ink-stained wretches," were part of the ballclub. With access unthinkable in the hyper-controlled-and-choreographed access world of a half-century later, where at-home media just have a 45-minute pre-batting practice window to talk to us, both ballplayers and writers in '69 had plenty of opportunities to really get to know each other. I think Chicago Tribune writer George Langford's rapport with Ernie Banks on personal issues was at a depth Mr. Cub did not even share with me, his road roommate, as a prime example of the relationships possible in that era.

Even with the platforms of WGN-Radio's booming 50,000-watt, clear-channel signal covering every game and sister WGN-TV airing 144 contests, newspapers were still the primary way fans followed us in '69. And we had an advantage compared to all other big-league teams in how we were personalized and thus popularized in print coverage. Chicago was the only two-team market of the four in existence – then and now – where one team played all its home games during the deadline friendly day while the other played at night. For teams playing after dark, writers scrambled to get the play-by-play of game accounts, sprinkled with quotes for the final newsstand editions.

Such a huge advantage in publicity was best summed up by Tribune columnist David Condon, remembering Sam "Toothpick" Jones' no-hitter against the Pittsburgh Pirates at Wrigley Field on May 12, 1955. Since the contest was a day game, Condon recalled he had the luxury of a number of hours before his home-delivery edition deadline to track down Jim "Hippo" Vaughn, the last Cub to have thrown a no-hitter in Chicago in 1917. Had the Jones hitless gem been tossed at night, Condon would not have been able to reach Vaughn in time.

Much of the tension between writers and the Cubs in '69 revolved around Leo Durocher. A controversial and acerbic personality like The Lip was needed to put teeth into what was described in 1969 – and many decades later – as softer-than-average local sports media. The scribes were much gentler than their tougher counterparts in Boston, New York, and Philadelphia. No Ted Williams character flipping off the writers had come to Chicago by '69. The sometimes flamboyant, sometimes stoic but always "star" personalities, like the Dave Kingmans, Albert Belles, and Milton Bradleys of the world, respectively, wouldn't arrive in Chicago until a decade or more later.

In his controversial career coming into Chicago, Durocher had innumerable conflicts with those Eastern Seaboard writers. He was no media politician unless it suited his business interests to do so. As the years wore on in Chicago, Durocher simply got older and more crotchety with the traveling writers, and even more conflict erupted. But in the clubhouse, you did not have any Cubs players zipping their lips or outright flipping off the media in the manner of slugger Dave Kingman, hard-throwing reliever Antonio Alfonseca or moody outfielder Milton Bradley in later decades.

In 1969, the four traveling writers from the pair of downtown Chicago morning and afternoon dailies each traveled with us on our chartered flights and team buses from airports and hotels. I thought that arrangement was really good. Present-day media are on the clock, observed by team media-relations personnel, when they talk with a player in the clubhouse – or if lucky on the bench -- to get in-depth material instead of quickie quotes. We had the advantage of those hours-long plane rides, lubricated if necessary by drinks, to chat with the writers in a far more relaxed manner.

All the time, writers would come up to you in the usually cramped locker rooms throughout the National League to ask if we had more time on the plane to talk. Once airborne, we'd speak of our performance goals or our expectations for the upcoming series. There was no time limit with the locker room closing – only the plane landing and maybe the spigot being turned off on final approach. But by the early 1990s, the writers were unwelcome on team flights and the steady decline in media access began.

What I said was for publication, on the plane or in the locker room. I was not an off-the-record guy. Neither was someone like closer Phil Regan. When I was asked years later, as Cubs pitching coach, if he threw "Vaseline balls" during his pitching days, Regan said, "I don't talk off the record."

Overall, it was a good era for player-writer relations. The player trusted whoever was doing the story. Otherwise, it was a face-to-face confrontation if you were misquoted. You'd see the writers the next day and they didn't want that hassle.

One qualification was necessary though for the scribes – getting along with clubhouse chief Yosh Kawano. The locker room, especially the broom closet at home, was his domain. Yosh did not like a lot of people crowding in, so staying on his good side was a good talent to possess.

But while our quotes were important in boosting our popularity with fans, they were, in relative contrast, a new innovation in baseball writing. Through the mid-1960s, game stories for all editions were typically play-by-play from start to finish. If anything really important or a robust personal performance took place, it was broken off into a "sidebar" or supplementary story.

When Adolfo Phillips slugged four homers in a June 11, 1967, Wrigley Field doubleheader, Jerome Holtzman's Chicago Sun-Times game story did not feature any Phillips' quotes. He segregated Phillips' comments into a sidebar. Holtzman, later called "The Dean" of baseball writers, was a late convert to the quotes' style. But with TV increasingly expanding its sportscasts on half-hour news shows and radio reporters beginning to work their way into the locker room, the predominant print end of baseball reporting had to keep up with the times by personalizing players and managers.

About the only time the stories did not feature quotes was a "getaway" day on the road. Since the writers traveled on our buses and planes, they had to make our departure from the ballpark. Durocher surely was not going to hold the bus for a tardy writer. They were forced to do an old-style play-by-play story and had to allow time to hand off to a Western Union teletype operator, who would retype the story for transmission to their home offices. Again, in the pre-computer days, there was no instantaneous transfer of text from press box laptops to faraway copy desks.

As we roared off to a fast start in 1969, the newspapers cleared out plenty of prime space for us every day. The Tribune and Sun-Times were the big blowtorch morning dailies, each with a huge reach of at least 600,000 daily circulation, even more on Sundays. Already in decline but still influential for baseball fans were the afternoon tabloid Chicago Today (owned by Tribune Company) and the prestigious Chicago Daily News (owned by Sun-Times parent Field Enterprises). The Today folded in 1974 and the Daily News in 1978.

All the papers put out multiple editions per day, framed around our games, with varying kinds of coverage. Avid fans waited for the "sports finals" of the morning papers, going to press around 1 a.m. or so. These editions went to bed late enough to not only have a complete account with quotes of our day games and road night games, but also the West Coast box scores. But the quotes were important and a relatively new innovation in baseball writing.

The quotes were important, and a relatively new innovation in baseball writing.

Those impatient for these final editions could get earlier versions home-delivered or even read them the previous night in "bulldog" papers coming out at the end of the evening rush hour. The 'bulldogs' featured a play-by-play account, but with no quotes, of our home day games. Otherwise, they'd contain either an old story of the previous day's night road game or a preview of the following after-dark contest. The "green streak 'bulldog" would appear around dinnertime Sundays, back in the day, editions shipped out to our far-flung fans throughout the Midwest for next-morning consumption.

The deadlines of the afternoon papers permitted a more in-depth, feature-like account of our lives as ballplayers. The first editions of the afternoon papers – the 5-Star Final in Today and Blue Streak for the Daily News – had deadlines around dawn, permitting their beat writers not to perform a rush job on a Cubs night game. These deadlines especially came in handy for West Coast games. The writers had hours to craft quotes and observations into a feature-like story and even more time after a day game, home or road. These initial editions got the same out-of-market circulation to Peoria and beyond as the morning papers' 'bulldogs.'

The final editions of the "PM" papers – Green Streak for Today and Red Streak for the Daily News – were both timed for the stock-market close at 3 p.m. Central time, or for the Eastern horse-racing results. That permitted pre-game news woven into shreds of the earlier feature-like story and a partial line score of the game. On 1969 afternoons, local sports fanatics would mob red-colored Daily News trucks before the newsstand operator could get to unload them when they delivered Red Streaks..

All but the Today had an age-old tradition in 1969. The papers rotated their writers between the Cubs and White Sox at each All-Star break. The rotated scribes would cover the second half of the season, then spring training and first half of the next season. Only James Enright of Today, about a 25-year Chicago baseball-beat veteran, stayed with us the entire season.

Langford began the year at the Tribune, then handed off to Richard Dozer, whose tenure dated back to the late 1950s. For the Sun-Times, Holtzman – elevated to baseball in 1957 -- switched off to Edgar Munzel, the most senior of the writers, with service dating back to 1929. Munzel, then 62, threw out the first pitch prior to the 1969 home opener in honor of his 40th anniversary on the beat. Meanwhile, comparative newcomer Ray Sons of the Daily News yielded to George Vass for the stretch run.

I got along pretty well with Enright, who would come to be a Durocher antagonist. He had covered Banks his entire career and became a real good friend of his. Enright came to your locker prior to games and after games to see how you felt and how you'd pitch against specific teams and hitters. He wrote what you told him and put it the way you said it. No writers used recorders at this point, and amazingly, Enright didn't write his notes in shorthand. He wrote in longhand.

Enright already had been a legend as a basketball referee. He even was pulled away from Cubs spring training to officiate at an important Big Eight game. Retiring from the hardwood before he could see me play for the Harlem Globetrotters, Enright eventually co-authored Banks' first book, "Mr. Cub," in 1971. Eighteen years earlier, before the Cubs purchased Banks from the Kansas City Monarchs, Enright also wrote in the Chicago American, the Today's predecessor paper, about the lack of promotion to the majors for Gene Baker, who would eventually be Banks' double-play partner with the Cubs: "Why are the Cubs delaying a move to bring up Gene Baker, Los Angeles shortstop? Is it because the 28-year-old Negro isn't ready--or are there other reasons?" Had the Cubs promoted Baker, in their system since 1950, during that time, they might not have signed fellow shortstop Banks.

After Today folded, Enright stayed a part of the daily Wrigley Field scene. He succeeded legendary PA announcer Pat Pieper, who died after the 1974 season. Enright took over for the next seven seasons, but was memorable for the wrong reasons. One malaprop was announcing shortstop Ivan DeJesus as "Ivan De-GEESUS."

Meanwhile, Vanderbilt product Langford, whose assistance with this book is welcomed, was a big believer in going into the locker room for quotes. Just 30 in 1969, Langford built great relationships with players. He was so much a part of the regular scene at Wrigley Field by 1969 that Durocher asked him to be an extra in his Schlitz TV commercial, Stricter ethics in coming years would have prevented Langford from appearing in a commercial with the manager.

Dozer was an underrated guy for scoops on what Langford called a very competitive beat. Back in late May, 1964, Dozer reported that Lou Brock was being shopped for a St. Louis Cardinals pitcher, who turned out to be Ernie Broglio when the deal actually was completed, on June 15. He had beaten everyone else by a country mile.

Meanwhile, Holtzman was distinctive in a number of different ways. He probably was the roughest-cut of any of the scribes. I remember Holtzman with his bad breath and cigar, which I'm sure were related. He'd get up in your face with a cigar in one hand and he'd be writing with the other. Langford, who eventually hired Holtzman when the former became Tribune sports editor in the early 1980s, admired his reporting style. Holtzman would ask a seemingly stupid, disarming question in a group of writers. When that group dispersed, Holtzman would circle around and come back to the player one-on-one to get an inside-baseball angle. I witnessed that tactic, where he'd come at you with different, more-informed questions.

Holtzman could also have been the most combative of the beat men. After one game in 1969, he and Durocher got into a heated dispute and a fight seemed in the offing. Former World War II Marine Holtzman refused to back off and Durocher fortunately cooled down. Holtzman eventually was inducted into the writers' wing of the Hall of Fame. After retirement from the Tribune, he became baseball's first official historian under Commissioner Bud Selig.

Holtzman thus joined Munzel in Cooperstown. Named to the writer's wing in 1977, Munzel was just about the lowest-key writer in the group, with his nickname as "Mouse" thus deserved. He was real quiet and to the point. Munzel wanted to hear what your thoughts were. He did not want to pick your brain. He just wanted the basic quotes.

With more time to do his Daily News stories, Vass, by contrast, was able to get a little more personal with his quotes. I developed a good relationship with him. One time, Vass came out to my house for a feature and had his photographer snap photos of my daughters. After my sixth straight 20-win season in 1972, Vass co-authored "Like Nobody Else," my first book. He later co-authored "The Cubs Encyclopedia," with Holtzman.

Today, with quotes and up-close-and-personal looks at us now mandatory, the four newspapers' columnists could not afford to just sit back in the press box and pull opinions out of their nether regions. They also had to come down to the clubhouses, but two distinctive columnists who were personally White Sox fans stood out.

The portly Condon, the Tribune's lead columnist and successor to All-Star Game conceiver Arch Ward, writing "In the Wake of the News," was the stereotype of the old-time sportswriter. Condon liked me. A lot of times while he blew his cigar smoke your way, he'd come into the clubhouse, never with his tie on and usually as a kind-of-sloppy dresser. Of course, as a regular at the Billy Goat Tavern, Condon was a mainstay in promoting the myth of the billy goat curse touched off by our team.

Another certified member of the cigar columnist crowd was the Sun-Times' Bill Gleason, who on several occasions proclaimed, "All Cubs fans come from Peoria because that's where their broadcasters (Jack Brickhouse, Jack Quinlan and Vince Lloyd) come from." Gleason wrote some great stories about me and I really liked him. He phoned me a lot at night to just get a personal side from me, I think. We thought we'd get together to write a book, but Vass ended up with that assignment.

Although Today columnist Rick Talley ended up renowned for his conflict with Durocher, refusing to name him in his copy and calling the manager "Whatshisname" instead, he had little to do with me. Talley did not get a lot of quotes from pitchers because, for some reason, he went to the everyday players. He acquired the nickname "Rick The Ripper." A self-professed Cubs' fan from southern Illinois, Talley ended up penning The Cubs of '69, the first book on our team, on the 20th anniversary in 1989.

You'll notice that the list of writers and columnists is all male, as the thought of a female baseball writer in 1969 was close to science fiction. But one day in June, Linda Morstadt, the sole female writer for Chicago Today sports, was assigned Cubs coverage and so Morstadt appeared on the field. A ladies man, often crudely, off the field, Durocher reacted with near-horror. "What? A broad covering sports? Some of the men are bad enough. Tell her to get off the field. I don't want her distracting my ballplayers."

Veteran broadcaster Red Mottlow encountered some of the resistance experienced by Morstadt, but for different reasons. His tools of the trade were different than the writers, as he had the ability to get post-game interviews from players on the air for Top 40 rocker WCFL-Radio, many hours before the writers' first stories with quotes came out. And so, the writers did not want broadcasters sitting among them. "I had to talk to the writers to let the radio guys sit in the press box," said Chuck Shriver, the 1969 Cubs media relations director.

Mottlow, who had recreated baseball games via Western Union ticker in both Minneapolis and Chicago in the 1950s, thus became a regular in Wrigley Field in the late 1960s. Overall, Mottlow was the first man to bring a tape recorder into the locker rooms for Chicago sports events. He once had George Halas all to himself at Bears practice. Red thus mimicked the legendary Howard Cosell, who had been the recording ice breaker a decade previously in New York.

Although Regan as 1969 player rep began setting a price for recorded interviews of any length, Mottlow broke through that defense. I did not mind radio interviews – I wouldn't be misquoted. And Mottlow knew his Cubs baseball. The Marshall High School alum on Chicago's West Side had attended one of Dizzy Dean's first starts as a Cub in 1938. Twenty years later, he watched from his bleacher-seat perch as Stan Musial slashed his 3,000th hit against Cubs' reliever Moe Drabowsky.

Mottlow was still the only radio man on duty when Ken Holtzman began spinning his strikeout-free no-hitter on August 19, 1969. Brad Palmer of WBBM-Radio raced to the ballpark for game's end when he heard the hitless gem unfolding. Mottlow's big challenge was not getting our sound bites – it was delivering them on-air, on-time. He did not yet have the ability to feed the tape via phone to WCFL. But Mottlow had to hope the game ended before 4:30 because he had several routes to knife through rush-hour traffic to get back downtown to the station's studios at on the Near North Side's Marina City and get his engineer to rack up his tape for his 5:45 sportscasts.

Mottlow had no Shriver as an advocate in New York. Properly credentialed by the New York Mets for the fateful September 8-9, 1969 series at Shea Stadium, Mottlow was barred from sitting in the main press box by writer Jack Lang, head of the New York chapter of the Baseball Writers Association of America. "This is my press box," Lang proclaimed to Mottlow, who simply took a seat elsewhere and dutifully covered the games. Eventually, he got an assigned press box seat, covering the Cubs through 2002 until shortly before his death at 76, and co-hosting Castle's "Diamond Gems" baseball radio show.

While Mottlow was a Wrigley Field regular, TV crews wanting your thoughts weren't as common each day. The clubhouse was so small it could not accommodate a reporter, camera operator, light man and soundman, the complement of each station's' crew. They typically had to record us out on the field. We got paid for our WGN pre- and post-game appearances, so we also believed we'd get some kind of compensation for filmed interviews. The Reds' Jim Maloney had asked TV sportscaster Jim Brosnan, his former Cincinnati teammate, for $25 for a requested interview after his August 19, 1965 no-hitter against the Cubs at Wrigley. Me? My comment was, "Are you taking me out to dinner?" I never asked them for money, but eventually we got accustomed to the camera crews and did not request compensation.

One man accompanying WGN film crews from time to time was Wendell Smith. We were happy to intersect with history via Wendell. He had accompanied Jackie Robinson as his "Boswell" throughout baseball during his breakthrough 1947 season. Wendell was barred from press boxes, so he was forced to set up his typewriter in the grandstands. Yet he followed Jackie as a barrier-breaker. In 1948, Wendell moved to Chicago as a sportswriter with the old Chicago Herald-American (which had evolved into Today in 1969). He also became the first African-American member of the Baseball Writers Association of America. Brickhouse, always advancing the image of players of color on WGN, hired Smith as a sports reporter on the station, thus doubling his newspaper salary in 1964. Within three years, Smith was the first regular African-American on a 10 p.m. news program in Chicago.

Smith also doubled writing a weekly Sun-Times column with a lot of baseball angles in 1969. I remember talking to him a few times, knowing his history all along. He'd ask good sports-related questions and I'm happy Smith got the exposure he deserved with thousands changing the channel to WGN in time for the Cubs highlights he narrated around 10:20 p.m. He'd join Holtzman and Munzel in the Hall of Fame's writers wing. Unfortunately, like his old traveling companion Robinson, Wendell never saw old age. He died of pancreatic cancer at 58 on November 26, 1972, just a month after Robinson's seemingly premature death at 53.

Smith and his sportswriting and broadcast colleagues would not have earned present-day athletes' trust in the way we did, which was unfortunate. They were our conduit to the fans and we benefited from their coverage. You can't really say the same about a modern blogger who doesn't have direct contact with the players. Opinions are a sugar fix of a dessert, but perspective and relationships are really the protein-laden main course in how fans consume baseball and other sports.

As we embarked on an 11-game home stand that began with Holtzman's no-hitter on August 19, the writers with whom we were close began asking questions and writing about our physical and mental states. We couldn't answer them to their satisfaction – and Durocher flatly would not.

We Played 'Til We Dropped –
By Our Choice

You might say on many sunny, blisteringly hot summer days in 1969, the perfect storm had arrived at Wrigley Field.

On one hand, we had a manager who felt withering pressure to win it all with the best team in the National League. Leo Durocher also was first among supposed equals in Cubs management, a rascal/charmer who held a Svengali-type hold over owner Phil Wrigley. Straight out of old-school baseball central casting, Durocher ruled with an iron fist and a resolute verbal put-down for failure or malingering, or even personally risqué behavior he'd consider child's play for himself. He had the almost unanimous support of the Cubs Universe, in other words, all the fans throughout the Midwest and beyond thirsting for a pennant after a 24-year dry spell.

All the while, Durocher may have subtly become more conservative and even lost his best mental "fastball" compared to, say, 1967. He would not experiment with new concepts, such as Mets Manager Gil Hodges did with a five-man starting rotation, two late-inning relievers and use of a bench to counteract weaknesses in some lineup regulars.

On the other hand, Durocher had a ready, willing and supposedly able batting order and rotation. I expected to go 9 innings and so did Bill Hands. Lefty Ken Holtzman wanted his complete game wins while fourth starter Dick Selma volunteered to pitch with two days' rest in August. Phil Regan thought he had a rubber arm in the bullpen. '

Bill Hands on the play.

193

The joy of Ron Santo.

Meanwhile, outfielder Billy Williams had no intention, just yet, of breaking his National League record consecutive games-played streak, begun in 1963, that would reach 1,000 in a row in 1970. With only one exception, a week off in 1966 due to a beaning that fractured his cheekbone, team captain Ron Santo played at least 160 games each season since 1962, in spite of dealing daily with Type 1 diabetes. And remember, we had a beloved Ernie Banks, whose catch phrase, even at 38, was "Let's play two." Mr. Cub once had a 717 consecutive games-played streak, played in 163 games at 34 in 1965 and logged at least 150 games in each of the 1967 and 1968 seasons, as Father Time crept up on him.

Randy Hundley had set the major-league record of 160 games as a catcher in 1968. He never asked out of catching doubleheader and was a bear straining at the bit on the bench if he somehow sat out. Don Kessinger played 160 games in 1968. Only a broken thumb in the spring of '69 prevented Glenn Beckert from reaching Kessinger's workload. All of us remembered the challenges of making the majors and winning a job, whether it was in the days of talent backed up to Class D ball or under taskmaster Durocher. If work was offered, work was gladly accepted. And now there was a pennant to win.

"They hustled, they played hard," recalled Jim Colborn, a rookie pitcher in '69. "This wasn't a coasting-type team."

Only Banks was aging. Williams was the second oldest, having just turned 31 on June 15, 1969. The others were what could be called "young veterans" in their primes – Santo was 29, Beckert 28, Kessinger and Hundley 27 by mid-season.

Lean and lanky with hardly an ounce of body fat to give up during the heat of the season, Kessinger spoke for Durocher's core with this remembrance, even with the hindsight of 50 years:

"Would I like to have some days off? Answer is no. I wanted to win a pennant. If Leo had come to me and asked if I wanted a day of rest, I'd say no. That's the way all of our guys felt. We felt we were the best team in the league."

Double-play partner Beckert recreated the tenor of the times, not only on the Cubs, but with most other big-league teams:

"Back then, there was a feeling in baseball if you weren't in the lineup playing, your job was in jeopardy. It's not like today where players take for granted they're going to be rested. If your name wasn't in the lineup, you went up to the manager and asked why am I not playing today? There was a different atmosphere. Only a manager who didn't have the talent in the starting lineup used backups. The Mets had great pitching, but they didn't have the talent we had at the everyday positions. And that's why they utilized everybody on their team. They had to. The Cubs had a set lineup and so did other teams in that league."

Santo and Williams were the true ironmen of all position players with all those 160 game-plus campaigns. They even went to the extreme of playing 164 games in 1965, when two games were called due to ties and not resumed from the point of suspension, as per the rules of the time. The pair of contests were replayed from the start and Santo and Williams played in both. Looking around the NL, only a handful of stars endured multiple 160-or-more game schedules. The Cardinals' Curt Flood and the Reds' Tony Perez each logged a pair, to their everlasting credit in the brutal heat and humidity of St. Louis and Cincinnati.

Our pitchers largely were of the same mindset. Remember, the front end of the staff was leaned on heavily by Durocher. The back end, via lefty Rich Nye and three to four other relievers, cried for work. The latter group, in my opinion, would have adhered to the old axiom, "Put me in coach, I wanna' play."

At the time, I don't think any of the regular players or starting pitchers were thinking about being overused or wanting days off," said southpaw starter Holtzman. "We were in first place the whole year and we couldn't wait for the next game to begin in front of (big crowds) every day. Of course, the playing of day games all the time has to take something extra out of any player and we were no exception. Leo went with the players who got us into that position and he was reluctant to make any changes, a sentiment that we all agreed with at the time."

The likes of Kessinger and Beckert, logging extra at-bats at the top of the order, both have said through the decades they had challenges adjusting to different sleep and meal times going from all-day games at Wrigley Field to many night games on the road. Santo could set a routine for insulin injections and regular mealtimes for his Type 1 diabetes at home, yet had a constant battle for physical stability with managing the illness with the changing schedules on the road.

And don't underestimate the impact of cramped facilities at Wrigley Field. Our cubbyhole locker room was smaller than the visitors' clubhouse at then 3-year-old Busch Stadium in St. Louis. We had to walk down the left-field line to get to the locker room in mid-game from our cozy dugout, which could not comfortably accommodate all the players. We did not exactly have a decent lunch to stoke our blood sugar for long afternoon labors. Remember, in this era, we also took infield practice after the visitors' batting practice. With less free pre-game time, we could have benefited from some more spacious facilities.

We had no shortened work days, as manager Joe Maddon imposed for his Cubs starting in 2015. Maddon's canceling of mandatory batting practice so players could sleep-in proved to have a positive effect on the Cubs' strong second halves in three consecutive seasons that extended at least into the National League Championship Series. Of course, the Holy Grail was achieved in that long-awaited World Series title in 2016 we thought was in our sights 47 years previously.

Recriminations have haunted the 1969 Cubs for a half-century about tiring players in the stretch and Durocher refusing to enforce any rest, starting with Hundley and moving to Kessinger and beyond. Later, out of the heat of battle, Durocher realized he erred badly. He remarked if he knew we were dog-tired, he'd have thrown nine pitchers into the lineup. But, every day, the packed Wrigley Field houses clamored for more Cub Power and long-delayed gratification from their matinee idols. The "magic number" ticked down into the low 30s, and then descended into the 20s. Any consequences beyond winning that day, that inning were put on the back burner of manager and players.

Performing a forensic examination of the 1969 season, we'd find all wasn't as recalled or stereotyped, although not every player overtly wilted. Hundley did not backslide from season-long overwork, but from coming back too quickly from a hospitalization. Modern measuring sticks available online show if anything, our pitching – so effective overall going into late August – faltered the most and likely was mishandled by Durocher and pitching coach Joe Becker, in my opinion, carrying out his orders.

With his handling of the players, Durocher felt crushing expectations to win.

"Leo definitely felt the pressure," said then-Chicago Tribune beat writer George Langford. "The Cubs hadn't won for forever. Being in a position to win was natural pressure." After moving players around in 1966 and continuing to experiment with pitchers through 1967, he now had a lineup of the NL's best players at their positions, a Big Three starting rotation and a two-time Fireman of the Year closer. To be sure, he had holes in center and right, and little flow of big-league ready players from the Cubs minor-league system to fill them. But in Durocher's mind, he'd ride his talented regulars to the World Series.

The contrast of Durocher handling players in his grab-bag first year and the sudden solidification of 1967 was best described by Hundley, a chief beneficiary of the manager's trust in his core of position players and pitchers:

"You knew he was in charge. My first year with him, he drove me nuts. I thought man alive, if this is the big leagues, I don't know if I want this. I feared the guy. As a rookie catcher, it was my fault for everything the pitchers did wrong. But it was a tremendous learning year.

"My second year, he turned me loose. He depended on me to be his manager on the field, to handle the pitchers and move the fielders around. He put me on automatic pilot behind the plate. I loved it."

Mind you, Durocher had been no ironman shortstop of the Cal Ripken Jr. mold. His top games-played season total was 146 in a 154-game season with the 1934 Cardinals. In 13 seasons as a regular or semi-regular, he exceeded 140 games played just three other times. But the ole gambler felt he played a good hand with prime talent. He did not have to move players around, as on the 1951 and 1954 Giants, when he carefully kept a colorful clutch hitter like Dusty Rhodes away from lefty pitching.

However, he morphed into a more-stodgy manager by '69, comforted by a set lineup with some of his daring younger days likely tempered by age and health. As Dodgers third-base coach seven years earlier, he had seen the transformation of the game, waving around a Maury Wills, who had just destroyed Ty Cobb's stolen-base record with 106. LA offered additional speedsters like Willie Davis to steal runs and set the table for RBI men like Tommy Davis and Frank Howard.

But Durocher offered up a hint of LA-style base-paths derring-do through his first two seasons. He let Adolfo Phillips steal 56 bases in 1966-67. But he pulled in the reins severely by 1968 and 1969. The team stolen-base totals dropped from 76 in 1966, 60 in 1967, 41 in 1968 and just 30 in 1969. The 1967 sights of a Ted Savage stealing home, followed by an unsuccessful theft of the same destination by Phillips, would not be repeated the next two seasons, even as speed became mandated with bigger, multi-purpose road ballparks and the advent of artificial turf. Yet, Durocher's strategy devolved to a pre-Wills thinking of not taking the bat out of the hands of big hitters with a risky theft attempt.

As the Cubs showed they were firmly on the rise, he gave an indication how he'd work his roster during the marathon Labor Day weekend of four consecutive doubleheaders in '67.

Durocher started Kessinger, Beckert, Williams, Santo and Banks (one through five) and Phillips (batting eighth) in all eight games. Hundley started seven of the contests, but came in to catch the final three innings, replacing backup Johnny Stephenson, in Game 2, a 5-4 loss to the Mets on Saturday, September 2. Work was offered without a break by Durocher to his regulars, and work was gladly accepted in spite of the brutal schedule that has not been repeated since.

Six weeks earlier, on July 23, 1967, the regulars' attitude toward asking out of the lineup for a breather under taskmaster Durocher was best summed up by Hundley. Not quite yet the ironman receiver, the Rebel admitted: "Maybe having a little less energy…but don't you go saying I'm tired. That gets back to the 'skip' and he might not let me play."

Periodically over the next two seasons, various Cubs – including the consecutive-games streak-building Williams – admitted to mid-season fatigue, but the statements prompted no follow-up. Hundley's 160-games-played record was considered more a mark of distinction and dedication by the budding team leader. Unlike Johnny Bench, who sometimes played doubleheaders but often moved to third or left for the nightcap to keep his bat in the lineup, Hundley dutifully stayed behind the plate to handle his pitchers, no matter how dog-tired he'd become. The only noticeable plan of resting a regular was not playing Banks in a day game after a night game. But at 38, Banks still played doubleheaders. After seeing Durocher trying to unsuccessfully replace him, Mr. Cub was not asking out of the lineup.

The issue of a fatigued ballclub in 1969 actually was first raised after the All-Star break when Durocher came under pressure to play his regulars in the annual mid-summer Cubs-White Sox Boys Benefit charity exhibition game scheduled for Monday night, August 18, at old Comiskey Park. We were flying back from a two-week Houston/West Coast road trip, with an off-day at home on August 18. Durocher stated he'd keep Kessinger, Beckert, Williams, Santo, Banks and Hundley completely away from the South Side ballpark for a full off-day at home.

Still, pressure mounted for at least cameo appearances for all the Cubs stars in front of the expected huge crowd. Facing a daily near-empty ballpark for his floundering team, Sox owner Arthur Allyn roasted Durocher for the projected absence of Cubs stars. Two days before the game, Durocher relented, the regulars made their starts, played 4 innings and Banks and Williams homered as the Cubs won 2-0. Many Cubs fans were thus thrilled in the turnout of 33,333, more than double the size of the largest regular-season home Sox crowd of '69. Allyn had recalled how as many as 52,000 had shown up, in 1964, for the benefit game, and thus craved the star power his own team could not provide. Some $72,500 was raised for youth baseball in Chicago from the August 18 event.

Given what was percolating, Durocher might have simply taken the heat and let the team's core stay at home with their families with a day game the next day at Wrigley Field. The boys could have used maybe a week off, but revving up in his hottest month ever, Jim Hickman was holding the Cubs up almost single-handedly in August. The team had not scored more than 4 runs a game since August 6 in Houston. Hickman and good pitching had kept the team afloat through the often-run-starved West Coast swing.

Gentleman Jim carried the weight.

On the second-to-last day of the road trip in San Francisco, utility infielder Paul Popovich got his 7th pinch-hit in 13 at-bats to help me notch my 17th win and seventh shutout of the season. He batted more than .300 with the Cubs in his best offensive season since coming over from the Expos in the Adolfo Phillips trade two months earlier, as he was equally adept defensively at second, third and shortstop. "The big thing is the confidence Leo has shown me," Popovich said after the August 16 game. "And all of sudden, I'm confident, too. Sure, I'd rather be playing every day. But when you're battling to get in an All-Star infield, you can't feel too badly about it."

Popovich's availability, and lack of use, eventually attracted the attention of Wendell Smith in his weekly Chicago Sun-Times column on September 2, 1969. The in-studio narrator of our taped highlights six nights a week on WGN-TV's 10 p.m. news, Smith knew a good story. After all, he was Jackie Robinson's traveling Boswell and minder in 1947.

"Sometimes it is very easy to identify a utility man from the regulars," Wendell wrote. "His complexion, compared to the every-day player's, has a pallor similar to a penitentiary inmate's. (Popovich) is neither frustrated nor weird. He waits in the wings, anxious to play third, second or shortstop. The durability of Ron Santo, Don Kessinger and Glenn Beckert can be exasperating at times, but he has trained himself to be patient. It's like his (West Virginia) daddy said: 'It sure beats the coal mines.'"

Like fellow utility infielder Nate "Pee Wee" Oliver, who filled in for an injured Beckert earlier in the season, the Popovich of August, 1969, had to wait with the patience of Job for his pinch-hit chances and maybe late-game defensive duty in a double switch. He even logged a cameo appearance in center field in a double-switch on July 26, the day Durocher went AWOL to see his step-son at Camp Ojibwa. There would be no starts to switch up the lineup through the hitting lull, even with Popovich's .347 overall average (35-for-101) with the Cubs and Dodgers in '69, through August 16.

Oliver, meanwhile, had been a lifelong bench guy from his days with the Dodgers. He understood the concept of regulars doing anything to stay in the lineup. A younger player without Oliver's perspective would have had more difficulty understanding grabbing some bench day after day. Oliver could daily commiserate with Willie Smith as a Hyde Park roommate, "Cub Power" singing partner about their roles coming off the bench – if at all.

"There was never a thought or consideration about resting anybody," said Oliver, who got into 44 games with 49 plate appearances after coming over from the Yankees in late April 1969. Oliver previously had spent two years with third-base coach Durocher in Los Angeles in 1963-64.

"It was not tough to accept. In every walk of life, everybody does things different. That was Leo's style. He was a great asset to us.

"It was just like any other baseball job. If you had no specific assignment, you still needed to be prepared. Do your early work, and just prepare like we were going to start."

Popovich, Oliver and the rest of the overlooked bench-warmers dutifully did their work as the lineup remained unchanged during the August offensive lull. And the Cubs regulars weren't the only ones working every day without a break, as the newspaper beat writers covered every game of the hitting slumber. The Chicago Tribune's Richard Dozer began putting it all together. Always underrated for his reporting and sourcing, compared to the Chicago Sun-Times' more-celebrated Jerome Holtzman, Dozer put two and two together after the 8-2 loss on Friday, August 22, as we got just 4 hits off Astros starter Larry Dierker. While Durocher was shaving in his office, Dozer asked Durocher, "Are you going to rest any of the players in view of the fact the club's not hitting?"

Half-shaved, Durocher put down his razor, led the assembled beat writers out of his office and into our cubbyhole clubhouse and remarked, "Don't ask me – ask the players those silly questions. Here, let's go in and ask them. All you guys, ask the players if they need a rest."

The manager then acted like a commandant rousting a POW camp: "I want all my players out here. Turn off the showers! Come on in here!"

Durocher then turned to Dozer and barked: "You said to me, 'Are you going to rest anybody on this club?' Now don't ask me, ask the players."

None of us in the cubbyhole locker room or showers knew just what was transpiring. George Vass of the Chicago Daily News described our stunned reaction to Dozer's forced question as "bewildered silence." If none of the regulars would admit to Durocher their tiredness, they certainly would not publicly confess to a writer. After Durocher marched back to his office to complete his shaving, Williams did take Dozer aside for some one-on-one truth-telling. After playing in his 945th consecutive game, Williams revealed the attitude that covered the entire team, having held first place since Opening Day and with the finish line in sight:

"Sure, everyone's a little tired. But we just got to keep battlin.' This is as far (in first) as we've ever gone. No one's goin' to quit for a minute in this race. We'll just hang in there."

Four days later, Ray Sons of the Daily News returned to write a feature on us after switching off the beat two months previously to move over to the NFL's Bears. Nice-guy Sons was able to spot a difference in our on-field comportment.

"We left them June 27 when they were as carefree as 25 hippies with sacks full of pot," he wrote in an August 27 top-of-the-sports-age piece. "Their road trips were a constant ripple of laughter and song. And they came to each game like 10-year-old boys to a class picnic."

In contrast, the 8-7 home loss to the Reds that Sons witnessed prompted him to write: "They were uptight. And they were tired. The fun was gone. Winning a pennant had turned out to be hard work that rubs your nerves raw and ties your stomach in a knot."

Even the ever-loyal, loud fans helping the Cubs set their all-time attendance record were perceived to possess fraying nerves on this home stand.

"When the Cubs were sailing along comfortably ahead earlier in the year," wrote D.J.R. Bruckner of the Los Angeles Times, "you could see the fans tumbling out of the elevated trains and off buses, running to the gates. Now they march off the vehicles in columns, like a mean mob."

By then, a diminished Hundley gamely had returned to the lineup on August 23 after leaving a sickbed and Durocher had been in near-panic due to his absence. Hundley had missed the Boys Benefit Game and the drooping loss to Dierker. In fact, the Rebel had not played since a cameo appearance at the end of the first game of the August 17 doubleheader. He had injured his finger on Padres catcher Chris Cannizzaro's shin guard a few days earlier on the road trip. The damaged digit made it hard for Hundley to swing the bat. However, as we flew home, Hundley also developed an ear infection and was hospitalized. He missed catching Holtzman's no-hitter on August 19, then was still laid up the next three games.

Making matters even worse in Durocher's mind was lefty-hitting backup Bill Heath breaking his hand during the Holtzman no-no. Gene Oliver, a jovial guy and impresario of our singing on Cub Power records, was little used at the end of his career. Good for quotes and booking the Cubs' mid-season chorus on our records, Gene Oliver was not trusted to handle pitchers despite his decade of experience, but now was the No. 1 catcher in Hundley's absence, with rookie Ken Rudolph, whom Durocher also kept chained to the bench, his backup.

Rudolph caught the August 21 game while Oliver worked the August 22 contest, the same day Hundley finally was discharged from the hospital. The team leader, who admitted he thought and breathed baseball all day and all night, could not stay away from the ballpark.

"Nurse says to me at 7:00 A.M., 'do you want a pain shot?'" recalled Hundley, who asked for the injection. "My wife (Betty) picks me up, and I asked her to drop by the ballpark to get my mail. I walk into the clubhouse, Leo's in middle of the room, and asks me if I can play."

His answer should have been as obvious to Durocher as Hundley's was to newsmen who caught up to him in his impromptu visit: "I've lost eight pounds, and I feel very weak. I haven't eaten hardly anything for a week. I've got to build myself back up."

Nevertheless, Durocher had the Rebel back in the lineup on August 23. Today, he'd return slowly or even go to minor-league rehab, but Durocher only trusted his regulars, haggard or not.

"They put a ball in my hand, and I played," Hundley recalled. "First time up, I bunted, and we won the game. I caught every game after that. It was a frustrating season to say the least."

Hundley came back and tied with Banks for team leadership in homers with 16. He had 59 RBIs and was batting .284. Memories of '69 had him worn out and wearing suspenders from loss of weight from playing every day for many weeks in the second half. But the truth was he had lost the better part of a week in the hospital and was rushed back by a Durocher desperate after going to the end of his

Hundley at bat.

depth chart with Oliver and Rudolph. Hundley started both ends of the August 24 doubleheader against the Astros the day after his return, getting only some late-inning relief from Oliver in Game 1. In his weakened state, his spirit was as strong as ever, but his flesh was weakened. After the doubleheader, Randy sat in pain with his head in his hands by his locker. His batting average steadily plummeted to .255 and he slugged just 2 homers with 5 RBI the remainder of the year.

"Leo would call me in and say how you feel?" the Rebel said. "I said, 'Skip, look at me, how you think I feel?' He said, 'You're all right. I said, 'Skip, I'll give you everything I got. If I don't do something you expect me to do, don't rag on me. I'll give you all you got.' I didn't want to lose my job to someone else. All I knew to do was play the game, get hitters out, score runs.

"I went to the ballpark to play baseball, that's all I thought about. I didn't think about anything else. I'd go home to be with my family, but I'd think baseball. It consumed me 24-7."

But Hundley still had the energy to ride herd on we pitchers. He knew his primary duty was handling the staff and his offense came second. Even if his bat slowed under the workload later in the season, the Rebel's self-proclaimed solemn duty was to take his place behind the plate. We knew not to cross him too much.

Lefty Rich Nye even classified Hundley as our real team captain, the on-field leader, above and beyond Santo.

"When he was behind the plate and not happy with the way I was pitching, I'd know it, the way my hand would burn (on Randy's return throw)," Nye said. "One day I bent over and it'd go out to center field. He always talked about when he's catching me, when am I going to catch one of your pitcher?"

And Hundley had a quick retort: "I never caught one of his pitches. It'd go nine miles."

But based on Durocher's track record of allowing Hundley to catch most doubleheaders and play in a record 160 games as a catcher in 1968, rest for the weary and weakened was not on the docket. Common sense, whether 1929 or 1949 or 1969, or in any of Durocher's baseball incarnations would suggest giving Hundley a break at the most physically and mentally demanding position. But the manager seemed to be in a trance, in a spell, in regard to his on-field manager, trusting no one else in the desperate quest to win.

Rudolph was the same kind of youngster to whom Durocher gave chances just three years earlier. But even with a team of All-Stars and the league's hottest hitter in Hickman, in Durocher's all-consuming desire to win, he simply could not trust Rudolph with catching responsibilities while Hundley properly recovered.

"If I was there, I'd have the skills to give Randy a blow," remembered Rudolph, who lives nearby from me in Anthem, Arizona. "Leo was so worried about not putting his best product out on the field. The ultimate goal is to use all the players on the team. It's nice to give somebody a break. Randy was just a hard-nosed guy wanting to play. He won't say to Skip, I need a day off. Randy was a durable, strong guy, but I do remember him wearing suspenders (from losing weight after his return).

"I appreciate the fact his decision to let me be on the club, but why not let me in a game or so? I was with the team almost the whole season, but I just sat on the bench.

"Leo came from a pedigree. He had enough history to warrant where he was. He had a lineup to provide contention. Had full reign to do what he wanted to do. It goes back to Leo and his coaching staff. I could not believe Leo did not sit down with his coaches. How we should handle it? I don't know what the input of these coaches was. Joey Amalfitano was a young coach (35 in 1969), so he would not rock the boat."

Rudolph would not get a break either when Gene Oliver was de-activated and made a coach on August 26, 1969, when Durocher and General Manager John Holland opted to prematurely promote Double-A center fielder Oscar Gamble and throw him straight into the lineup amid a pennant race. At nearly the same time, they also brought up Triple-A catcher-outfielder John Hairston, son of legendary White Sox scout and coach Sam Hairston. The younger Hairston had batted .451 in 25 Tacoma Cubs' games.

But Durocher was not about to rest Hundley in favor of a pair of rookies. His incumbent would start for the duration even if Durocher had to find a buttress of some kind to prop up Hundley behind the plate. Hairston would earn a footnote as the first black catcher in Cubs history, starting the season finale on September 2, 1969, at Wrigley Field. True to Durocher's form, Hundley found his way into the game, replacing Hairston by the fifth inning.

A great handler of pitchers was a pennant necessity, and we had one of the best of the era in Hundley. Durocher also knew from his own playing days, a winner needed even more strength up the middle. "Nobody ever won a pennant without a star shortstop," was one of the manager's pet sayings. And, indeed, we had the NL's two-time All-Star at the position in Kessinger.

But Durocher apparently had a poor recent memory in Kessinger's handling of a season without rest. He had finished on the upswing at the plate in 1966 and 1967, the former year the introduction of his switch-hitting. He played 150 and 145 games, respectively, missing some time due to a slump and military reserve commitments. Then, in 1968 as a first-time starting NL All-Star, Kessinger played in 160 games. In our mid-summer 33-14 surge that excited Chicago, he rose from .250 to .264 on August 15. Continuing to play without a break, Kessinger dropped to a season-ending .240, not the kind of average a manager, old-school or not, wants from his leadoff man of two-plus seasons.

Kessinger displayed a similar pattern in 1969. His offensive numbers held up going into September. But also telling was Kessinger making several critical errors, fatigue can affect reaction time and even concentration. Kessinger started every contest until September 16 in Montreal, going out late in a double switch on September 15 in favor of Popovich. The under-used utility player then started the next three games at shortstop. Kessinger's average had slumped into the .270s. Durocher realized, albeit a little too late, that Kessinger needed rest at the second most-demanding, non-pitching position.

"At the time, we were all doing the best we could," said Kessinger.

Popovich had recently gotten his first 2 starts down the stretch, filling in for Santo at third on September 3 in Cincinnati and September 5 against the Pirates at Wrigley Field. Santo missed his only 2 games with a right-knee injury September 2 against the Reds. He felt so apologetic for missing time that he walked out to left field before the Pirates game to inform the Bleacher Bums that the Cubs' doctors, not him, mandated the extra day of rest for the knee.

Santo's durability in the face of playing with Type 1 diabetes was well-known. But in 1969, the underlying illness must have crept up on Santo in the dog days. He slugged his 27th homer, good for his 108th RBI, on August 27 against the Reds at Wrigley Field. For the final five weeks, he had just 2 homers and 15 RBI, narrowly losing the RBI crown to Willie McCovey of the Giants.

Even though he was 38 with sore knees, Banks played in his most games (155) since 1965. Getting his wish with "Let's Play Two," he started both ends of most doubleheaders, once in a while getting a late-game break at first base from Willie Smith. Sitting out the nightcap of the July 20, 1969 twin bill at Connie Mack Stadium in Philly was an uncommon rest for Mr. Cub. On several other occasions, he was given the day game off after a night game.

But after ranking as one of the few Chicagoans to best Durocher in a battle of wills, Banks was not about to slack off. Durocher should have had the last word, though, with the oldest regular in the National League. Smith should have given him more of a blow against lefty pitchers to preserve him for the stretch. Like Kessinger, Banks' production had tailed off at the end of the 1968 season and history was repeating itself. He had just 27 RBI after the All-Star break out of his season total of 106. With 79 RBI on just 15 homers with a .267 average, Banks surely ranked as one of baseball's top clutch hitters when he was added at the last minute to the NL All-Star team at the insistence of NL President Warren Giles.

Beckert probably was the last of Durocher's core to slump. Limited to 131 games due to early time off after being roll-blocked by Mike Shannon at second and later suffering a broken thumb, Beckert should have been fresher than the others. But he played without a break down the stretch and still was hitting .300 (after batting .309 on September 2) when double-play partner Kessinger was benched on September 16. Only then did Beckert's production tailed off to a .291 finish.

The only one of the core who did not slump was Williams. Whistler had been batting .293 on September 2, and that's exactly where he finished. On that day, Hundley was hitting .276, having dropped from .285 at one point. Kessinger was hitting .287, finishing at .273. Santo only lost 5 points off his average for a .289 final, but his run production decrease was key. Banks was at .262 and dipped under .250 at one point, before finishing at .253.

The concept of a fixed every day lineup took a beating in the eventual final standings when Mets Manager Gil Hodges platooned at four positions.

No Mets regular played more than 149 games. No Mets pitcher started more than 35 games, with five pitchers making at least 21 starts. Starters in the late 20th and 21st centuries working on four days' rest typically do not work in more than 33 or 34 games. By the time Greg Maddux established himself with the Cubs by 1990, he was the NL's endurance man, pacing the league with 35 to 37 starts – but no more – four years in a row. Additional starts probably took away from a starter's effectiveness, in my opinion.

Durocher was in affect a 1930's manager going against a 1970's (or later) skipper in Hodges.

Decades later, Swoboda used metaphors, including military, to describe the personnel match between Durocher and Hodges. We had quality, they had quantity. The concept of our core of siege guns were eventually outflanked by their mobile unit of riflemen. Every Met was called on to contribute, while our bench men sat around and wondered when they'd next be used.

But the difference in personnel may have been even more striking on the mound. Hodges went deeper and more regularly on his pitching staff than Durocher did. The Cubs skipper, in fact, tried to get too much of a good thing. Oddly enough, ex-Met Dick Selma could have been the most overworked man on our staff.

Durocher and pitching coach Joe Becker working key hurlers to the bone and did not get the publicity or criticism, in 1969 nor in ensuing decades for the use of the everyday players. All starters were accustomed to working with three days' of rest, throwing batting practice between starts as a workout. But Durocher often shortened up the normal rest in non-crisis situations, desperately trying to win the next game if there was a perceived pitching shortfall. Another famed Durocher philosophy apparently governed his handling of pitchers: "You don't save a pitcher for tomorrow. Tomorrow it may rain."

Meanwhile, Durocher virtually ignored the last three pitchers on the staff – lefty Nye, right-hander Don Nottebart and a rotating cast of rookies taking the manager's backward-moving truck to Triple-A Tacoma. They called themselves the Dead Man's Brigade for lack of work.

Nye was ready, willing and able to work as the staff's third lefty, but his statistics with an ERA above 5.00 were worse than they should have been through lack of regular work. A fifth starter was only employed for second games of doubleheaders or when the schedule was jammed up. But certainly Nye could have worked more in the way southpaw Mike Montgomery was used for the 2016-18 Cubs, in my opinion.

"People have asked me why I didn't push harder with Leo in 1969," Nye told the Chicago Tribune in 1997. "I'd won 13 games as a starter in 1967. My arm was healthy. I was young. Why didn't I go to Leo and tell him I could try to give the team 200 innings? The answer is Leo himself. Leo was unapproachable. He had his tough-guy image to maintain, and you just didn't question him. And part of it had to do with me as well. It wasn't in my nature to go to a manager that way."

At the end of his career, 33-year-old journeyman Nottebart got into just 16 games in relief after coming over from the Reds at the end of April, 1969. Nottebart was a virtual batting-practice pitcher with a WHIP of nearly 2.00 – not big-league capable. The onus was on General Manager Holland, not Durocher, for keeping an ineffective pitcher around the balance of the season. Once Durocher saw a pitcher could not get outs, he'd cast him aside as if he was a non-person. A rookie could be optioned to the minors, but a veteran taking up space when we had just a 9- or 10-man pitching staff was the general manager's call.

Among our tight little group of regular workers, I was the only Cubs pitcher to refuse short-rest work the entire season. On two other occasions, I was the first arm to try to come back with no rest in a tight spot on Saturday, June 14, 1969, in Crosley Field in Cincinnati. Fortunately, I had to get just one out. I had gone 5 innings, giving up 5 runs, in the 14-8, 10-inning triumph the night before in Cincy that included Jimmy Qualls' famed somersault over catcher Pat Corrales to score. The June 13 game also was a high-scoring affair where we again rallied to take a 9-7 lead in the top of the 10th. Nye, the Cubs' fifth pitcher of the night, started the bottom of the 10th and yielded a 2-out Lee May homer and then walking Johnny Bench. Durocher warmed me up on no days' rest with these right-handed sluggers up and he took no chances, pulling Nye and putting me in to face Tommy Helms, who grounded out to end the game. That's why my '69 line is 43 games, an NL-leading 42 starts, 21 wins and 1 save.

Usually asking a starter to try to pitch in relief the next day simply does not work, in my view. On Saturday, August 23, 1969, Holtzman worked long and hard in a complete game, 11-5 victory over the Astros at Wrigley Field. He gave up 8 hits and 5 runs, 4 earned, while walking 4 and striking out 10. That meant well over 100 pitches, to say the least. The next afternoon, in the first game of a Sunday doubleheader, the Cubs and Astros engaged in a run-fest. I was off my game, going 3 2/3 innings and yielding 6 runs on 8 hits. Durocher went on to use six more pitchers. But with the Astros rallying off Phil Regan and another game to play, Durocher ordered Holtzman and fellow starter Bill Hands to warm up. Holtzman cut short the effort – he could not get his arm loose after pitching the previous day, so lefty Hank Aguirre finally got the last out in a 10-9 victory.

And Durocher really ran Dick Selma into the ground in the same Astros series. He was called upon to work 2 innings in relief in each game of the Sunday doubleheader. The double-dip, in which 'Looney Tunes' Selma did not give up a run, came with one day's rest after Selma started the opening game of the series on Friday, August 22. In that game, he took the loss after working 5 innings with 6 walks and 5 strikeouts. With that line, Selma did not have a low pitch count by any means. So would Durocher give Selma a few days off after his weekend-series marathon? No rest for the weary on a Durocher team. The manager brought back Selma on one day's rest to start against the Reds at home on Tuesday, August 26. He lasted all of 1 inning-plus, getting battered.

But like his everyday-lineup teammates, Selma gave his manager the impression he wanted work, and more work. On Monday, June 16, in Pittsburgh's Forbes Field, Richie Hebner slashed a liner off Selma's ankle in the first inning and he had to leave the game. Today's standards would have Selma under a trainer's precaution and his next start five days later questionable. But Selma iced the ankle and was brought back to pitch the second game of a doubleheader on the night of June 17 after I lost the opener, 1-0. Obviously, my two hours of work gave Selma the "extra" rest he needed. He went 7 innings, giving up 3 runs with 8 strikeouts, for the victory.

The rubber-arm routine with quick recovery from the sore angle gave Durocher ideas. In 94-degree heat at Wrigley Field on Thursday, June 26, Selma recorded a no-decision over 7 innings, giving up 8 hits and 4 runs against the Pirates No, not another low pitch-count day. Durocher had seen Selma baffle hitters with his fastball in the shadows of the second game of doubleheaders. So on two days' rest, Leo brought him back to start the second game of the Sunday, June 29, Billy Williams Day twin bill against the Cardinals.

Selma said afterward he was "dead tired" before taking the mound, but he somehow got a second wind to stifle the reeling Cardinals on 4 hits and 1 run, fanning 10 in the complete-game win. Pitching coach Becker had asked if Selma had worked on two days' rest previously with the Mets. Replying in the affirmative, Selma agreed to start.

"It was a credit to (Becker) I went nine innings today," he said afterward. "If he hadn't run me as hard as he had since I came to this club, I never would have made it. I was tired after warming up for 15 minutes before the game and by the third inning I was physically exhausted. The only things that felt strong were my legs and my arm." Selma added a third-inning call from Becker from the bullpen counseled that he was "reaching back too far." He made the adjustment and "hit the groove."

And so Selma may have convinced himself he was Superman. On Sunday, August 3, at Wrigley Field, he beat the Padres 4-3 with an 8-inning, 10-strikeout effort. And when Durocher needed a starter for Wednesday, August 6, at the Houston Astrodome, Selma volunteered, but Durocher declined his request to start, opting instead for Nye. But 'Looney Tunes' Selma did get half a loaf after all. Nye went 6 innings for the final victory of his Cubs career, Selma swooped in for a spotless 3-inning save. But it turns out he robbed the proverbial Peter to pay Paul. Selma was hardly fresh down the stretch when, staying in the rotation, he lost his final six decisions in a row while making an infamous, ill-considered pickoff move toward third base in a crucial game in Philadelphia.

Selma's abbreviated August 26 start after his marathon of work against the Astros originally had my name on it. Becker, obviously acting on behalf of Durocher, had asked me to pitch on one day's rest after I threw 72 pitches in the Sunday, August 24, doubleheader that prompted Selma's relief work. I had declined because I already had 250 innings under my belt. Previously, after a Willie Crawford liner hit my thumb on Sunday, July 25, I came back to pitch ineffectively on Sunday, July 27. And I answered the short-rest call under the gun to pitch the Black Cat game against Tom Seaver on two days' rest on September 9, as Holtzman's turn had to be fashioned around the Rosh Hashanah holiday. I gave up 7 runs in the loss at Shea Stadium.

The other pitcher whose workload proved too much was Regan. Durocher was thrilled to get his hands on Regan early in 1968 after Chuck "Twiggy" Hartenstein had only short-term success as a closer in 1967. Sinker-baller Regan supplemented his dry pitches with others adorned with a moist substance.

He was nicknamed "The Vulture" for swooping in to take some Dodgers starters otherwise apparent victories in a 14-1, NL Fireman of the Year season in 1966. Durocher would bring in Regan as early as the fifth inning and definitely would not hold him out past the sixth if needed. He apparently did not care how frequently or how long Regan threw. The stage was set for his burdensome '69 workload during our mid-summer '68 hot streak.

On Saturday night, August 10, 1968, at Crosley Field in Cincinnati, Durocher inserted Regan with 2 out in the sixth in relief of starter Joe Niekro. He pitched the rest of the game, earning the win while giving up 2 runs, as we rallied late for an 8-5 victory. Sleep fast, Vulture and massage your arm loose quickly.

On Sunday afternoon, August 11, Regan again was summoned to save a tiring Holtzman with 1 out in the seventh and a 5-3 lead. But the Vulture served up Johnny Bench's 2-run homer to tie it in the eighth and he even kept pitching, and pitching and... He ended up working longer than Holtzman, who had started, – 7 2/3 innings – through the 14th. But Williams slugged a 3-run homer in the top of the 15th for an 8-5 lead. Finally, Durocher gave Regan his leave with Jack Lamabe saving Regan's second straight win. Regan got all of two days off before being summoned to pitch 2 innings against the Cardinals at Wrigley Field.

Regan would not have that kind of endurance test to that extreme in '69, but you get the picture. He used his closer early and often, and would not switch out for any matchups. And the longer Regan worked, the more chance he'd give up runs, as he pitched to contact. Right out of the gate in '69, Regan relieved me on Opening Day after I gave up a game-tying, 3-run homer to Don Money in the ninth. He pitched a full 3 innings, giving up the lead run on a Money double in the 11th. Our mutual generosity to Money set up Willie Smith's memorable 2-run pinch homer to win the game in the bottom of the 11th.

The overwork likely caught up with Regan by late August. He was summoned again to pitch 2 innings, the latter in a save-situation after an eighth-inning rally, on Sunday, September 7, 1969. Durocher would sink or swim with Regan, and got dunked at just the wrong time. With 2 out in the ninth and the Cubs clinging to a 5-4 lead over the Pirates, Durocher could not think ahead of his time and cut down Willie Stargell's power with a lefty. Aguirre had worked two consecutive days, but what about the under-used Nye? Durocher reflexively kept Regan in and Stargell powered his hanging pitch all the way onto Sheffield Avenue as a real shock to the collective Cubs system. We went on to lose 7-5 in 11 innings.

Submariner Ted Abernathy, in whom Durocher lost some confidence in the second half of '69 after several poor performances, certainly could have shared some late-inning burden off Regan as an experienced closer himself. Underworked, Abernathy turned in poor performances in the first two games of the home Pirates series on September 5-6, and further buried himself in Durocher's bullpen food chain. After the Cubs let him go for the second time in 1970, Abernathy went on to have two more good seasons as a closer for the Kansas City Royals. But what is most remembered was his short analysis of 'bullpenning,' 1969-style, in his North Carolina drawl:

"He wore out poor ole Phil Regan," said one half of Brickhouse's under-used "Ab and Ag Show." Later, Durocher admitted to Abernathy he had not worked him enough.

Years later, Ken Rudolph computed the starters; Regan, Abernathy and Nye logged some 1,300 innings. "The rest of the pitchers threw 82 innings," the back-up catcher said. We're not about to quibble with his numbers at this late date, but again, you get the picture.

Compressing an entire staff's work into six or seven pitchers took its toll down the stretch. My ERA and Selma's went up one-half of a run down the stretch, while Holtzman's went from 3.12 after his August 19 no-hitter to 3.58 at season's end. Regan's ERA was 2.83 on August 3 but finished at 3.70, high for a top reliever of the era. I went from 17-9 to 21-15, while Holtzman – 14-7 after his August 19 no-hitter – finished 17-13. And Selma's 10-2 Cubs start simply disintegrated with a huge slump.

And so, the busiest of we pitchers, working on short rest, were bushed. Despite the aborted attempt to warm up on August 24, Holtzman had escaped such urgent calls, yet later classified himself as "physically and psychologically drained" in the "overwhelming" season. He claimed he had lost 23 pounds, going from 185 to 162 by season's end.

"You can always go back and second-guess," Holtzman said on the 25th anniversary of our team, in 1994. "The (Oakland) championship teams I played on later made much more use of all 25 players. I don't know if a different manager would have helped. I think Leo knew a lot about the game. He was a stubborn guy. He wanted to play the same eight guys, the same three starting pitchers and the same relief pitcher 'till we collapsed. I think, not necessarily a different manager, if Leo would have been a little less stubborn and gone with all the players we had, the outcome would have been different."

"Fergie, Bill Hands and I (each) pitched close to 300 innings apiece. You start getting into late August and September playing all day games, it does take its toll. We just didn't have anybody to fall back upon because they hadn't been used in April and May."

Added Beckert: "I agree with Kenny. Utilization of the 25-man team definitely would have helped."

Kessinger also believes that perhaps strategic rest here or there would have headed off the September downslide, which actually began after Holtzman's no-hitter, but then was interrupted by a 6-game winning streak against the Reds and Braves. Durocher would have had to send a starter one by one to the bench, perhaps beginning with Hundley and Kesssinger, because they weren't going to beg out of action on their own.

"I can say without reservation, we'd have done several things different," Kessinger said. "Maybe we should have done this, maybe we should have done that."

After we finished in second place with a 92-70 record that would have won the division many other years, Durocher had to issue numerous mea culpas. In September, he had realized too late he handled the team incorrectly. Vows to change filled his comments in spring training, 1970. No matter, as the bloom was off the Durocher rose, surely with Chicago media and with many fans.

Durocher was slowing up physically and mentally, after our historic season, though. A funny story circulated that Durocher, dozing mid-game in the dugout, suddenly awoke and shouted for Willie Smith to grab a bat to pinch hit. Hickman then came up to Durocher with this response: "Skip, we traded Willie, but if you want me to go get him, I will."

So TV voice Brickhouse had been correct after all. Durocher had seen his best days as a manager, while we were in our primes as players and not about to let up. Durocher craved to win and so did we. But the old saying applied here: Everything in moderation.

Dirt from the fans...

No "son of the South Side" (the "Sox-Side") who was around in 1969 will ever forget that year. However, I am not a South-Sider, though I sometimes ask myself why, since my life-long allegiance to that underdog team has been from afar. I endured a terrible time until September, when the Cubs completely unraveled. I must confess that having endured so much hazing and ridicule all that summer from my Cubs fan "frenemies," the stunning Mets' stampede to the National League pennant came as a bolt out of the blue, a gift from God and sweet music to the ear. Call it what you will. I watched those Cubs-Mets games in September with unabashed delight.

-Rich Lindberg, Chicago

Knockdowns, Black Cats, Errant Pick-Offs,
And A "Gamble" That Backfired

"It's From Wrigley Pan To Shea Fire."

That Chicago Tribune main sports-page headline of Monday, September 8, 1969, said it all. After the brutally long five months in which we held serve in the new NL East, we now had a true showdown series with the upstart New York Mets, whose confidence grew like the proverbial snowball rolling downhill.

As we stumbled through the finale of an 11-game, make-hay home stand, going 3-7, the Mets had gone from 10 games back on August 13 to just 2 ½ in arrears on August 28. Then we built our lead back up to 5 games by winning 6 in a row in capturing the final home stand game against the Reds, sweeping the Braves in Atlanta and taking 2 of 3 with the Reds.

But then the Pirates manhandled us, sweeping a 3-game series in Wrigley Field. Losing 10 of our last 14 games in front of packed, adoring crowds was the last thing we needed. Willie Stargell slugging a 2-strike Phil Regan pitch onto Waveland Avenue to tie the September 7 game at Wrigley before we lost in 11 innings was the proverbial icing on the cake. The Mets had regained all their lost ground, standing 2 ½ games back before we came into Shea Stadium for a Monday-Tuesday prime-time series with the entire baseball world watching.

Normally, that's the type of series making your season. You can hitch up your stirrups and show who's the better team, or you can give further confidence to a team that had finished in ninth place in 1968. The Mets were expected to improve for 1969 – but not so much as having a shot at first place in September.

But as a right-field Bleacher Bum bookie would tell us, what would happen from September 8 onward, via game results, unbelievable plays and recriminations, would forever frame our lives and shadow the Cubs franchise wherever it finished in the standings well into a new millennium.

Amid the tumult of two big-market teams clashing and heading in opposite directions was the sidebar of a young player brought up too far, too fast and without the proper life coaching who went from the next Willie Mays to a pariah with management because of his party-hearty activities.

Leaving for New York Monday morning, September 8, we had even more baggage on our hands than the ones on the plane. Leo Durocher had scolded me for leaving the cubbyhole clubhouse after a mediocre mound performance early on Saturday, September 6, and made a reference to me – although not by name – in a team meeting prior to the Stargell-clouted contest the next day. And we had plenty of food for thought if we caught up on our reading heading to the Big Apple.

The Tribune headline was only the appetizer. The Chicago Sun-Times hit the newsstands on September 7 with a huge Midwest Sunday magazine story and what I believe was a hit job on the game's most controversial man: "Countdown at Wrigley Field – or will Chicago ever learn to love Leo Durocher?"

Fitzpatrick, 42 in 1969, would win a Pulitzer Prize a year later for a story on running with the radicals during the October 1969 "Days of Rage" in Chicago.

But Fitzpatrick's thousands-of-words piece was not done in a day. More likely, given advance magazine deadlines, he was commissioned to write the story after Durocher went AWOL to Camp Ojibwa to see his step-son in late July. And so, in my opinion, Fitzpatrick went out to condemn, not praise, "Caesar." Even as Durocher was still lionized by most fans for the franchise's firm revival and first-place standing, Fitzpatrick picked up on every inside story, every negative thread involving the manager. Some were true and some were proven to be exaggerated or off-base, but it was must reading for anyone who cared a whit about the Cubs.

"A man with knowledge of baseball history would be hard put to recall a time when a major-league manager in this town was more feared and more disliked," Fitzpatrick wrote. He quoted "one of the town's most prominent telecasters" as ripping Durocher as "the most unprincipled man in all of sports," desiring to fire Durocher if the Cubs won the first three games of the World Series and not even let him buy a ticket for the fourth game. Putting two and two together, the anonymous quote likely came from Jack Brickhouse, three years into a behind-the-scenes feud with Durocher.

The problem with the story was most of the quotes were anonymous and Fitzpatrick did not name players and coaches who purportedly had conflicts with Durocher.

Almost unbelievably, one player supposedly told a "friend" before the wedding that a team revolt was imminent because Durocher could not properly handle the pitchers. But as the ace pitcher, I would have known if a revolt was brewing. One did take place, August 23, 1971, when Durocher and Ron Santo had their famed locker-room confrontation – but not in 1969. To be sure, Durocher did not handle us properly when all accounts were settled. Yet, we were so focused on winning the division that we did not rebel against authority, which was firmly backed by ownership and management in the pre-free agent era.

Given the fact Fitzpatrick snooped around Wrigley Field and probed around the edges talking to "friends," he did not cause any disquiet among the players.

Of most immediate concern was our stretch run. In the September 7 sports section, distanced from the Midwest color insert, the Sun-Times offered contrasting viewpoints from Brickhouse and then-Cardinals announcer Harry Caray on our prospects.

Brickhouse, always sunny in his outlook, opined that, "The Chicago Cubs are a team of destiny. I think they're going to win. The Eastern Division. The National League pennant playoff. The World Series. The works. There have been repeated times when it appeared the Mets had captured that same lightning in a bottle (as the Cubs), and their tenacity has to be admired, but until now the Cubs have responded to the pressures of it all with the most memorable baseball in this city's history."

Caray, always opinionated, sometimes to a fault, responded, "What happened to the Phillies in 1964 might happen to the Cubs during the final weeks. I'm not saying it will, but it might. If the Cubs should prevail, the first words of congratulations will be mine, and nobody will have appreciated what they have accomplished more than I. Meanwhile, I will leave you with this comforting thought for next season: 'The Cardinals are coming, Tra, La, La, La!'"

Caray never broadcast that St. Louis "next season" that he forecast, as he was fired after 1969, amid reports he had a liaison with owner Gussie Busch's daughter-in-law. But it is interesting he brought up the Phillies' infamous '64 collapse, of which I feel I might have braked had I been called up a year earlier.

Meanwhile, in the early Sun-Times editions of September 9, columnist Bill Gleason summed up the all-the-marbles nature of the two games in New York: The Cubs, like the Yanks of old, were running first, and all they had to do was win two. Not just any two. These two … the two that could end the dream for the Mets."

Gleason weighed in on the "tired" player theme that had been circulating for two weeks. Who would you rather put out there in a showdown: "(Gil) Hodges has two third basemen – Ken Boswell and Bobby Pfiel – and two second basemen – Wayne Garrett and Al Weis. Most managers would prefer to have Ron Santo and Glenn Beckert, weary or not."

And more Gleason: "This is the time of year when baseball isn't fun in any form. It is drudgery, and the motivation is money…This is the time of year when the players can press the button of the deodorant spray can long and hard, but the armpits never are going to be as dry as the commercials promise to make them. The palms at the hands are always clammy. If a pitcher wants to throw a wet one, he can borrow the moisture from any teammate. Everybody is a little soggy. And the weather has almost nothing to do with it."

But our palms and other body parts weren't particularly sweaty going into Shea Stadium on a drizzly, cool evening on Monday, September 8. Some 48,000, less than the expected capacity throng, assembled in Queens with millions watching on TV at home both in the New York and Chicago markets. In the future, the showdown would have been on national TV, but NBC did not carry a prime-time game at that time of the year on Mondays, as it did sometimes in the summer.

Newspapers, still a predominant way to follow baseball in 1969, were well-represented. Writers from 27 papers from seven states and Washington, D.C., packed the press box. Red Mottlow, the pioneering radio reporter taking his recorder into locker rooms for Chicago's WCFL-Radio, was refused admittance to the main press box by Jack Lang, head of the local Baseball Writers Association chapter. But Mottlow simply sat in auxiliary seating and relayed his staccato-laced reports back home. Meanwhile, Bill Wrigley, son of Cubs owner Phil Wrigley, took a seat next to the Cubs dugout for the 2-game series.

Bill Hands, our starting pitcher, already had been entangled centrally in the budding Cubs-Mets rivalry. 'Froggy' had been involved in a beanball battle with Tom Seaver in May at Wrigley Field and had beaten the New Yorkers twice in July – including by a 1-0 score – in the only games we had won in a pair of 3-game series. But he'd be forever linked with Mets leadoff man Tommie Agee, who'd turn the evening into his own virtuoso show with what I believe was the help of a rookie umpire.

However, Hands wasn't going to back down from anyone under pressure. After Jerry Koosman retired us in order in the first inning, 'Froggy' prepared to face Agee. He did not wait to send a message, old-school style. In a sequence right out of early 20th-century baseball, Hands simply knocked down Agee, who went sprawling at the plate. Batterymate Randy Hundley was not in on the plan.

"Bill doesn't tell me he's going to throw at the first batter. But the first bloomin' pitch is right at Agee's head," the Rebel recalled of the surprise move as he had to leap to try to catch the high, inside serve.

"He doesn't indicate to me one iota this is going to happen. He's going down on the ground and I think, 'Oh, baby, this is baseball.' The baseball goes back against the screen. I absolutely loved it. He's trying to intimidate Agee to no end."

Nearly two decades later, 'Froggy' told author Rick Talley in The Cubs of '69 book that he was not prompted by Durocher to deck Agee. No matter how the Mets could respond, Hands was the toughest-minded man in Shea Stadium that night.

"I was not told to do it. I just did it," Hands said. "Right. Let's go, gentlemen. Right on his ass. I didn't hit him, did I? I just did what I wanted to do. And you know, here's the funny thing about Tommie Agee. He had that kind of arrogant swagger about him. All through the minor leagues I owned him. But in the majors I just couldn't make good pitches against that mother. I was constantly hanging sliders over the middle of the plate, and he was constantly hitting the shit out of them."

And the Mets acted immediately to retaliate. Santo, first man up in the second, was drilled in the arm by a Koosman fastball. The message pitch stung to the point that trainer Doc Schueneman had to spray-freeze the arm to dull the pain. Santo took his base, but many in the ballpark wondered why neither he, Cubs players nor Durocher were enraged enough to start a ruckus against Koosman.

Later, calling the lack of Cubs counter-action a "degrading incident," lefty Rich Nye, from his perch in the outfield visitors' bullpen, realized how the Mets were prepared to fight fire with fire, only come in hotter.

"I could hear Santo screaming going up to first base holding his wrist," Nye said. "That's intimidation. Koosman had a fabulous game (13-K). He came right back. Agee got knocked on his ass and Koosman said you're not going to do that to my team. In those days, you didn't have to be told by the manager to do that."

Adding insult to injury, a hyper-motivated Agee came to bat in the third inning to do his frequent damage against Hands, apparently rising above even his considerable talent to power a 2-run homer off a slightly high slider for a 2-0 Mets lead.

"The pitch he hit out of the ballpark, I never ever saw him hit that particular pitch," Hundley said. "But he stayed on that bloomin' thing and he took it nine miles. After this, this is major-league baseball."

The pain dulled enough for Santo to tie the score 2-2 with a sacrifice fly after 3 consecutive singles. Yet, the beast in Agee apparently had been awakened. In the bottom of the sixth, Agee shot a ball past Santo at third and tore hell-bent-for-leather for second, sliding in safely for a double.

Then came the most controversial play at the plate to that point in Cubs history.

Third baseman Wayne Garrett shot a line-drive single to right. After two bounces, Jim Hickman picked up the ball and fired a perfect strike to Hundley, waiting up the line for Agee steaming around third. The ball and Agee arrived at the catcher at the same time as Hundley quickly turned to make a swipe-tag on Agee. Umpire Dave "Satch" Davidson, in his first season as an NL arbiter, positioned in foul territory to make the call, ruled Agee safe. His back turned to Davidson, Hundley thought Agee was out and prepared to throw to first if Garrett strayed off the bag. Then the safe call registered and the Rebel then repeatedly leaped up into the air as if his feet were on fire.

The play came 45 years too soon for replay review. Only one replay angle was available – the actual live shot rerun – in an era when local TV stations' baseball production crews only had one replay machine. Agee appeared to be out on that angle. A mass audience viewing the setback on WGN-TV was alternately angry and depressed.

Watching from the Cubs bench, I thought the throw beat Agee and that Davidson probably made the call too quickly. That's a frequent umpiring error.

I rated Davidson just a fair umpire over his career, although certainly not among the game's elite. He had a knack of being involved in famous events, working behind the plate for Hank Aaron's record-breaking 715th homer in 1974 and Carlton Fisk's walk-off homer in Game 6 of the 1975 World Series. He retired in 1984, working as a police officer in London, Ohio, and as a Big Ten basketball referee. Davidson died at 75 in 2010.

Hundley did all he could to restrain himself in jawing with Davidson, who I believe displayed a verbal comeback much better than his umpiring judgment.

"I jumped straight up and down," The Rebel said. "I knew I wanted to bop him right in the bloomin' kisser. I knew if I just touched him, I'd be gone the rest of the season. I tagged him so hard I almost dropped the ball. He was on the wrong side of me. I stayed right with him and tagged him up on his body. I looked down at first base. Garrett looked disgusted because he sees the bloomin' tag."

"The ump said is that all you gotta say? I say no, I want to bite your head off. He said if you do, you'll have more brains in your stomach than you have in your head."

Agee knew he got away with the play, in my opinion. But when a team goes on a wild run like the Mets did, it will benefit from almost every call going its way. He made the admission to The Rebel's son, Todd Hundley, when the latter became the Mets' slugging centerpiece in 1996.

"He's out," the younger Hundley said in '96. "I've talked to Tommie Agee, and he told me he was out, too. (But) the umpire made the call."

The blown call was all the Mets and Koosman needed. Staked to the precious 1-run lead, the lefty mowed us down with 13-strikeout pitching. Our post-game mood was sullen. The mob of writers could not get more than a handful of words out of any of us. Gene Oliver, tagging along as a coach, tried to discourage the scribes from asking questions. Durocher zipped his lips, then paced the clubhouse in what was described as a "well-tailored" blue sports coat.

Chicago Tribune columnist David Condon, always a cheerleader and management backer, ended his September 10 column: "It's up to the Mets to do the catching! They won't." Maybe in the back of his mind, Condon began recalling the old billy goat curse story from 1945 that he heard in long nights and early mornings at the Billy Goat Tavern. And when Condon began publicizing successor goats' attempts to gain access to Wrigley Field, he no doubt based his ongoing curse narrative partly on Satch Davidson and a Hundley previewing a future Michael Jordan vertical leap.

Even before the barnyard-horned animal became an adjunct to the Cubs' narrative, another symbol of bad luck overwhelmed the play-by-play of the September 9 game. Going for my 20th victory for the second start in a row, I again fell short, as homers by Donn Clendenon and Art Shamsky off me staked Tom Seaver to his 21st victory, 5-hitting us in a 7-1 win that cut our lead to a half-game. The details of this game are not remembered as much as the appearance of a black cat walking past Ron Santo in the on-deck circle toward our dugout in the first inning.

Unlike William Sianis' billy goat publicity stunt in 1945, in which one newspaper photographer was stationed at the Wrigley Field turnstile, multiple film cameras ground away in color at the Cubs-Mets duel. So when the cat appeared, it was preserved for all time. Not a year has gone by ever since – at least not until 2016 - when the film of the possibly scared kitty has not been replayed in connection with the Cubs, past or present.

Immediately, editors had fun with the cat image, which was the lead photo in many newspapers the next morning. The Tribune took note in the photo caption that the loss was my 13th, and that Clendenon's and Shamsky's homers off me were the 13th for each.   I always believed the cat–or more specifically a kitten–was turned loose by the Shea Stadium ground crew, or perhaps jokester Mets pitcher Tug McGraw, from the double doors behind home plate. Ronnie [Santo] was still swinging his bat, getting loose, and the cat was right behind him. The cat's pose was something nobody ever forgets. I saw it and the other guys on the bench were laughing. The cat just walked past Santo, past the dugout and it was gone. Boom! It was there and it was gone.

The timing was perfect, with Santo closest to the cat, if one was a Mets player or fan.

"He ran in front of me, stopped to stare and headed toward our dugout, where he glared at Leo, who was stooped on the front step of the dugout," Santo recalled in his Love of Ivy autobiography. "I don't like to walk under ladders; I throw salt over my shoulder and don't light three cigarettes on one match. I especially don't like black cats in my path."

You can be sure the Mets also took notice.

"Say, did you see that black cat on the field tonight?" Hodges asked newsmen after the September 9 game. "I thought it might be bad luck, but apparently the cat visited the Cubs dugout before it visited ours."

No one really got the Mets off the hook for the cat's appearance until much later, when Hundley had a more specific explanation.

"(Mets catcher) Jerry Grote asked me 30 years after, 'Did you guys think we sent that cat out on the field?'" The Rebel recalled. "I said, yeah. But Jerry said they didn't have anything to do with it; those cats lived underneath the stands chasing rats all the time. Holy Cow, can you believe that? We came down the runway from the clubhouse. There was a hole by the seats next to the runway, and the bloomin' cat came through the hole."

Mets Closing In On Cubs!	# The Heckler	GROOVY SINCE 1967

VOL. MLVI WEDNESDAY, SEPTEMBER 10 1969 NO. 227

Cubs Not Phased by Mets or Little Black Cat at Shea

Santo Insists:'The Mets Are A Fluke ... Will Never Catch Us!'

Quirky Banks:'For The Love Of God, Let's Not Lose Two!'

Cubs Claim Themselves Lucky To Not Be Superstitious

REPORT ON THE CUBS

The Cubs' stranglehold on the NL East lead has dwindled to nothing, as the pesky upstart New York Mets have finally caught up with them, however Chicago and doesn't seem worried. But should they be, particularly after a black cat ominously strolled past slugger Ron Santo in Shea Stadium's on-deck circle last night?

"Maybe if I was superstitious, sure," said a confident Santo, wearing an "I Love NY" T-shirt and mired in a month-long slump. "Let's be honest, the Mets are a fluke.

They will never catch us."

Meanwhile, normally optimistic shortstop Ernie Banks took a different approach, pleading with his team. "For the love of God, let's not lose two. Please, sweet Jesus. This is probably the last chance I'll ever have at winning a title. Look at this roster. We have no depth. We'll never be this good again."

ABOVE: A silly black cat crosses slugger Santo's path

OTHER NEWS FROM THE N.L. EAST PENNANT CHASE

* Downtrodden Cubs fans: 'We've waited 51 years for this title. Can't wait any longer?'
* Billy Williams: 'When the heck are Santo and Banks going to start hitting again?'

* Fan who says 'Woo' all the time never more popular at Wrigley Field
* Fans outraged by scalpers' demands for $5 for front row tickets to next home stand

The concept of cats calling ballparks their home-made absolute sense when, decades later, stories of a family of feral felines also chasing rodents at Wrigley Field were published. Co-author George Castle also remembered a black cat getting on the field late in the 2003 season at Wrigley Field.

Long after the cat disappeared, the sounds of the night added to the unforgettable sights. TV cameras relayed the image of the full house serenading Durocher, while waving handkerchiefs and towels, to the tune of "Good Night, Ladies: "Good-bye, Leo. Good-bye, Leo. We hate to see you go." If any doubts still existed that Durocher was viewed throughout baseball as the main anti-hero of 1969, the serenade ended them.

And just as momentum is usually that day's starting pitcher, but unfortunately, we had a reverse "mo" going by now, busing down to Philadelphia. Starting with Opening Day, we had the Phillies' number – but now it was time to turn the tables. Our half-game lead coming out of New York disappeared in a 6-2 loss, the seventh in a row, in gloomy Connie Mack Stadium on September 10 in front of fewer than 5,000 fans. Now seemingly unstoppable, the Mets then swept a doubleheader against the expansion Expos to snare a 1-1/2-game lead. Then the comic-tragic finish of our Eastern swing took place as we tried to recover our equilibrium in Philly on September 11.

Starting pitcher Dick Selma tried to outsmart the baseball gods, but such a tactic does not usually work. With a 1-0 lead in the third inning, Dick Allen came to bat with Tony Taylor and Johnny Briggs on second and third, and 2 out. Selma ran the count to 3-and-2, but did not particularly want to throw another pitch to the feared slugger in that situation.

He recalled being taught an avante garde pickoff play by Roger Craig in spring training with the Padres, prior to Selma's trade to the Cubs. With the full count, the runners would be off with Selma's motion. But instead of pitching to the plate, he'd wheel and throw to third to get Taylor.

Months before, Selma told Santo how he'd signal the play was on. "Knock the ball down, 'Dag,'" was the verbal prompt. Santo would acknowledge the play by shouting "OK."

But so much time had passed that Santo did not recall the prompts. He concentrated on the hitter. The situation logically would not be the time to employ an unusual pick-off play. When he heard Selma yell for him to knock the ball down, that's exactly what a Gold Glover would do with Allen – keep the ball from getting into left field.

"I missed the sign," Santo said in For Love of Ivy. "Sure, I'm thinking – knock the ball down. I had forgotten that was the signal for the play. Selma wheeled and threw toward me; the ball went over my head and soared out to left field. A run scored."

On TV, the image of the ball sailing into left field, no one taking the throw at third and Taylor scoring nailed down the idea that if it rains, it pours in this strange twist of the '69 season.

Ernie Banks did homer in the eighth to give us a 2-1 lead, with Selma still on the mound. But he allowed consecutive doubles to open the bottom of the eighth, with Allen coming up again. With first-base open, Durocher had the option of walking Allen and then replacing Selma to allow southpaw Hank Aguirre to face lefty-swinging Johnny Callison. But he stayed with Selma, whose fear of Allen with men in scoring position had been demonstrated disastrously. Sure enough, Allen boomed a two [2]-run homer to right to give the Phillies the lead – and enough runs for the 4-3 final, our eighth loss in a row.

Hands, our stopper, finally would break our fall the night of September 11 against the Cardinals at Busch Stadium with a masterful performance. But behind the scenes, away from the gaze of media and even some of us veterans in St. Louis, our most overhyped prospect was lurching around like a frat boy turned loose amid constant parties and girls. Outfielder Oscar Gamble, just 19, had been promoted at least a year ahead of schedule in my opinion, and tossed into center field in the middle of a pennant race. He had grown up on a farm and was just a year-plus out of high school in Montgomery, Alabama. In his situation, Gamble should have trodden lightly, been all eyes and ears as the rawest of rookies and been strictly business. The ill-considered promotion to Chicago would turn out to be the basis for his exile to Philadelphia, then the NL's Siberia.

Gamble would go on to a nice journeyman's career, always more noted for sporting baseball's most luxuriant Afro in the mid-1970s than any of his on-field play. He was not the five-tool, Willie Mays-type player Durocher and General Manager John Holland touted him to be in spring training, 1969.

Gamble was signed by the legendary Buck O'Neil out of Carver High School in Montgomery. But Carver did not have a baseball team. Gamble's teenage experience was first for the sandlot Oakwood Clowns, then for the Montgomery Mets semi-pro team. In 1967, O'Neil first saw Gamble, telling the kid he'd keep an eye on him. "And he'd come back," Gamble told George Vass of the Chicago Daily News in a September 5, 1969 article, "and sometimes after a game, he'd tell me about my mistakes and how to correct them."

Gamble signed with O'Neil for a "small bonus" as a 16th-round draftee in '68, but was far from even O'Neil's top pick of 1968 in a Holland front office that never drafted the legendary scout's finds No. 1. Speedy infielder Matt Alexander out of Grambling University was chosen No. 2 after the Cubs made the University of Oklahoma outfielder-pitcher Ralph Rickey their top choice. Interestingly, Alexander and Gamble were the only '68 Cubs draftees to ever make the majors. Only two from 1967, No. 1 pick Terry Hughes and No. 2 choice Jimmy McMath, an O'Neil signee, also made it all the way to the show.

Gamble was dispatched to the bottom of the minor-league food chain – rookie level Caldwell, Idaho, where he batted .266 in 34 games.

"It was the first time I'd ever been away from home and I was homesick," Gamble told Vass. "There wasn't much to do in Caldwell and I'd call home twice a week. I'd talk to my mother, my brothers and sisters and to girls."

Then Durocher and Holland got reports of Gamble tearing up the 1968 Arizona Instructional League with a .355 average. He displayed his hitting skills again in spring training, 1969. As he did with other promising prospects, Durocher compared Gamble with Mays. But Mays was a little older when called up at 20 and had experience in the Negro Leagues.

"He's got an arm like a cannon and can run like the wind," Durocher said of Gamble. "Sure, he's young and hasn't any experience. But did you ever hear of (Mel) Ott and (Frankie) Frisch? They didn't need any experience. They came right up to the big leagues."

But Gamble was not in the same ballpark as Hall-of-Famers Ott or Frisch, as reality set in for his career.

As it turned out, in my opinion, Durocher and Holland believed their own press clippings. O'Neil contributed to the overhype by proclaiming Gamble was "the greatest prospect I've signed since Ernie Banks." Buck was a Hall-of-Famer, to be sure, but at that point, had he forgotten Lou Brock? Instead of sending Gamble to low Class-A with his minimal pro experience, Holland bumped him all the way up to the Double-A San Antonio Missions of the Texas League. Gamble had a "nice" year, hardly dominating, hitting .298 with 7 homers and 32 RBI in 119 games. If he could run like the wind, the Cubs did not green-light him much, with just 8 steals in 13 attempts. Given the lack of prime position-player prospects – a perennial weakness in the Cubs system, Holland typically rushed him. The impatient general manager never showed any hesitation on promoting a 19-year old to the Cubs, given his past record with McMath, Rick James, Kenny Hubbs and Danny Murphy, who actually was a true teenage Cub at 17 in 1960, straight out of high school.

Meanwhile, the Don Young experiment finally was concluding in center while Jimmy Qualls was injured colliding with the outfield wall in our final, trouble-filled home stand in August, 1969. Holland could not wait any longer. He called up Gamble and Durocher threw him into center, cold, for our August 27 game against the Reds at Wrigley Field.

Writers picked up on management's profuse enthusiasm about their only good-looking prospect.

"There is no false humility or artifice in this boy of 19 who has come to the Cubs and found a home in center field that he may not vacate for 15 years to come," wrote Vass.

Even Ernie Banks got ahead of himself in projecting Gamble's stardom. As we moved about the clubhouse, unable to comment on the September 8 loss to the Mets in Shea Stadium, Ernie Banks brought Gamble to talk to writers with the invitation, "You ought to talk to Oscar. He'll be around awhile."

But even with his thin level of pro experience, Gamble was not overmatched on the field. He helped me gain my 19th win in Cincinnati on September 2 with a run-scoring single and 2-run triple. "I'm ready to play right now," Gamble said. "I want to get my swings." Away from the ballpark, though, Gamble must have felt he was the kid who fell into the cookie jar.

He later told Rick Talley in The Cubs of '69 that females mobbed the eligible, young first-place Cub from every direction, knowing he was staying at the Executive House, like all other rookies. Any 19-year-old guy often would behave in the same manner if women simply offered themselves up rather than having to work for their affections with clever lines or dinner and a movie. In Gamble's case, he apparently reasoned he was not in Montgomery anymore, where he grew up with the vestiges of Jim Crow law, with interracial relationships strictly forbidden, and San Antonio had been cut from the same discriminatory cloth. The virulent racism caused Williams to jump the Missions exactly 10 years earlier and return home to Whistler. Alabama, only to be coaxed back by O'Neil's clever politicking in his own visit to Whistler.

But if Gamble felt the coast was clear north of the Mason-Dixon Line to fraternize with girls of all races, he was mistaken, as a country kid thrown to the sharks in a big city. I viewed Chicago as being known for its own special kind of segregation and prejudice. As we played out the 1969 season, white construction workers battled with Chicago police, angered at a Labor Department hearing near downtown on discrimination in hiring and apprentice programs. In the cloistered world of baseball, Gamble played for an ultra-conservative Cubs organization run by Holland, whose own father ran a Triple-A team in Jim Crow-based Oklahoma City. Phil Wrigley himself was not outwardly prejudiced, but the slavishly loyal Holland acted to spare any possible embarrassment to the owner.

Meanwhile, Bleacher Bum Randy Anderson, the deejay of left field with his portable record player, quickly made friends with Gamble. One off-day, he picked up the rookie at the home of a fellow teenage white girl who had been friendly with big leaguers. "They made out in the back seat of my car," Anderson said of his 1955 Chevy, "and made out in my basement when they listened to my record collection." Given the mores of Chicago at the time, Gamble was probably fortunate, I believe, that a patrolling police car did not notice his public display of affection and stop Anderson.

As a too-young, new arrival, Gamble could not have known the lay of the land, no pun intended. If players of color wanted to pursue interracial relationships in 1969, they had to be extremely discrete. Guess Who's Coming to Dinner had come out just two years previously, but attitudes toward black-white romantic relationships had not significantly evolved. And the Cubs themselves would prove to be behind the times, before, during and after 1969.

Starting pitcher Ray Burris, nicknamed "Little Fergie" when he first came up in 1973 as my teammate, was told by a management person not to be seen again with a white woman Burris conversed with outside the ballpark, as I understand it. The woman happened to be president of Burris' fan club, chatting with him in the most positive, innocent manner possible.

Word of Gamble's budding connections with white girls soon filtered back to Durocher, who did not mind trying to legislate players' personal lives while enjoying an enthusiastically carnal existence himself, and so he called a team meeting before the September 21 home game against the Cardinals. Apparently, he had talked to Gamble privately, but per Durocher's style, he blasted another player in front of his teammates, threatening to send Gamble to "outer Mongolia" if he kept up his carefree liaisons. Around the same time, Williams mentioned to me that Gamble would lose his job if he kept up his off-the-field behavior.

Amazingly, like other objects of Durocher's public wrath, Gamble did not grab some bench. He started all but 3 games the rest of the season. He even batted leadoff twice when Durocher rested a tired No. 1 hitter, Don Kessinger, and played Paul Popovich in his place at shortstop. But after we played out the string to finish 92-70, Gamble was sent to the

Arizona Instructional League. He batted just .182 while Holland and Durocher heard more stories of interracial dating. That was the last straw. The man over-marketed as a Cubs savior was packaged with Dick Selma -- once as coveted as much as Gamble but who also fell out of favor – and was hustled off to Philadelphia in what I thought was a bad deal for outfielder Callison on Nov, 17, 1969.

If Williams and I had more time and we weren't immersed in fighting for survival in a pennant race, we probably would have counseled Gamble to cool it with some of his hookups and perhaps parts of this book would have been written in a different way.

My 20th and 21st victories seemed somewhat anti-climactic as we finished up. Given the circumstances, not as many players like Gamble and Selma would've been dealt, as you'd figure after the season. The storylines, soap operas, triumphs and tragedies that riveted the Cubs Universe in 1969 would continue over the next few years, to add new chapters to an unforgettable era.

Chapter 23

They Kept Our Ole Gang Together...
For A While, At Least

Almost to a man, our 1969 veterans will say no matter what we could have done, the New York Mets likely would have won the first-ever NL East divisional race.

To be sure, we needed to play better...a lot better...in September, 1969, but the Mets pulled off a once-in-a-generation run, going 38-11 down the stretch, fashioning a 19-game swing from August 13 to October 1. Fighting fire with fire, we would have needed to play our best baseball in September to have fended off the 100-win Mets.

The cryin' shame is that the Tom Seaver-led Mets team never again approached its '69 feats.

Stardust '69-style did return, however, in 1973. The Mets were 58-70 and mired in last place in the NL East in late August. They had life, though, because none of the other divisional opponents were playing much above .500 and we had frittered away a 15-games over-.500 advantage on July 6 with an interminable slump. This time, with the likes of Rusty Staub and John Milner in the lineup, the '73 Mets went 24-9 down the stretch to nose out the Pirates and Cardinals. They finished 82-79, lowest winning percentage of any first-place team to that date. And the magic continued well into October. The Mets upset the Big Red Machine in the NLCS and took a 3-2 lead in the World Series over Reggie Jackson, Ken Holtzman and the Oakland A's before Charlie Finley's boys restored order to their mini-dynasty.

The Mets never returned to the 100-win level until the Darryl Strawberry-Doc Gooden-Gary Carter teams of the mid-1980s. The 1984 Cubs had the good timing of knocking them off in the August-September stretch just before the New Yorkers hit their prime.

Thus, timing is everything in baseball. But looking back, we had chances to do the same between 1970 and 1973 and fell short for reasons different than '69. Each season is almost self-contained with its own challenges and soap operas. The fact we did not book a World Series trip in that time after falling short in '69 is worthy of another book. But we're in the eighth inning of this book here, so all we can do is summarize our next four post-'69 seasons and how much longer we kept together our never-to-be-forgotten bunch.

Before we reassembled for spring training in Scottsdale in 1970, Leo Durocher had to dodge investigators throughout the off-season. Suspicion had arisen that Durocher had some kind of debt to gamblers and whether that had affected his managing. Investigators from the IRS, Better Business Bureau and the Chicago Tribune knocked on Durocher's Lake Shore Drive apartment door and were turned away by his wife Lynne Walker Goldblatt Durocher.

Baseball Commissioner Bowie Kuhn's radar had been activated in September, 1969, and he kicked the tires on his own investigation. He asked Chicago Today sports editor Rick Talley not to write about the pending probe for the good of baseball. Talley complied, which would never happen in our scandal-mongering 21st-century media. Eventually though, Kuhn met with Leo and Lynne Durocher in Scottsdale, Lynne getting angry for getting her shoes soggy in the early morning wet grass. But Leo's explanation was good enough for Kuhn and it was case closed.

Meanwhile, two name contributors from 1969 had been dispatched in an off-season trade that did not help the Cubs, in my opinion. Fallen wunderkind prospect Oscar Gamble and right-hander Dick "Moon Man" Selma were trundled off together to the Phillies for right fielder Johnny Callison. Durocher and General Manager John Holland no doubt sent Gamble and Selma away, partially due to their personalities and off-the-field behaviors. But I felt snaring a past-his-prime Callison was wrong-headed, as my former Phillies' teammate had not racked up a quality offensive season since 1966.

The majority of our cast members returned for 1970, with rookie Joe Decker slotted as the fourth starter in place of Selma. But as we did a '69 redux in a fast start by running off an 11-game winning streak in April, by mid-June we were back in first with a 35-25 record. Then, like a bolt out of the blue, we had the mother of all Wrigley Field pratfalls.

We lost 7 out of 8 on a home stand against the Cardinals and Mets. We dropped a Sunday doubleheader to the Redbirds and then were swept clean in a 5-game series against the hated-team-du jour New Yorkers, including another twin-bill loss. The Mets, never muscle-bound, scored 44 runs in the 5 games. The losing streak reached 12, the most in Cubs annals since 1944, before I stopped the bleeding with a shutout in steamy St. Louis, July 1. While I was working up a sweat, Durocher whacked the side of the dugout with a bat to intimidate a photographer aiming his lens the manager's way. The collapse reached 15 out of 17 games when we dropped 3 out of 4 to the Pirates in Wrigley Field after our return home. We had given back the advantage of that 11-game winning streak, and then some.

The biggest casualty of the losing streak was Durocher. In February, he signed a $40,000 annual deal to co-host a nightly sports-talk show with Bill Berg on WIND-Radio. Unless a night game interfered with the scheduling, Durocher would go on the air between 6:30 and 8 p.m. Owner Phil Wrigley did not like the time commitment and inevitable controversy, so he tried and failed to get Durocher out of his contract with WIND parent company Westinghouse Broadcasting. WIND did suspend Durocher from the show near the end of the losing streak. In reality, WIND wanted to rid itself of a hot potato and the feeling was mutual.

Behind the scenes, the floor under Durocher got shaky. The losing streak, wasting the talent at hand, made Holland believe that Durocher's best managing days were behind him. With the hubris from 1969 still floating around like a ghost, Holland floated the idea of replacing Durocher to Wrigley. Later reports said the owner was leaning Holland's way until a five-part newspaper series highlighted Durocher's faults. Wrigley did not like to be dictated to, so Durocher kept his job.

Meanwhile, Santo was caught up in a mega-slump while his relationship with Durocher began to deteriorate as well. Off to a slow-ish start, Santo was benched in both ends of the Mets doubleheader, Santo ended up being demoted – without explanation – to the No. 7 lineup spot during an August series in Montreal. Despite all those negatives, Santo still drove in 114 runs in 1970.

Management got rid of underused '69 bullpen holdovers Ted Abernathy and Hank Aguirre by midseason 1970, even as it appeared the bullpen needed even more help than the previous year. Also departing the organization in '70, without seeing a day at Wrigley Field in the new season, were '69 outfielders Don Young and Jimmy Qualls and infielder Nate Oliver. Holland plugged a hole for the fourth starter – Joe Decker had displeased Durocher to no end – by purchasing Milt Pappas from Atlanta in June and trading shortstop prospect Roger Metzger to Houston for Hector Torres and acquiring Joe Pepitone on waivers from Houston in July.

The lineup was the most power-laden in my Cubs career. We belted 179 homers, second in team history to that point. Hickman and Billy Williams combined for 74 homers and 244 RBI, batting in front of Santo. But we had a feast-or-famine team. We either pummeled opponents into submission or lost 1-run contests due to an inability to play "small-ball" and manufacture runs late in games.

With all the glittering numbers and veterans filling the lineup and the rotation, no wonder many of us believe we actually had a better chance to win the NL East in '70. The Pythagorean rating of our run differential (806 to 679) stated we should have gone 94-68. The computation, of course, did not take into account the problems with close games or the bullpen.

We had plenty of regrets when we simply could not overtake what I considered to be an average Pirates team in September. The Buccos were 89-73 while we finished second again at 84-78.

And management still believed the Cubs fielded a strong core going into 1971. Traveling Secretary Blake Cullen, serving as de facto assistant general manager, recalled how he, Holland and the scouts rated our regulars against comparable starters in the league, handwritten on index cards. Individually, the Williamses, Santos, Kessingers, Beckerts and Hundleys were still rated as best at their positions, respectively. But even as something you couldn't put your finger on was just falling short, Holland opted to stand pat.

Although I started to put together a pitching portfolio for my Cy Young Award season, the Cubs started off slowly at 22-27 in 1971. Suffering another knee injury, Hundley was lost for most of the season, ripping open a lineup and leadership role. Yet, for a while, we seemed to overcome the Rebel's absence. Holtzman's second career no-hitter on June 3 in Cincinnati was a dividing line. We played much better for the next 2 ½ months. By August 20, after a doubleheader sweep of the Astros at Wrigley Field in which I won my 20th in the opener, we were 68-55 and just 4 ½ behind the pace-setting Pirates. We had cut into a double-digit deficit, prompting Sports Illustrated to make me the cover-guy for its August 30, 1971 issue, entitled, "Here Come the Cubs."

But the infamous clubhouse rebellion against Durocher on August 23 stopped all forward progress. Durocher began a team meeting prior to a game against the Reds by ripping Pappas for his pitch selection in a loss to the Astros the day before. One thing led to another and soon Durocher was questioning whether Santo had prompted Holland to stage his special day, scheduled for Saturday, August 28. Santo lunged toward Durocher and got his hands around his neck. Durocher threatened to quit and Holland was called down to the cubbyhole clubhouse for a further explanation of the Santo Day. Santo apologized to Durocher while cooler heads soon prevailed. We actually beat the Reds, 6-3, in front of a big Monday crowd of nearly 32,000. Yet, our '71 run, for all intents and purposes, was over.

Wrigley inflamed the situation on September 3 by writing an ad himself, placing it in the sports sections of the four Chicago dailies, as he blasted the anti-Durocher faction on the team. He said Durocher would continue as manager. I labeled the ad "a bunch of junk" when asked by beat writers.

We finished 83-79, in third place. But the only significant Cub to find a "happier home" in the off-season was Holtzman. He had feuded with Durocher in the second half, moving out of the rotation at times while he finished his worst season at 9-15, after which he was dealt to the Oakland Athletics for center fielder Rick Monday, as Chicago-based A's owner Charlie Finley by now had become a frequent trading partner of Holland. The Cubs' general manager filled another longtime outfield hole by landing Jose Cardenal from the Brewers, sacrificing young right-hander Jim Colborn in the process.

Although Monday proved to be a tremendous producer at bat and in center over the next five seasons, we also had speedster Bill North coming up. Sidetracked from playing time due to Monday's and Cardenal's presence, North eventually was snared by Finley a year later in another what I believe was a lopsided trade, bringing in aging reliever Bob Locker. Our ponderous team developed a two-time AL stolen-base champion for the Athletics in North, just as we had done for the Cardinals a decade earlier with Lou Brock. Meanwhile, Holtzman matured in a championship atmosphere, earning three World Series rings. He no longer had Durocher or Wrigley Field's short fences and winds blowing out playing on his mind.

Holland kicked the tires on a Santo-for-Cesar Tovar trade with the Minnesota Twins at the 1971 winter meetings, dominated by the White Sox's Tommy John-for-Dick Allen deal. But he opted to keep Santo in an uneasy relationship with the rehired Durocher.

Fans had to wait a week to see Burt Hooton because of the first-ever player strike in 1972. He did not disappoint, no-hitting the Phillies at a chilly Wrigley Field on April 16, as I tried to forecast, alongside Jack Brickhouse in the WGN-TV booth, how he'd work Phils' final batter Greg Luzinski. Fittingly, the Phillies loser was old '69 friend Selma. Meanwhile, Durocher at least superficially, had tried to portray himself as a bit kinder-and-gentler chap in a year he'd turn 67. He was filmed doing agility drills with the baseball, dropping it at my feet for me to quickly retrieve in spring training, calling me "big fella" in the process. The clip was shown in a Canadian TV documentary, "King of the Hill," about me in my Cy Young Award aftermath, shown almost two years later and now available on YouTube.

While Williams and I were fly-fishing in my native Chatham, Ontario, on July 24, Wrigley and Durocher agreed the manager should step down after 6 ½ seasons. And while there were claims that Wrigley outright fired Durocher, the owner would never label his decision as such. He owed too much to Durocher for reviving the Cubs from 1966 onward. At the same time, as he hired player-development chief Whitey Lockman as manager in his "next man up" style, Wrigley threw out a challenge to the players to prove they could play at a contender level.

Initially, Lockman proved to be a bit of fresh air – although as time moved along, he had his conflicts with me and my teammates. We finished 39-26 under Lockman, ending up 85-70 in second place. Williams won his long-coveted NL batting title with a .333 mark and finished 3 homers and 3 RBI short of the Triple Crown. I nailed my sixth consecutive 20-win season, but could not add to the total in the final two weeks due to a sore shoulder.

And Holland further subtracted from the '69 remnants by trading Bill Hands to the Twins.

By now all the regulars expect Monday, Cardenal, Hooton and second-year starter Rick Reuschel were 30 or older. Holland's decision to again stand pat proved to be yet another error, in my opinion, for the Wrigley loyalists. We seemed to defy our collective ages by playing well in the first three months, staking as much as an 8 ½ game lead in the division and sporting a 50-35 record on July 6. But the truth was we were an undermanned lineup with Williams having an off season, Santo's power production in decline (despite a .300 average in mid-summer '73). Beckert, who had a 26-game hitting streak early, was increasingly forced out of the lineup by a bone spur in his left heel as his average plunged into the .250s.

And the entire team fell into a hitting slump in July, which the increasingly stressed rotation couldn't erase by pitching shutouts daily. Typical was a 1-0 loss suffered by Reuschel in August in Cincinnati. I was off my game as my streak of 20-win seasons was broken.

We went 6-29, including an 11-game losing streak, from our July 6 season high point into mid-August. The losing seemed interminable, right out of 1966. The only salvation was the entire NL East played .500 or worse.

And so Wrigley mandated a housecleaning to obtain young players the farm system still could not produce on its own. I went first, to Texas for infielders Bill Madlock and Vic Harris. Beckert was dealt to San Diego for outfielder Jerry Morales. Hundley rejoined

Hands in Minnesota in exchange for burly catcher George "Baron" Mitterwald. After turning down a deal to the Los Angeles Angels for lefty Andy Hassler, Santo got to keep his home in Chicago with a crosstown trade to the White Sox, with pitcher Steve Stone and young catcher Steve Swisher the main commodities in exchange.

Holland waited for spring training 1974 to deal Hickman to the Cardinals – another favorite trading partner – and Popovich to the Pirates. That left Williams and Kessinger as the only remaining '69 players. Both joked with each other about who would depart first. Shuttled between first and left field by Lockman and successor Jim Marshall in the 96-loss '74 campaign, Williams was snared by Finley after the season to DH for Oakland. The Cubs came out even at least, landing second baseman Manny Trillo in return. Williams was fortunate to finally play in the postseason in '75. Kessinger was still the regular shortstop in his 11th season in 1975, but was assured he'd be traded afterward.

And then there were none. No physical remnants of 1969. Only memories, which fortunately grew stronger and more fabled as the years went on, and laid the foundation for the fondness between fans and players the Cubs enjoy these days, with the Holy Grail finally won in 2016.

1969 Plus 50

Time has taken its toll on the 1969 Cubs, as it does on all of the great sports heroes.
Some 18 players from that team, manager Leo Durocher, and all of the coaches except the youngest – Joey Amalfitano – passed away before this memoir could be recorded. First to succumb was bit-part young catcher Randy Bobb. A self-employed carpenter in Bullhead City, Arizona, Bobb died of injuries suffered in a June 13, 1982 auto accident while on a camping trip to Lake Tahoe. Oscar Gamble was the youngest 1969 Cub, promoted from Double-A at 19. He died of a rare tumor of the jaw at age 68 on January 31, 2018. In between, I watched many other teammates leave the field.

The beloved bullpen coach, Verlon "Rube" Walker, was the first uniformed figure from the team to pass away. Walker contracted leukemia while an active coach, went into remission, and then suffered again from the disease. After being named pitching coach early in January 1971, Walker died at Wesley Memorial Hospital at age 42 on March 24, 1971.

Living or deceased, the 1969 Cubs are long remembered . . . never forgotten. Their story will keep going simply because of its impact on a generation and those told the tale by succeeding generations.

What happened long-term to many of the major contributors to the 1969 Cubs? With a year in which players, fans, staff, and media all connected as family, it's hard to keep up with everybody, but I've managed to know of few of my old team's post-1969 Cubs lives.

You can come home again . . .

Some of us were miffed when we asked to leave the Cubs in the 1970s. Ken Holtzman had conflicts with Leo Durocher; ditto with me for Whitey Lockman. But too much good had transpired in our Wrigley Field days to hold grudges forever. The lure of coming home always lingered and, for many of us, it was satisfied.

Holtzman, Randy Hundley and me ended our careers with the Cubs. Holtzman was a fifth starter-type in 1978-1979; his effectiveness was essentially gone at age 33 after going rusty as a Yankee under Billy Martin, also one of my former managers. Hundley was a backup's backup when he returned to Chicago in 1976 behind All-Stars, Steve Swisher, and George Mitterwald. He took his last wraps in 1977, becoming a coach under manager Herman Franks, and then was a minor-league manager and scout for four more seasons. I was the Cubs' first major free-agent pitching signee, coming back for two seasons starting in 1982. I called it quits after 284 wins in spring training in 1984 under manager Jim Frey. I would have loved to have pitched for the NL East champions that season – but it was too little, too late.

Billy Williams, Phil Regan, Hank Aguirre, and I returned to the Cubs as coaches. Nate Oliver came back for three years as an instructor and minor-league manager in the farm system.

Amalfitano returned to his old job as a baseline coach, but first fulfilled his ambition to manage finishing out the 1979 season and then serve the better part of 1 ½ seasons as the last manager under the Wrigley family regime in 1980-81.

Amazingly, Durocher had pangs of a comeback. Phil Wrigley considered a Durocher return – as general manager.

Holtzman was traded cross country to gain three consecutive World Series rings in Oakland, starting in 1972. Despite the distinctive run of championships, he still derives his main identity as a Cub a half-century later.

Leo The Lip sniffs a grand return . . .

Durocher managed longer – 6 ½ seasons – than any other Cub since Charlie Grimm's three tours at the helm. In fact, Durocher's time as my dugout boss – all but two weeks of my first go-'round at Wrigley Field – was longer than any of 'Jolly Cholly' Grimm's terms.

In modern Cubs history, only Frank Chance (7 ½ seasons) managed longer continuously than Durocher. You'd have to go back to baseball's antediluvian, pre-1900 history to see Cap Anson (18-½ seasons) for a longer continuous run than The Lip.

Seeing how Durocher got the Cubs from Point A to Point B (but always eluded Point C in the form of a championship or even the postseason), the Houston Astros summoned him back to duty one and a half months after Phil Wrigley asked Durocher to step down during the 1972 All-Star break. He managed the final 31 games of Houston's season, then the complete 1973 campaign. The Astros, who had flirted with contention starting with 1969, ended up 82-80 in their full season under Durocher. But they were stuck at Point B, not to reach the postseason until 1980.

At age 68, Leo returned to his Palm Springs stronghold, along with then-wife Lynne Walker Durocher. He liked life at his club and left the dugout for good.

Wrigley's mandated rebuilding program would soon break up the 1969 team. And John Holland, turning 65 in 1975, was ready to step down from full-time general manager's duties.

So why not Durocher? Wrigley's post-Holland plan apparently was two-fold. Durocher would return as general manager with the assistance of Blake Cullen, the longtime traveling secretary who had performed assistant general manager duties, including negotiating contracts under Holland. But the catch was a big one – WGN broadcaster Jack Brickhouse, already closely entwined with the organization – would become team president.

When Durocher heard he'd report to Brickhouse, any advancement of the new deal was off. Without a real Plan B, Wrigley then elevated park operations chief Salty Saltwell to general manger. He would continue to do both jobs with Holland helping as a "consultant."

Now permanently retired from baseball, Durocher authored his autobiography and, perhaps realizing his own mortality, began making some amends. His appearance at a Hundley Fantasy Camp in 1983 to apologize to Santo for past hurts and take responsibility for the 1969 nosedive astounded all attendees. He spent the last few years of his life alone and in relative seclusion.

Durocher died October 7, 1991. Like backer-turned-critic, Santo, his reward would only come posthumously. The Veterans Committee elected Durocher to the Hall of Fame in 1994. His third wife, Laraine Day, spoke on Durocher's behalf at the induction ceremony. Lynne Walker Goldblatt Durocher lived long enough to see the Cubs World Series winner her ex-husband coveted so badly. She passed away at age 89 on August 11, 2017.

Ronnie's long 'walk'. . .

Santo's efforts to cut into diabetes' debilitating effects on millions went into high gear on August 28, 1971, at Wrigley Field. "Ron Santo Day" not only publicized his affliction, but also drew attention to diabetes and was important in public awareness. The special day in front of nearly 35,000 began Santo's lifelong connection with fundraising for diabetes research.

Nine years later, his name was attached to an annual lakefront walk to raise money for the Juvenile Diabetes Research Foundation (JDRF). "The Ron Santo Walk For the Cure" would raise tens of millions of dollars over the next four decades as a high-profile annual event. And Santo's own struggles with managing diabetes on a daily basis got even more publicity when he joined the WGN-Radio Cubs broadcast booth in 1990.

"Obviously (medical handling of diabetes) is 100 percent better thanks to all those walks," said Ron Santo Jr., who managed his father's business affairs in his post-Cubs career. "They average $4 to $5 million raised each time."

But the money almost was secondary to the countless people Santo met and advised on handling diabetes and amputation of limbs. His own journey was shown in graphic details in the "This Old Cub" video production by his other son, Jeff Santo. Scenes of Santo dealing with his prosthesis after his legs were amputated were included.

"That showed people you could not only live with diabetes, but you can also have a job like my dad," Ron Jr. said. "It was a story that needed to be put out there."

Santo witnessed his son Jeff's wedding before he succumbed to complications from bladder cancer he contracted later in life. He died at age 70 on December 3, 2010. Interestingly, he lived far longer than diabetics' projected life spans when he was first diagnosed late in his teenage years. Those too young to have witnessed his career can now see him, bronzed and in typical aggressive throwing pose, via his statue dedicated in 2011 outside the northeast corner of Wrigley Field.

The Santo name is no longer attached to the annual fight-for-the-cure walks. But the family involvement in diabetes research continues.

Vicki Santo promotes diabetes-monitoring dogs, who work in the same manner as canines who anticipate epileptic seizures or help sniff out bouts of cancer. Santo's own companion canine was named Joker.

Older and ill himself, Joker died soon after Santo. Vicki figured he wanted to rejoin "This Old Cub." Meanwhile, 1 percent of all sales from the new Ron Santo 10 Ale are being donated to JDRF.

From most durable to the eternal Cub . . .

Williams could not project he'd be the eternal Cub in 1956, when scout Ivy Griffin gave his father a cigar and his teenage self a contract to start at the bottom of baseball's food chain at Ponca City, Oklahoma.

But in a total of 57 seasons ever since, "Whistler," my best friend on the Cubs, simply rolled on and on like Old Man River. He survived some virulent Jim Crow experiences, set the National League record with 1,117 consecutive games played, slugged 426 homers to make the Hall of Fame in 1987 and served the team in every position except the one he most coveted in 1987 – manager.

Williams was the ultimate man for all positions – minor- and major-league player, minor-league hitting instructor, big-league hitting and bench coaches, speaker's bureau coordinator and special assistant to the president.

You might say it's more distinctive to list the years Williams has not been employed by the Cubs. He moved through many roles across the leagues, with the Cubs always his heart's desire through the Seventies and Eighties. In conjunction with his Hall-of-Fame enshrinement, his No. 26 was retired at Wrigley Field on August 13, 1987. Soon afterward, Williams expressed his ambition to manage to Green.

With his big-league acumen, he felt he was ready to pilot a team without an apprenticeship. But Green insisted Williams put in some time in the minors before being seriously considered. Williams was ready to comply – until Green was fired and replaced by Jim Frey, who hired buddy Don Zimmer to run the Cubs. Williams had to put his managerial aspirations aside. He worked in the Cubs' marketing department until more management upheaval led to his return to the coaching ranks as hitting coach under Jim Lefebvre in 1992.

Thus we were back together for the third time in our Cubs annals when I was named pitching coach in 1995 under Jim Riggleman. Imagine if, in 1969, General Manager Holland had been transported 26 years into the future to see Williams and me on the coaching lines! My tenure was just two years, but Williams simply continued on. Again, an old 1969 Cub came aboard – my successor, Phil Regan. We veterans of 1969 just kept crossing paths.

As the 2000s proceeded, Williams got off the road and into a special assistant's role. He was still part of the daily rhythms of Wrigley Field home games and spring training. Many hitters still benefited from his counsel on their approach to hitting. And like sitting around the cracker barrel, Williams became a top storyteller from his perch in the dugout, pre-game. In 2010, Williams got his own statue, the third one erected at Wrigley Field after Harry Caray and Banks. Meanwhile, June 15 became an annual celebration – Williams' birthday. In 2018, he turned the big 8-0.

We may not have enjoyed a World Series together as buddies and teammates, but Cooperstown at the start of August is a decent consolation prize. We've been up on the podium during induction ceremonies since my own entrance in 1991. For more than a decade we were a threesome with Banks. Then we became a quintet in a true Cubs Alumni Association on the stage with Ryne Sandberg (2005) and Andre Dawson (2010), until Ernie "Mr. Cub" Banks' passing in 2015.

From shortstop to manager . . .

If you made book on which of us would be the first to manage in the majors, Hundley would have likely drawn the best odds.

Hundley never got that opportunity though, stalling out at Triple-A in the Cubs farm system. Instead, another son of the South, Don Kessinger, got the first shot to run a team.

After late-career service as a starting shortstop, first with the Cardinals, then the White Sox, budget-conscious Bill Veeck asked Kessinger to do double duty (under one salary) as a player-manager of the White Sox in 1979. But Veeck's Sox were talent-deficient and even wore those non-descript and inappropriate softball-like uniforms at times, something long-retired by the time Kessinger arrived.

College coaching was more to Kessinger's liking. In 1991, he was named head baseball coach at the University of Mississippi, where he had been a two-sport star before signing with the Cubs in 1964. He had the joy of coaching both of his sons, shortstop Keith and center fielder Kevin. The old man made Ole Miss an SEC powerhouse with four 30-win seasons. Kessinger amassed a 185-153 record in six seasons before moving on to become Ole Miss' associate athletic director for internal affairs.

The generations followed in his wake, as his sons couldn't help but catch the baseball bug.

The Vulture's permanent baseball perch . . .

Phil Regan did not waste much time getting into coaching after he threw his final big-league pitch for the White Sox in 1972.

The Vulture moved home to the Grand Rapids area and became head coach for Grand Valley State University for a 10-year run starting in 1973. He has hardly stopped ever since. He was the second 1969 Cub to manage in the majors – and experienced good timing as well – as Baltimore Orioles skipper in 1995. He oversaw Cal Ripken Jr.'s stretch run to bust Lou Gehrig's record of 2,130 consecutive games, culminating in the national hoopla for the historic 2,131st game on September 6, 1995. Always with an eye toward history, Regan ensured he made out two lineup cards that night for the once-in-a-lifetime event.

In 2018, at 81, Regan still dispenses counsel to baseball up-and-comers. He is a pitching coach with varying assignments in the Mets system after officially retiring as Class A St. Lucie pitching coach after the 2015 season. He was proud of throwing batting practice at his advanced age. Regan has worked for practically everyone, including back with the Cubs in 1997-1998 as pitching coach, overseeing Kerry Wood's 20-strikeout game and Rookie of the Year season. He also was pitching coach for the Cleveland Indians and Seattle Mariners, advance scout for the Los Angeles Dodgers, and a minor-league manager for the Dodgers and Detroit Tigers. Thus he made coaching and scouting comebacks for all the big-league teams for which he pitched . . . except the Sox.

Regan does not appear to want to retire.

A Fantasy (Camp) come true . . .

Hundley was not allowed to serve an apprenticeship at the big-league level after working under Franks. He was told to get experience managing in the Cubs farm system. Dutifully following that classic path, he began working his way up. In 1979, he alighted at Double-A Midland (Texas), and provided a lesson for eager youth baseball player/son Todd, then 10.

The Midland Cubs had a hard-throwing, but sometimes wild right-hander named Lee Arthur Smith. Todd Hundley challenged himself to catch my future Cubs teammate and riotously hilarious buddy in good times during and after our careers.

"I just wanted to get back there and see what it was like," Todd said. "To catch him as hard as he was throwing, it got me over the fear of the baseball, which a lot of Little League kids have a fear of, getting hit by the baseball. It got me over the hump of being afraid of the baseball. I played with Mel Hall and Scott Fletcher, and they're hitting bullets. And I'm out there (in the outfield during batting practice) trying to catch them and field them. And I know if I don't catch them, they're going to go right through me."

By 1981, Randy Hundley had advanced to managing Triple-A Iowa. But after two months, farm director Davis, with whom he did not get along, came to town to fire him. A short while later, Franks, who had returned as Cubs general manager, made Hundley an advance scout. But when Green replaced Franks in the fall of 1981 amid Tribune Company's takeover of the team, Hundley was canned again.

Unable to connect with another organization, Hundley steadied himself and began conducting kids instructional camps. The concept morphed into adult Fantasy Camps in 1983. The program was an immediate hit as middle-aged would-be baseball players rubbed shoulders with their old Cubs' heroes in both Arizona and at Wrigley Field. The quality of baseball was not exactly crisp, but the camaraderie was priceless. Hundley conducted camps for other teams. His franchise became a stable cottage industry he still runs as a senior citizen. And Cubs of various eras, including the 1969 bunch, love getting together to tell old war stories. It's like our own informal Alumni Association.

Hundley has joined me as a great-grandfather among the 1969 regulars.

A different kind of trade . . .

Glenn Beckert was legendary as the Cub who borrowed and bummed and zipped his money belt for many of his daily necessities. He was fortunate he hung around with the open-walleted Ron Santo, who sported a roll of big bills after hours.

That's' why we all thought Beckert ended up the wealthiest 1969 Cub. He, of course, denied such a rating for years.

"No, no, no," he said in 2003. "Maybe I get teased about that. I was somewhat frugal. You just try to save everything up."

But the one time he really borrowed to the hilt turned out to be a daring, but successful gamble for the man we called Bruno, and the best man for my 1993 wedding to Lydia Farrington. After Beckert's big-league career crawled to a conclusion in San Diego in 1975, he had to find something to do with his life. He had a mortgage on his suburban Palatine home and a young family to support.

Beckert broke into the Chicago Board of Trade in 1976 with longtime trading executive Hank Shatkin lending him $130,000 to purchase his seat. Shatkin bet on a winner. Beckert attacked the world of trading in the wheat pit, which features daily setbacks, just like baseball, but he traded with the tenacity of slashing pitches to right. In just three years, as the loan was debited from Beckert's earnings, he paid back Shatkin's stake. He'd go on to trade full-time, earning a good living for 15 years until deciding to lease out his seat in 1991.

One Sunday, September 4, 1983, a day off from trading, Beckert paid his first visit to the Wrigley Field bleachers. As you'd figure, he immensely enjoyed himself, from the still-empty upper-center field section before the game, he looked out on the panoramic vista. So many countless thousands looked straight at his crouched batting stance and the No. 18 back of his uniform from that angle.

He spread his arms and said, "I can't believe the view you get from here." **Gentleman Jim on the farm and in the field . . .**

Everybody's friend, Gentleman Jim Hickman, simply went back to a farmer's life in his native Henning, Tennessee. Hickman's base property was 250 acres on which he raised cotton and soybeans, with an additional 1,400 acres leased.

The strong man did all right until, starting in 1980, land prices crashed from $1,500 an acre to $5 an acre. Gentleman Jim was in hock for $75,000 for the purchase of new tractors, but the agricultural depression prevented him from paying back the notes. In 1983, Henning's People's Bank foreclosed on the Hickman farm, allowing the family to stay on the property while paying rent. At the low point, the family lived one winter on $700 earned from Gentleman Jim working at Hundley's Fantasy Camp. He also was forced to take his baseball pension 'early,' $1,000 a month, at age 45.

"I enjoyed it, farming was a good life," Hickman said in 2003. "It was a decent living (until the crash). I got out of it because I didn't have any money to pay off (debts)." He discouraged his four sons from pursuing farming.

His first preference in any return to baseball was the Cubs. But regime change thwarted that goal; nobody was around anymore who remembered his clutch-hitting feats and clubhouse presence. Fortunately, Gentleman Jim had old connections in the Cincinnati Reds organization. Ted Kluszewski had retired as minor-league hitting instructor in 1987 and Hickman got the gig and held it for 20 years. Gentleman Jim also was inducted into the Tennessee Sports Hall of Fame.

Hickman died at 79 on June 25, 2016, never to be forgotten by his teammates and legions of Cubs fans. The Cubs organization sent a floral arrangement in the form of the team logo to his services.

Froggy wanted no relief . . .

Like me, Bill Hands always expected to the finish what he started. He completed 18 games in his 20-win season in 1969.

47 years later, contacted at his home at the eastern tip of Long Island, 'Froggy' was delayed in coming to the phone. At 76, he was outside mowing the lawn. No sense in hiring a kid to do the job if you can do it yourself.

He was a semi-retired squire at the time, living on Long Island during the warmer months, then bailing out to Florida in the winter. Hands never got back into baseball after throwing his final pitch in 1975.

Hands also never lost his opinionated status. Subjected to working for the Twins' Calvin Griffith in 1974, he let loose with both barrels at the alleged penny-pinching owner.

He was thrilled to see the Cubs finally get the monkey off their back in '16 after doing his part – and them some – with his 2.49 ERA in 1969. He still seemed so vital at the time. On March 9, 2017, he died after a brief illness in an Orlando, Florida, hospital.

Kenny the kids' coach . . .

Like 'Froggy,' Ken Holtzman did not stay in baseball after retirement. He worked in insurance for nearly two decades, settling in north suburban Buffalo Grove, Illinois.

Then he decided on a change of life. The University of Illinois alum went back to DePaul University to get a teaching certificate. He student-taught at Francis Parker High School in Chicago and enjoyed helping out with the girls softball team.

In the late 1990s, Holtzman moved back to his native St. Louis. He became supervisor of health and physical education at the new Marilyn Fox Jewish Community Center in the affluent western suburb of Chesterfield, where he became both coach and groundskeeper. "During the hot weather (one year), he'd be out on the field, picking up rocks and sweating his butt off," said then-JCC official Jeb Margolis. Inside, Holtzman helped boost the youth basketball program participation from 140 to 850.

Baseball, of course, remained his pride and joy. Chesterfield was a destination for Cardinals players' homes, so several worked out at the Fox Center in the off-season.

Holtzman used his connections to get former Cardinals Andy Van Slyke and Bob Forsch to serve as guest instructors. Albert Pujols signed autographs there for him as a rookie in 2001. He also coached the St. Louis-area team competing in the national Maccabiah Games – a kind of Jewish Olympics.

In 2007, Holtzman journeyed to Israel to coach in the short-lived Israel Baseball League with several other Jewish big-league veterans. The league was run by future Red Sox and Orioles General Manager Dan Duquette.

He has been retired in recent years, yet he has lived to see his long-time advocacies for more night games and modernization of Wrigley Field play out positively. Holtzman was not a prophet, but just a common-sense guy who was ahead of his time.

Moon Man back to earth . . .

We had a shaky bullpen in 1970, so sure enough, the traded Dick Selma saved a team-record 22 games with 153 strikeouts in 134-1/3 innings with the Phillies. I think we could have used Selma in '70, although Durocher might have been tempted to overwork him again.

An arm injury and a motorcycle accident helped cut short Selma's career, as he bounced from the Phillies to the Cardinals to the Angels to the Brewers. A new regime gave Selma a non-roster invitation to spring training in 1977, but he was essentially done by then. He retired after the 1978 season with a 42-54 record. He returned to his native Fresno, worked nights for the Fleming Food Company and went into amateur coaching. Selma served as assistant pitching coach at Fresno City College.

At just 57, Selma died of liver cancer on August 29, 2001.

The bird is the word for Nye . . .

A 1994 Chicago-area sports magazine cover photo had Rich Nye posing with a blue-and-gold macaw on his shoulder while he cradled a rabbit in his right arm and petted the shell of a tortoise with his left or former pitching hand.

No, Nye was not a zookeeper, although there were far more creatures where those came from, then and now. Nye was simply posing with typical patients of his longtime veterinary practice. Being an old southpaw, of course, there was a catch. As "Dr. Nye," he only treated "exotic" pets, not your own or your neighbor's dog or cat. That meant some patients, such as parrots, could talk right back to their sawbones.

When he decided to pull the plug on his career in 1972, his arm aching and vested for a big-league pension, Nye decided to turn an avocation into a vocation. He had grown up with animals and visited all the zoos on road trips. So he began the tough training to hang out a shingle as a veterinarian at the University of Illinois.

Nye became a standout, focusing on the non-mainstream four-legged pets. He and second wife Sue, a fellow veterinarian, opened Midwest Bird and Exotic Animal Hospital in west suburban Westchester, Illinois, in 1986. In his early 1970s, he still practiced several days a week, but was on duty 24/7/365 with his still considerable menagerie of dogs and other critters at his home, some 20 miles further west.

Qualls deals with Old Man River . . .

Jimmy Qualls could make a good catch in center field in his day and he continues that concept in another form now.

Living on 12 acres – where he raises chickens – 25 miles north of Quincy, Illinois, the former switch-hitter works as an inspector of grain being loaded onto barges on the Mississippi River.

Qualls was one of three 1969 Cubs, along with Regan and lefty pitcher Dave Lemonds, to play on the Dick Allen-fueled 1972 White Sox, which battled the Oakland Athletics well into September for the AL West crown. That was the wrap-up of Qualls' big-league career.

Eventually, Qualls worked on his own farm in very rural, far western Illinois, nicknamed "Forgottonia" for its overlooked status in the state . . . an ironic landing place for one of the *never forgotten* 1969 Cubs.

Don Young, from the desert to the mountains and back . . .

From Class A, to starting center fielder with the first-place Cubs, to obscurity again. Don Young sure knew how to bounce around.

The bespectacled centerpiece of one of the 1969 season's biggest controversial plays did not stay in one place, or one job, in the two decades after he faded out of baseball following his one full year in the majors with the Cubs. That's why rumors of his whereabouts and type of employment circulated so long.

Young finally showed up at the 1992 McCormick Place reunion of our team. In the Phoenix area, Young ran a milling machine, drove a truck delivering dairy products, and was a groundskeeper for the suburban Paradise Valley School District. Now in his 70s, he has faded back into obscurity.

Rudolph finally 'backed up' . . .

"Rudy" had to possess the patience of Job to finally get his chance to be primary backup catcher to Hundley. Despite the Rebel's knee injuries, which wiped out much of his playing time in 1970 and 1971, Ken Rudolph simply was bypassed by a parade of catchers the Cubs acquired from outside the organization.

Start with ex-White Sox J.C. Martin, who joined outfielder Art Shamsky as one of two '69 Mets to go on to play for the Cubs. Rudy became Hundley's backup in 1972, jumping ahead of Martin, while Durocher was still manager. But he got swept out with me in the housecleaning of Durocher-era players after the season.

Rudolph went on to back up Ted Simmons in St. Louis, had two stints with the Giants and finished up with the Orioles in 1977. He went on to work as a supervisor for United Parcel Service in the Phoenix area, then taught physical education while coaching baseball and golf at Arcadia High School in northeast Phoenix. 'Rudy' was 130-75-2 as baseball coach. After living in suburban Gilbert, he moved 40 miles north to Anthem in 2014 and we certainly cross paths.

Even with his backup-to-the-backup status in 1969, Rudy still gets four to five fan letters a week. "After 50 years, I'm flabbergasted people still want my autograph," he said.

Ollie 'survived' his fall . . .

Beckert suggested Gene Oliver must have used a parachute when he "supposedly" jumped off the John Hancock Building after we did not win the pennant in 1969.

Ollie flapping his gums like that was par for the course after he organized the Cub Power singalongs. He had a real-life soft landing when Durocher, who liked him, kept him on as a coach for the rest of the 1969 season. He thus got a better pension vesting after being bumped off the roster when Oscar Gamble was brought up on August 25, 1969. The day before, Oliver played his final big-league game at age 34. He returned to his native Quad Cities [along the Illinois-Iowa border] to assume the status as raconteur and sometime sportscaster. We'd see Ollie at Cub Conventions and Hundley's camps. He died at 71 on March 3, 2007.

Heath MLB farewell in no-no . . .

Turns out Bill Heath's final big-league game was catching most of Holtzman's no-hitter on August 19, 1969. A foul ball broke his hand in the eighth inning with Oliver finishing up behind the plate. He ranked as the only big-league catcher whose final game was during a no-hitter he caught. His four-team career concluded at 30 with 27 games, 32 at-bats and 1 RBI as a Cub.

Heath went on to earn a degree in accounting from the University of Chicago. He wasted no time using his sheepskin, establishing Barrington Financial Advisors in Houston in 1972. He branded himself a "financial coach," advising clients on handling their assets.

Heath lost second wife Patty and daughter Courtney, who were murdered in a home invasion in 1975. After that, he worked to rebuild his life with a new wife he eventually married, Linda – I hope his final farewell can be as strong as that he had with the 1969 Cubs.

Pee Wee teaches and still sings . . .

Amid a minor-league career, Nate "Pee Wee" Oliver came back to the Cubs as a rookie-league manager in 1998, high-A manager at Daytona Beach in 1999 and a minor-league infield instructor in 2000. Then he worked for the city and parks system of Oakland. He coached and only stopped refereeing (basketball!) at age 77 in 2018.

"I sing second tenor at church," said Oliver, still able to carry a tune after being a soulful mainstay voice of the songs in the 1969 "Cub Power" record.

'Ag' proud of his heritage . . .

Hank Aguirre, one half of the "Ab and Ag Show," returned to the Cubs as "information and services" coach in 1972, as a buffer and go-between for Leo Durocher and the media.

After Durocher stepped down as manager, Aguirre stayed on for 2-½ more seasons, moving to bullpen coach in 1973 and pitching coach in 1974.

Proud of his family's Mexican heritage, Aguirre founded auto-parts maker Mexican Industries in southwestern Detroit in 1979 to promote jobs for local Hispanics. He kept his company going until Aguirre died of complications from prostate cancer at age 62 on September 5, 1994. It was another seven years before Mexican Industries closed its plant, victim to the Detroit depression.

'Ab' two-time Cubs departee . . .

Ted Abernathy was twice traded away by Durocher. And, twice, he had good years in Cincinnati, and then in Kansas City, while Durocher tried to patch up a leaky bullpen. After his career, "Ab" tried in vain to get a coaching job. Thwarted, he worked for a building supply company for 16 years and was in the landscaping business with his son in his native North Carolina. He kept fields as green as Wrigly until he died at age 71 on December 16, 2004, in Gastonia, North Carolina.

Back home in Alabama . . .

"Wonderful Willie" Smith played one more season after the Cubs traded him to the Reds after the 1970 campaign. He returned to his native Anniston, Alabama, and worked as a material handler foreman for a microwave company. Smith died of a heart attack at 66 in Anniston on January 16, 2006.

Gamble a 'South Side Hit Man' . . .

Durocher hyped Gamble as the next Willie Mays before souring on him due to his personal life. He had him 'exiled' to Philadelphia at just 20. He did not play center field after 1971, nor did he steal more than 11 bases in any season. He ended up as a well-traveled platoon corner outfielder, earning good coin, ranging coast to coast from the Yankees to the Padres. He slugged 200 homers in 17 seasons.

Gamble became noted for two things: baseball's most luxuriant Afro in the 1970s and the leading slugger on Bill Veeck's rent-a-player, South Side Hit Men White Sox of 1977. After his career, he coached youth players in his native Montgomery, Alabama, before his death in 2018.

Popo still in Chicago area . . .

Paul Popovich continued to live in Chicago's northern suburbs and work in private business after his career ended with two seasons on the Pirates (1974-75). "All I can say is I wish I was playing baseball today," Popovich told the Beckley Register-Herald in his native West Virginia in 2014. "You ask whether my salary was ever close to a million — my answer is, 'Not really!'"

Popovich makes appearances these days doing signings at Chicago-area card shows.

Wrigley and Holland's final acts . . .

Phil Wrigley struggled with the idea of being the lovable loser Cubs, especially as he got on in age. In 1976, turning 82, he called the Cubs a "bunch of clowns" after a mid-season losing streak. He railed against the coming free-agent era and continually grasped for a gone era. His last major baseball act was the trade of two-time NL batting champ, Bill Madlock.

On April 12, 1977, with a new season upon him, Wrigley died at his Lake Geneva estate.

John Holland yielded his GM's job to Salty Saltwell just after the 1975 season, completing a 19-year run. Holland stayed on awhile to advise Saltwell, then retired.

The Cubs would prove to be his life's work as he died just a few years later, at age 65, in Chicago, on July 15, 1979.

Hey, Hey, Holy Mackerel, No Doubt About It . . .

Jack Brickhouse announced 1981 would be his final season on Cubs play-by-play at age 65. Moving over from the Pirates booth, Milo Hamilton was designated to succeed him. But after the 1981 season, Harry Caray made contact with Tribune Company executives to arrange a shift from 11 seasons with the White Sox to the North Side. Caray actually was two years older than Brickhouse, who hosted a WGN-Radio sports show and then became an unofficial storyteller and baseball historian.

Brickhouse emceed the pre-game ceremonies for Wrigley Field's first night game on August 8, 1988.

Brickhouse died at age 82 in Chicago on August 6, 1998. A statue commemorating him was dedicated on Michigan Avenue, a few feet from Tribune Tower, in 2000.

Yosh the Eternal Cub . . .

Figures Yosh Kawano would finally get a new clubhouse in 1984 . . . and soon players and others would proclaim it too small.

But the longest-running locker-room boss in Chicago sports history, just kept on going long, long after 1969. The Cubs were his life for 65 years, until he finally retired in 2008. He kept on running the home clubhouse for another 30 years. He was the one baseball person with lifetime job security. Bill Wrigley III had a clause in his contract to sell the Cubs to Tribune Company in 1981 that Yosh be accorded a lifetime job.

So Yosh kept on working, kept on recording what ballplayers owed him on the back of a piece of paper through the age of multi-millionaire athletes. When a new clubhouse administration headed by "Otis" Hellmann took over, the Cubs adhered to the 1981 contract and simply shifted Yosh to the visiting clubhouse.

He worked another 10 years. His trademark white sailor's cap was sent to the Hall of Fame.

Eventually, Yosh resided in a Los Angeles senior home with brother Nobe, a legend in his own right as Dodger Stadium home clubhouse chief. He was presented with a special Cubs World Series ring by his close friends, twins Carl and Tony Rudzicka, former ball boys. We don't know if Yosh fully comprehended the World Series triumph in 2016. Somehow, though, he knew. Yosh died at age 97 on June 25, 2018.

From one Cubs Hall of Famer to a bunch of others . . .

Hall-of-Famer Andre Dawson benefited from the intense, Cubs-loving atmosphere we created at Wrigley Field. A Montreal Expo, Bleacher Bums urged him to sign with the Cubs whenever his Expos player here. As if to demonstrate his interest in playing in Chicago, the Hawk went out and slugged 3 homers, 2 in a 12-run fifth inning, in a 17-15 Expos victory.

Dawson was aware of us at a great distance at age 15 growing up in Miami's inner city in 1969.

"I knew about (the Cubs) because of how the team was playing at that time," he said. "I grew up an LA Dodgers fan. That was kind of hard to do, because they were on the West Coast and you couldn't get the box scores 'til (two days later). You were always a day behind."

When he became a free agent amid the consequences of the owners' collusion efforts in the winter of 1986-87, he zeroed in on the Cubs, He agreed to a blank contract, which then-General Manager Dallas Green filled in for a base $500,000, plus incentives.

Well, Hawk earned every penny of the extra contractual money. He amassed one of the greatest seasons in Cubs history, earning the 1987 NL Most Valuable Player award on a .500 team through Labor Day that nosedived into last place at season's end. The vote went against the custom of choosing MVPs from contending teams. Dawson slugged an NL-best 49 homers – at the time the second-highest season total in Cubs history – and drove in a league-leading 137 runs.

Williams was Dawson's hitting coach in 1987, and again in 1992.

"Ernie, I always enjoyed being around because I just listened to him," Hawk said. "I never had to say a word and you gained a lot of knowledge just listening to him. Billy, he was quieter. It was more you listened to him and saw the wisdom that came out being the player he was. Ernie was a little more of a character. You enjoyed being around him.

"The one thing that Ronnie never really talked about was being or not being in the Hall of Fame. I knew how much that meant to him, when that day would come. I always tried to reassure him that time is going to show you're going to make it. It's just a shame he fell just (a year) short of being able to be here to witness it."

Then Dawson's turn to join us in Cooperstown came in 2010. Hawk credited his time in Wrigley Field, inspired by the fans, as crucial in making the Hall of Fame. Cubs Chairman Tom Ricketts hosted a ceremony at Wrigley to mark his induction. Finally, after he left his longtime employer, the Miami Marlins, Dawson was able to formally reunite with the Cubs as a team ambassador in 2018.

Long Remembered –
Never Forgotten

As of press time in fall of 2018, the following 1969 Chicago Cubs players and extended family passed away from this life, but not from our memories.

Rest in peace.

Players

- Ernie Banks
- Ron Santo
- Jim Hickman
- Bill Hands
- Dick Selma
- Willie Smith
- Ted Abernathy
- Hank Aguirre
- Oscar Gamble
- Gene Oliver
- Joe Niekro
- Don Nottebart
- Ken Johnson
- Joe Decker
- Randy Bobb
- Alec Distaso
- Manny Jimenez
- Charley Smith
- Manager and coaches
- Leo Durocher
- Pete Reiser
- Verlon "Rube" Walker
- Joe Becker

Broadcasters

- Jack Brickhouse
- Lloyd Pettit
- Vince Lloyd
- Lou Boudreau

Clubhouse Man

- Yosh Kawano

FERGIE JENKINS, *a 1991 Hall-of-Famer, is by all measures the greatest pitcher in Cubs history. He was 167-132 in 10 seasons in two tenures in Wrigley Field with an astounding six consecutive 20-win seasons from 1967-72. Overall, Fergie won 284 games in an 18-year career that took him to the Phillies, Rangers (twice) and Red Sox.*

Only Mordecai "Three Finger" Brown matched Fergie with his 20-win streak over six straight seasons in modern-day Cubs annals. Jenkins had his peak Cubs season in 1971 with a 24-13 record, 2.77 ERA and 30 complete games in 39 starts. For good measure, Fergie slugged six homers and drove in 21 runs in 1971, as well. He beat out the Mets' Tom Seaver for the National League Cy Young Award in his historic season.

Ranking as the first pitcher in big-league history to rack up more than 3,000 strikeouts with fewer than 1,000 walks, Fergie also is the Cubs career and season (2,038 career and 274 in 1970) strikeout leader. Jenkins also holds the Cubs' modern-day career record for career games started (347) and season games started (42 in 1969). He finished third in innings pitched (2,673 2/3), fourth in shutouts (29) and fifth in the categories of: wins (167), games (401), and complete games (154).

Fergie also won 25 games with the Rangers in 1974, after being traded from the Cubs for future four-time NL batting champ Bill Madlock. He is considered by many the greatest Canadian baseball player in history, too, and was the first from his country inducted into the Hall of Fame.

GEORGE CASTLE, *a native Chicago North Sider, never lived more than five miles away from Wrigley Field growing up. He lived and died with the Cubs. On September 3, 1969, his second day as a Mather High School freshman, he told a White Sox fan, "Me and a lot of other kids won't be here in October." "Where will you be?" asked the suspicious Sox rooter. "At the World Series, in Wrigley Field."*

George stayed in school while the Mets disposed of the Oriole s in five games in the Fall Classic, and he has wondered why ever since.

George attended 41 consecutive Cubs home openers starting in 1971. He witnessed Fergie outduel Bob Gibson 2-1 thanks to a 10th-inning Billy Williams homer in that first "lid-lifter" in '71 – in just one hour, 59 minutes!

He turned an avocation into a vocation. Castle covered the Cubs for more than three decades for newspapers, magazines, on-line sites and his syndicated baseball radio show "Diamond Gems." In 1998, he wrote the first post-mortem book on the legendary Harry Caray and has since penned 16 more books, including "The Million To One Team," considered a landmark book on Cubs ownership and management. In 2012, George wrote "Alou Makes the Catch," an alternate-history e-book on the team. He is widely regarded as one of the top baseball historians in the game today.

George has known Fergie, who contributed to "Diamond Gems," since the pitcher's second tenure in Wrigley Field in 1982. He pulled off the first-ever radio interview of Fergie and longtime rival Gibson together, in 1996 and is honored to share the historic 1969 Chicago Cubs story with him in these pages.

Acknowledgments...

This meaningful project could not have been accomplished without the extensive efforts, high-level skills, and genuinely passionate drives of many individuals and organizations coming together. I'd like to thank some of them, here.

Special appreciation to Publisher John Schenk, whose ability to put this fabulous team together is of a baseball-championship, general manager-like level. He kept everyone focused in direction and on a responsible schedule. He is at once professional and passionately engaged by this tale for the ages. Schenk is ultimately responsible for bringing this important work to market, recognizing the value of the story of what was at the time the Cubs' next great and rare run at breaking their World Series championship outage.

Further thanks to all the '69 Cubs alums who participated in a special time-tripping reminiscence: Randy Hundley; Don Kessinger; Ken Holtzman; Jimmy Qualls; Ken Rudolph; Nate Oliver; and Rich Nye. And we're not forgetting any other '69 Cubs, some of whom have since passed away, for sharing their memories over the decades.

Thank you for special contributions from the 1969 WGN play-by-play broadcast booth, as well as Cubs publicist Chuck Shriver and WGN Sports Editor Jack Rosenberg. My thanks to Rock Bottom Restaurant and Brewery in the Yorktown Plaza in Lombard, Illinois, for hosting a mini-reunion of several of my teammates, along with Shriver and Rosenberg.

The Jim Hickman family, namely Jim Jr. and Joey, shared impactful memories of Gentleman Jim while tapping into their photo archives. Another second generation of the Cubs family also gets credit. Veronica Cook, daughter of 1969 Cubs roving minor-league pitching coach Fred Martin, provided photos. A third '69 Cubs "child," Ken Holtzman's daughter Stacey, also was helpful.

Bob Waterman of Elias Sports Bureau in New York quickly looked up some telling stats about the '69 Cubs. Insightful 1969 Chicago Tribune Cubs beat writer George Langford doubled down with more memories and perspective a half-century later. Dr. David J. Fletcher shared his pristine scorecard from Ken Holtzman's August 19, 1969 no-hitter, and his memories of taking three trains each way – solo - at the tender age of 14 to reach Wrigley Field.

A big thanks to Bleacher Bums Karen Lindvig, Suzanne Grousl and her husband, Steve Podgorski, who almost got the former Left Field Bleacher Bum captain, Suzanne's brother Ron, to call us, and especially to yellow-helmeted Bleacher Bum Bugler and now Chicago sports radio personality and legend Mike Murphy

But I wouldn't be so involved with the Bums without my late friends and sometimes road hotel-crashing roomies Mike Haley and "Little Ray" Meyer, Jr.

And much appreciation to all the fans, former Wrigley Field vendors and ushers, and others who watched the '69 Cubs for writing up or dictating their memories.

Present-day Cubs officials also earn recognition here, led by Jeff Magee, the team's manager of team and family relations, for being the No. 1 go-to guy for me. Magee colleagues Jim Oboikowitch, Cubs manager of game and event production, and

Becca Wood, game and entertainment coordinator, were helpful for handling the logistical details for the debut of this book at the 2019 Cubs Convention. And the Wrigley Field security staff gets a nod for helping stage a bleachers photo while helping with access to the ballpark and the Convention.

Grant DePorter, impresario of Harry Caray's Italian Steakhouse, was a gracious host for the official book launch party with assistance from Harry Sherman and Mitch Dubinsky. Ditto for Linda Dillman, Bernie's Tap & Grill owner, for welcoming a mini-reunion of Left Field Bleacher Bums.

The mother-daughter combo of Nina and Laura Castle get kudos as usual for their assistance to and patience with the co-author, George Castle, without whom you're not reading this book right now.

You are immediately drawn in to this classic tale by John Hanley's fabulous cover artwork portraying yours truly and my teammates. Hanley was able to capture, not just a beautiful piece of artwork, but also the nostalgic feelings evoked by the 1969 Cubs.

Thanks to Howard Schlossberg, a 1969 Shea Stadium hot-dog vendor, for the editing of the manuscript and the keen understanding of which stories were most impactful to bring to print from a season printed on the memories of many. Lastly, to renowned author and writing coach, Reji Laberje, who masterfully nailed down the final manuscript. She also laid out this substantial literary effort.

Thank You,

Fergie Jenkins

"We were all winners; we were all World Series worthy, no matter what the final result says in the record books."

~Fergie

Made in the USA
Columbia, SC
01 April 2019